Off the Reservation

Paula Gunn Allen

Off the Reservation

※ ※ ※ ※ ※ ※ ※ ※ ※ ※ ※ ※ ※ ※ Reflections
on Boundary-Busting,

Border-Crossing

Loose Canons

BEACON PRESS ※ *Boston*

Beacon Press
25 Beacon Street
Boston, Massachusetts 02108-2892
www.beacon.org

Beacon Press books are published under the auspices
of the Unitarian Universalist Association of Congregations.

03 02 01 00 99 8 7 6 5 4 3 2

This book is printed on recycled acid-free paper that contains at
least 20 percent postconsumer waste and meets the uncoated paper
ANSI/NISO specifications for permanence as revised in 1992.

Text design by Lucinda Hitchcock
Composition by Wilsted & Taylor Publishing Services

LIBRARY OF CONGRESS CATALOGING-IN-PUBLICATION DATA
Allen, Paula Gunn.
    Off the reservation : reflections on boundary-busting, border-crossing
loose canons / Paula Gunn Allen.
        p.   cm.
    Includes bibliographical references.
    ISBN 0-8070-4640-x (cloth)
    ISBN 0-8070-4641-8 (paper)
    I. Title.
PS3551.L397038   1998
814'.54—DC21   98-21247

ETHEL HAINES FRANCIS

1916–1991

Thanks, Ma.

Contents

"Don't Fence Me In"

BORDER CROSSINGS

According to my people on the Laguna Pueblo side of the family, we emerged from the third world (*sipapu*, or "underworld") into the fourth world. That was long ago, so far, and when the people came out they had to wait until their mother, Iyatik^u, instructed them that the earth was ripe. Naiya Iyatik^u, our dear mother Beautiful Corn Woman, explained that the sun would rise four times but the people would emerge at the fourth, when it rose in the east. On that day, she herself would appear riding atop the sun, and Kokopelli, the humpback flute player, would lead the way, playing his flute from which multitudes of butterflies tumbled. Kokopelli is the Hopi Pueblo name for Humpback Flute Player and the most familiar form of his name. According to the petroglyphs as well as ethnological experts, Kokopelli is only depicted when the icon possesses three distinguishing characteristics: a humpback, a flute, and a rampant outsize penis. But poor Kokopelli! It seems that he ran afoul of Old Man Missionary and lost his joie de vivre, for he capers sadly about on wall hangings, tea towels, pot holders, tote bags, t-shirts, and pricey bronze cutouts sans his joyful manhood. Perhaps this sorry loss is symptomatic of all that is wrong with colonization, and indicative of all that fills Native hearts with rage.

Much of the sacred lore of the Keres Pueblo people circles around three major themes: creation, emergence, and migration. After creation and emergence into the fourth world, the great migrations began. This tradition, migration, is the strand I belong to; it is the dominant strand in the legacy of my gene pool's other parts. Like the old migration cycle, my line's tradition encompasses three major migration strands, most easily referenced as Laguna Pueblo, Maronite Lebanese, and Celtic Scots. All three are, I might add, Goddess-centered strands; whether this is through serendipity, cultural diffusion, or means we cannot yet identify, is not yet clear.

My pueblo, Laguna Pueblo, is itself a living artifact/expression of the migration cycle: Located on a major crossroads of cultural exchange from the early period of contact with Spanish explorers and colonials, Laguna emerged from the dislocations that Spanish arrival occasioned. When the Pueblos revolted against Spanish incursions and abuses, they drove the invaders hundreds of miles south of their lands. Then, a few decades later they invited them back, because when it's time, it's time, and all the wishings and revolts cannot change it. Or so they say. With the return of the Spaniards, their horses, and their garrisons came the founding of Old Laguna. Composed of a variety of mavericks – Pueblos, for the most part Keres, who had fled Spanish depredations, bacteriological plagues they brought with them, and, I should guess, the ravages of the Pueblo War against the invaders – the founders of Laguna Pueblo included Tewa, Tanno, Tiwa, and Navajos. It is rumored that my great-great-grandfather, Atseye, was himself Navajo. If so, his name would have actually been Atsitte, which, I'm told, means "silversmith." Laguna has from its inception been a mixed blood place, and to that distinguishing characteristic it owes not only its prospering survival, but its active and vital participation in many phases of American life. It was from Laguna lands that the uranium to build the world-changing bombs of the 1940s was taken.

According to my people's history from the Maronite-Lebanese side of the family, our origins are lost in the mists of Anatolia, from whence the proto-Celtic people migrated long, long ago to what would become Phoenicia, the red land. These were the people of the goddess Ishtar, sister of Egyptian goddess Isis. It is told that Isis consulted Ishtar and with her help located the remains of the beloved Osiris. They were stashed in his sarcophagus embedded in an oak tree in the Phoenician city of Byblos. Isis, sorceress, goddess, sister, mother, and lover of Osiris, resurrected him through her magic and impregnated herself. But his enemy Seth later found the body and hacked it into fourteen pieces; Seth tossed Osiris's penis to a crocodile for lunch; the other parts he scattered about the Nile valley. Isis found the pieces and reconstituted the god, sans penis. It seems Seth was an ancient form of Old Man Missionary, operating in the Mediterranean several thousand years before he found the homelands of the Keres. Maybe the other branch of my proto-Celtic ancestors, the one that would become Scots-

Irish, chose to migrate northwest in a doomed attempt to avoid his life-destroying, goddess-hating clutches.

There's an interesting confluence in these tales, hints of the braiding of the three strands that define me. Isis, sorceress, goddess of corn, goddess of sexual love, is reminiscent of Iyatik^u. According to Barbara G. Walker in *The Woman's Encyclopedia of Myths and Secrets*, ". . . 'In the beginning there was Isis, Oldest of the Old. She was the Goddess from whom all becoming arose.' As the creatress, she gave birth to the sun 'when he rose upon this earth for the first time.'" It is true that the apparent braiding has particular interest for me, stemming as I do from each strand. But the junctures of the traditions are not my doing: they are suggestive of something; – perhaps a global civilization that long predated what we think of as the ancient world; perhaps a paranormal link in which sorcerer talked to shaman, and they each talked to priestesses/priests over a spiritual "ethernet." Or perhaps the bumper sticker that announces "My Other Car Is a Broom" refers not to fanciful stories from a long-discredited body of thought as much as to an ancient mode of transportation. Maybe some rode brooms, some carpets, and some magic arrows powered by Spider Grandmother's magic pollen. Or maybe stories, like human beings, just get around.

My branch of the human family has been given to migration on every side. Migration, it seems, was in our blood from earliest times, for some of the people migrated across the trans-Alpine ridge into western Europe, thence to the British Isles, to eventually become the Celt-Scottish, Welsh, Cornish, Somerset, and Irish. Some found themselves on the Iberian peninsula, to eventually become the Spanish. And some would interrupt Odysseus and Aeneas on their journeys as goddesses bent on keeping the heroes from home and empire.

As time went on, some of the descendants of those first migrators made their way to the Americas. One of them was my mother's ancestor, John M. Gunn, and another his bride, Isabella Sutherland. They met in Canada and migrated south into Ohio Territory, where they set up farming in Hardin County. Family legend holds that Isabella named one lovely spot Belle Fontaine, because of its lake. It bears that name even now. Their descendants, all boys, migrated to New Mexico Territory where three of them married Laguna women; one continued on to the Coast and married an Anglo-American Valley girl.

Another ancestor possessed of the migrator gene was my father's grandfather, Elias buHassen (a.k.a. Elias Francis; "Don Francisco"). Grandpa

Francis came to the United States in the late nineteenth century, fleeing an avaricious uncle back in the home village, Rumé, located on the western slope of the Lebanon. He spent two or three years traveling as a peddler of rosaries, dry goods, and trinkets. After a time he returned to Lebanon, packed up his wife, Philomena, and young son Nacif, and migrated to New Mexico Territory, settling first in Albuquerque, then in the mountain village of Seboyeta, a Spanish land grant village not far from the Pueblo of Laguna. I guess they couldn't keep him up in the hills of Lebanon after he'd seen US.

I emerged from within my mother when I was "ripe," or "cooked," and the forces that move us opened her gateway, allowing me to emerge. Among the Keres and other Pueblos, "cooked," or "ripe," is a way of indicating maturity, or full human status. The people were able to enter the fourth world when the earth was "cooked," or "ripe." I was born in the closing years of that fourth world, just as the German Army entered Poland and the Second World War commenced. That was a few years before, and a few miles from the site in west central New Mexico, where, in a stunning and stunned nanosecond, about 4:45 A.M. Mountain War Time, July 15, 1945, the fifth world began. The day the sun rose twice, I was nearly six years old, and, true to my geno-history, I've been migrating ever since. As for the people, it seems we were all "cooked" that day.

I was born a mixed-blood Laguna girl on the border of the mixed-blood Laguna Reservation and the Cubero Land Grant, to a mixed-blood Laguna mother, grandmother, great-grandmother, and perhaps great-great-grandfather to Oak clan, to the Sunrise/Summer people; and to a Maronite-American father born and raised around the mountain to the east of Cubero, north of Laguna's mother village. Like his father and grandfather, he spoke many languages, told many stories, crossed many borders, busted many boundaries, loosened many canons—sometimes in spite of himself, because that was his heritage. My parents were both many-tongued and engaged in multiplicities of multilingual puns, their everyday common form of preserving their matrimony and their patrimony. As yet unknown, unnamed in the formalist world of the United States, deconstruction as cross-cultural jokes, ironies, puns, postures, gestures, and expressions fashioned our family life, sheltered as it was within the hollow of a sandstone mesa bounded by the main arroyo and the road to everywhere.

Being on the road to everywhere, at the crossroads of the modern, the early modern, the ancient, and the wilderness, Laguna Pueblo has from its inception been a way station for everything that goes on in the universe, sacred or otherwise.

Like my parents, I was born beneath the broad sheltering slopes of Tse'-pina/Kaweshtima, the Woman Veiled in Clouds/the Woman Who Comes from the North, a.k.a. Mt. Taylor. She, the Woman Mountain, soared seven or eight thousand feet above our village, fourteen thousand feet above the distant sea. She changed endlessly in the forever moving light of day, the forever changing times of year, and history changed her from woman to man, with a century or two of ambiguity between: from Pueblo feminine Tse'-pina to Spanish, mostly neutral, Cerro Pelones (loosely, "Old Baldy") to American masculine Mt. Taylor; anyone with eyes can see the womanly power-shape of that great entity. Anyone with ears can hear the woman-mountain song she sings.

I was born in a Spanish-speaking village of about sixty families, bounded on every side by Pueblo nations, Laguna and Acoma, and by wilderness, the Cibola National Forest. According to local rumor, the village, like others in the area, was founded by a mixed-racial couple: the husband, I think, was Spanish-American, and the wife, Laguna. Unable to live comfortably at either one's home village, they struck out on their own. Soon enough others came to build houses nearby, and thus Cubero, named for a Spanish army officer, was born. There in the shadow of the woman with very short hair, far away from the grind of Anglo-American civilization, nevertheless we were part of it all: among my relatives and close family friends were Spanish-Americans, Mexican-Americans and Anglos, German Jews and German Christians, Lebanese Maronites and Spaniards, Italian-Americans and Greek Americans, Basque immigrants, and Japanese-Americans fleeing the camps to the west. And as the years roll by, we take more and more of the human strains into the family lines: African-American, Chinese-American, Mexican immigrant, Salvadoreño immigrant—for all I know, there's even an Arab or two married in! We are global by blood, by law, and by injection. American through and through.

LOOSE(NING) CANONS

This re/collection of contemporary coyote Pueblo American thought is titled *Off the Reservation: Reflections on Boundary-Busting,*

Border-Crossing Loose Canons. I chose the name because if anything defines the American Indian peoples' post-Columbian situation, it is the freedom to leave and return to the reservation or local communities. Off reservation we are indeed a motley crew: carrying every variety of blood that has found its way to our ancient continent, faced with not only duality – that would be easy! – but with a multitude of complexities that are perhaps aptly summed up by our mixed blood, mixed-culture status. Yet however mixed in ancestry, heritage, and culture, we are all, all of us Indians, and have been "off the reservation" at all times.

"Off the reservation" is an expression current in military and political circles. It designates someone who doesn't conform to the limits and boundaries of officialdom, who is unpredictable and thus uncontrollable. Such individuals are seen as threats to the power structure. They are anomalies: mavericks, renegades, queers. Seen in its historical context, designating someone "off the reservation" is particularly apt. Originally the term meant a particular kind of "outlaw," a Native person who crossed the territorial border, called a reserve or reservation, set by the United States or a state government. In those days "the reservation" signified a limited space, a camp, to which Native people of various nations were confined. Those who crossed the set borders were deemed renegades. They were usually hunted down, and most often, summarily shot.

One of the major issues facing twenty-first-century Native Americans is how we, multicultural by definition – either as Native American or American Indian – will retain our "indianness" while participating in global society. It is the subtext of this volume. That we do not fit easily into pre-existing officially recognized categories is the correlative of our culture of origin. As Native Americans of the Five Hundred Nations never have fit the descriptions other Americans imposed and impose, neither does our thought fit the categories that have been devised to organize Western intellectual enterprise. In the ways that suit Native philosophical sets and subsets, each work in this re/collection seems, from a Western perspective, to be mixed in content and form. Each is a mixture of myth, history, literary studies, philosophy, and personal narrative. Each makes unspoken assumptions about the nature of human experience and the greater reality (or great mysteriousness) that surrounds and informs it, which suit a Native turn of mind rather than a Western inclination. Yet each is equally a product of Western thought, necessarily so.

Orthographic composition, whether poetry, essay, fiction, or renderings from the oral tradition, has its own laws and assumptions. Any orthographic text must partake of these. So, like the half-breed, hybrid, mixed-blood woman who has composed them, these essays resemble the oral tradition of the Laguna world and the essayist tradition of the orthographic academy by turns. They cross borders between and within paragraphs; bust boundaries of style, image, argument, and point of view; and at the best of times career wildly about the ship of utterance. Given their divergent and complementary sources, they can hardly do otherwise.

While many of the essays in the volume are clearly categorical, others could as well be placed in one category as in another – a peculiarity of contemporary Native American life and thought characteristic of its post-reservation and both pre- and post-Columbian nature. For while we have until recently been confined by other Americans' economic, philosophical, and cultural reservations, neither our thought nor our practice has been readily reconstructed into western modes. With the growing influence of Gambler on reservations, Old Man Coyote and the grand seducer Kokopelli riding freely the waves of popular consciousness, and Old Man Missionary finding himself fenced in by his own barbed-wire conventions, boundaries have grown permeable, wide open spaces abound. Gee, it's almost like old times!

Native civilizations have their boundaries drawn along lines that differ markedly from those that characterize other civilizations. Probably the tendency of my migration-conscious Pueblo mind to see borders as both liminal and transformational led me early on to choose "Don't Fence Me In" as one of my favorite songs.

I didn't know the word for "resistance" then, but I was raised in a family that assumed resistance to be the bedrock of its reality. The *fact* of it was so firmly integrated into my every moment that even in dreams I engaged in the pursuit of freedom. The pieces in this collection are my later articulations of that unspoken but fundamental way of being. Spanning thirty years, from the late sixties to the late nineties, each essay is, in its own way, an assertion that Indians are everywhere. On reservation and off, cross-border, boundary un-bound. Sort of like earth. Like the goddesses and gods. Neither fences nor reservations can confine us, for we are, as N. Scott Momaday has suggested, "an idea" as much as a deeply defining, living aspect of American life. Ideas can't be fenced. Or, for that matter, corralled.

It is the nature of orthographic writing to require some sort of linear organization. To that end, this collection is divided into three somewhat loose categories. The first section, "Haggles," might be understood to mean "*Gynosophies*" (gyne = woman; sophia = wisdom, and it's feminine). The essays here either focus on the feminine or arise out of a female-centered perspective. In the words of the famed anthropologist Bronislaw Malinowski, the Keres (my own Pueblo, Laguna, being one of the several Keresan communities in New Mexico) are "the last mother-right people" on earth. My mother's grandfather suggested naming my mother "Susan B. Anthony," I don't know why, other than that it was some sort of Scots-at-Laguna joke, but I like to think that Grandpa Gunn recognized the renegade boundary-buster in her; it was probably her most marked characteristic and most precious *heiress*-loom.

The work contained in "Haggles" is political, spiritual, and ecological in direction. The first three pieces, "Notes Toward a Human Revolution," "The Savages in the Mirror," and "All the Good Indians," were written in the sixties. In keeping with the tone of those turbulent times, they are political, devised as questions about the nature and foundations of Western civilization and its relationship to human life and history, specifically in regard to a western/American Indian interface. The next, "American Indian Mysticism," was written at the request of a colleague, Donald H. Bishop (*Mysticism and the Mystical Experience East and West*), and is in many respects a political study. This is because the way the world and life of Native peoples are viewed from the perspective of Western American culture needs correction so that discussions about our life and our vision of reality can be discussed with as little distortion as possible. While this task is all but impossible for a variety of reasons, it is one that is necessary. It becomes increasingly imperative that we realize that there are as many varieties of human social consciousness, of community in its largest sense, as there are varieties of life in the universe. And that in that recognition we grope for means of articulating each view, in and of itself, as truthfully as we can. For our future good depends as much on our recognizing our vast differences as on recognizing our powerful similarities.

Having firmly situated the terms of the discussion in the past and the politics of Indian country in the first four essays, the next group moves to the heart of the matter. From "Haggles" through "The Woman I Love Is a Planet," the ideascape reveals its formally woman-centered, gynosophic nature. Deep within the borderlands that form the boundary between old and emerging civilizations, opponents are engaged, skirmishes detailed, the lines of battle drawn. The discussion in "Father God and Rape Culture" provides a ripening of ideas that are explored in "Notes Toward a Human Revolution," "The Savage in the Mirror," and "All the Good Indians," indicating that the western world's relation to women powerfully mirrors its relation to Native people; certainly the language used to designate the one is frequently employed to designate the other. Both are close to nature, irrational, intuitive, mystical, culturally focused, domestic, dependent entities, at one with flora and fauna, and best kept silent, dependent, and enclosed – for their own protection.

In "The Anima of the Sacred," "'Indians,' Solipsisms, and Archetypal Holocausts," and "Radiant Beings," the discussion is transposed from the political to the spiritual, wherein it becomes clear that boundaries between Indian Country/Herland and Western Civilization/hisland are more a spiritual site than a geopolitical or gendered one. The profound knowledge of the true nature of earth, the land, and all that exists upon and within it, which once characterized gynosophic societies as it now characterizes American Indian societies, is the true site of conflict. The differing definitions of reality and the accompanying values those definitions imply are what is at stake. And the outcome is the fate of the planet and multitudinous forms of life thereon. Which takes us to the final essay in the first section, "The Woman I Love Is a Planet; The Planet I Love Is a Tree." Thus, the first four essays are reprised in the final five, with "Haggles," in which an older woman speaks at the Gynosophic Gathering in Oakland in the 1980s. Divided into two sections, the essay serves as modulation from one key to the next, exploring the concept of "gynosophy" in its textual ancestry: the sophia of woman.

The second section, "Wyrds/Orthographies," follows on the final paragraphs of the previous essay, beginning where it leaves off: "Our Mother, in her form as Sophia, was long ago said to be a tree, the great tree of life. . . . " The Great Tree is also known as the Tree of Knowledge (gnosis), and since time immemorial, inscribed knowledge has been the text. In "Wyrds/Orthographies," the text is the literature of contemporary times; the essays in this section deal mainly with American Literature, most frequently but not exclusively with that variety of American Literature produced by American Indian writers.

The method of inquiry I employ can be defined as applied gynosophy;

and while a number of the essays in the second section of this volume qualify as such, the most clearly thea-retical is "Thus Spake Pocahontas." The editors of the volume in which it originally appeared (*Introduction to Scholarship in Modern Languages and Literatures*, The Modern Language Association of America) changed the title of the essay to "Border Studies: The Intersection of Gender and Color" to fit the overall design of the volume. As is the case in "Haggles/Gynosophies," the essays on literature contain much that is classifiable as ecological, spiritual, and political. The opening, "Iyañi: It Goes This Way," which introduces the Southwest writers section of the first and only-of-its-kind collection, *The Remembered Earth* (edited by Geary Hobsen and published in 1979), speaks forthrightly to literary, spiritual, and ecological matters. Its opening statement, "We are the land," can be applied profitably to thousands of novels, plays, short stories, and music written by American Indian authors. It is an assumption, an underlying concept, that informs every Native American text. Similarly, the idea contained in the word *iyañi*, a Keresan (Laguna Pueblo) term for "sacred" – literally, "it goes that way" – points to the dynamic underlying many American Indian texts, traditional and contemporary.

The three main strands of American Indian literature in the modern era, history, politics, and the great traditions of the Native world, inform the texts in the way Simon J. Ortiz describes the rain lying in wait for its time "underneath the fine sand . . . cool / with crystalline moisture . . ." In my mind, critical essays – indeed, "nonfiction" writing in general – is simply another way of telling a story. Each has a narrative line, a plot if you will, and that line must unfold in accordance with certain familiar patterns, just as any story must. An essay contains all the elements of a good plot: conflict, crisis, resolution. Concepts take the role of character, and, of course, the unities of time, place, and action must be respected. The second section of *Off the Reservation* reads much like a novel: it has chapters, and as they unfold, as the plot thickens, the terms of the discussion, the dialogue, the dialectic are expanded, examined, and explored. From the opening paragraphs of "Iañyi: It Goes This Way," in which the basic situation is set forth, and through the ensuing plot developments, twists, and subplots, a journey through American Literature is detailed. It is a journey whose guide is not exactly American, at least not in the ordinary sense of the idea. A partial outsider, a maverick narrator completes the whole: for who but a maverick on a quest most closely approximates the American, journeying through lands as yet unfamiliar to western society. By the time the adventurers reach the final chapter, the "borderlands," they can, one hopes, discover that the nature of literature, like the nature of life, is at bottom perplexing. In a word, there are so many discoveries to make, so many strange new lands to explore; questions rather than answers, information and insight rather than "fact" and "authority" become the goal and the source of human experience.

There is something about stories that hooks humans into culture, that make human psyches and human societies all but indistinguishable from texts. The intertwined nature of literature and human beings has not escaped the notice of the old Indian peoples; it has, at last, come to the attention of their younger relatives, writers and critics of the Western world. The old ones' recognition of the intrinsic identity of text and human consciousness informs the structures of the whole of the oral tradition, and critical theory in Indian Country consists of the often subtle junctures of story cycles. Stories, whether narrative or argumentative in nature, tell us not who we are, not who we are supposed to be, but instead describe and define the constraints of the possible. Admittedly, what is possible for human thought is, in the oral tradition, quite a bit larger than it is in the Western rational tradition. The growing interface between the two, indigenous American and contemporary American, is the central narrative of the literary essays in the second section of *Off the Reservation*. This preoccupation culminates in the final essay, "Thus Spake Pocahontas," in which I argue that we, writers on the interface/frontier between modern and timeless, are the void, the place of endless possibility. It is that site – which is a dynamic flux rather than a fixed point – that is identified as Iyañi. It is power-sacred, informed by the great mysterious being known as Thinking Woman, Old Spider Grandmother, the Keresan version of Sophia.

BUSTED

The third section of the collection, "*La Frontera*/Na[rra]tivities," centers on my personal journey through my portion of the oral tradition, which, in keeping with Western formulations, I call "my" life. While it is not clear to me whether such articles are recountings of the oral tradition from a personal (read "constructed") perspective that I call "myself" or if they are narratives of the land, the earth herself rendered through the energy/information gestalt I take so personally, it can be seen that the essays possess the characteristics of narrative in the autobiographical sense. That is, they are stories in which the principal character is "I." The first, "Autobiography of a Confluence," is just that, an autobiographical narrative, but, like all such narratives, it is not so much the actual me as the me I have constructed within the wit and editorial limits given me. The next two, "*Yo Cruzo Siete Mares*," and "My Lebanon," address my life as my father's daughter. They point beyond themselves, within the context of the volume, to a larger issue: What IS "Indian," what is "White," and thus, "What is America/American?" It has perplexed Americans writing since earliest Spanish, French, and English colonial times to find Old World narratives inextricably bound up with the Nativity of the land from which the newcomers took their being and, consequently, their identity.

Life demonstrates that American Indian people remain curiously difficult to categorize outside of museums of natural history where we exist, frozen in time, as nostalgic accompaniments of American flora and fauna. Identifiably distinct in history, culture, style, and thought, Native people are also as American as fried chicken (a Cherokee recipe applied to a Celtic ingredient) and apple pie. Most of us wave the American flag as enthusiastically as any "redneck" (redneck and redskin, more alike than not); most of us are Christian, church-going, and devout; and more of us serve in the armed forces of the United States than, percentage-wise, any other demographic group in the country. We have the shell-shock, post-traumatic stress syndrome, Agent Orange Disease, Gulf-War Syndrome, and other side effects of military enterprise to show for it.

The habits of mind and activity common to the majority of American Indian people are perplexing to other varieties of Americans, most of whom, should they give us any thought, lump us in a box marked buckskin-and-feather-first ecologists-cum-natural phenomena. Despite commonly held notions about the state of the Five Hundred Nations, American Indian boundary lines occur where Old World Americans don't expect them. Most of us, given the opportunity to learn the words, would probably choose "Don't Fence Me In" as our pan-Indian anthem. And perhaps, as our traditions have always been about liminality, about voyages between this world and many other realms of being, perhaps crossing boundaries is the first and foremost basis of our tradition and the key to human freedom and its necessary governmental accomplice, democracy. Certainly, as both our literature and lives attest, that's how it seems to be.

The final essays in the final section are cross-category pieces. While each contains much personal narrative material, they verge into impersonal territories. "The Lay of the Land" is a threnody to *mi país*, "my land," which is, finally, the measure and spirit of who and what I am. Whatever writings center on it must, of necessity, be autobiographical, for in the "Indian" way I see myself a composite of land and myth, the oral tradition and its grounding. As for these two final pieces, each in its way is a candidate for inclusion in the first section of the volume, and both address themes and myths that characterize contemporary American and global literature. As such, they could also be included under the heading of Literature.

The old narrative cycle of the Pueblo peoples is traditionally divided into three sections: creation, emergence, and migration. Each of these portions is applicable to the community, to each clan within it, and to each individual member of the clans. In terms of our story as indigenous people in the contemporary era the story could be told thus: In the beginning was Thought, and she was Grandmother; the people emerged into the fourth world guided and led by our dear mother, Beautiful Corn Woman; under the continued guidance of Thought Grandmother, we migrated from wherever we were to our present homelands. Then there was a reprise of that cycle (one of many, and this one not the first): The people were created as Pueblo by the coming of others from the east; we migrated in Thought and custom from where we had been situated to where we are situated now, and our thought migrated over the globe, sending Grandmother Thought/Consciousness outward upon the web of life (again). The stories, the understandings, the figures, the significances remain as they ever were, even as they morph. Transformation is, after all, the heart of the people, the heart of the tradition, and the heart of the life process of Thought.

There's more than one way to skin a cat, as those of my grandmother's generation used to say, and in their spirit, let's agree: There's more than one way to be an Indian, to categorize an essay, and to organize a book.

A-Ho!

I.

Haggles

gynosophies

1.
Notes Toward a Human Revolution

For several hundred years at least, Europeans have staged a series of foredoomed revolutions on the European and American continents. The 1970s are merely a continuation of the 1770s in America: The revolution is fought and argued over and over, but life goes on as usual in the West. The big fish eat the little fish and the little fish starve. Or, as a four-year-old of my acquaintance put it, the good guys kill the bad guys and the bad guys kill people.

The revolutionary rhetoric of Berkeley in the 1960s sounds depressingly similar to that of Russia in the late 1860s: The critiques, the strategies, and the results are alike. The problems we faced as a human race two hundred years ago remain, and each failure to solve them, to at least set them to rest so we can get on with life itself in human terms, increases their urgency. And yet the means to effect a *human* revolution elude us, century after century, conquest after conquest, war after war. We think and think, argue, debate, struggle, incite, rebel, plunder, issue directives, publish, murder, and die, but what was true in colonial America is true today, and there is no end to it, no way out of the labyrinth of thinking and talking and slaying and murdering on an ever larger, ever widening scale.

THE WHEEL SURVIVES THE MYTH
Perhaps the flaw in the concept of revolution, and thus in its consequences, stems from the flaw in phallocentric thinking. Perhaps the wellsprings of Western civilization are the source of the pollution that strangles our breath and our spirit until there is nothing left but the machinery of death that orders our ever increasingly futile lives. Perhaps the uni-

versal law that requires a peony to grow only from peony seed is a law as applicable to revolutions as to plants.

If this is the case, if phenomena necessarily arise out of pre-conditioning or pre-programming of inter-related phenomena, if life really is a circle that lives and breathes in circular, inexorable terms, it becomes imperative that we examine the roots of the civilization we wish to turn, to change, and see what basic pre-conditions in that civilization create our present and seemingly eternal miseries.

If there is to be a meaningful, significant turn in the wheel of the civilized state, it must be semantic, linguistic, and semiotic. Three dimensions of the stance toward reality that characterizes Western civilization are: proprietorship (ownership as a concept), literacy (reading/writing as the power and glory of man), and separatism (the great and only heresy; splintering the biota). A true revolution, a lasting turn and transformation in human institutions and relationships, must begin with a reorganization of these basic values that have characterized Western civilization since the days of the ancient Egyptian pharaonic empire. We must abandon our faith in the myth of property, the superstition of literacy, and the heresy of separatism. We must abandon the essential paradigm of Domination/Submission in all of its forms.

DEFY THE METAPHOR THAT MURDERS METAPHOR

The need to put aside the private ownership of property, at least in capitalistic terms, may seem evident. But I am not suggesting that we do away merely with private ownership per se. I am suggesting that human beings do not naturally think in terms of ownership, but rather in terms of use. The idea that one can own a piece of land or a piece of productive enterprise is actually incomprehensible, except as a concept. It is not really possible (perhaps "executable" would be more appropriate here) in human behavior, because it implies the capacity to stop the automatic, natural flow of living. This is a very hypnotic illusion, but it is nevertheless illusory. I can only relate to land or money as a living thing, because I am living and because relationship is process. I cannot own a relationship. I cannot stop the process of relationship. But I can use land; I can use capital – both as a means toward expressing my aliveness and of maintaining it.

The concept of ownership is what led to the terrible difficulties of the Native Americans in their dealings with the European transplants to this continent. The Native Americans did not understand how a piece of land could belong to someone in some absolute sense by virtue of a piece of paper. They did understand quite clearly that the Earth takes care of us, naturally, and that each person and each people was entitled to such land as they needed to maintain their lives. A number of tribes would share or cooperatively use "hunting grounds," but the cultivated fields belonged to those who cultivated them. If those farmers moved, for whatever reason, that land was up for grabs; the next farmer to use it "possessed" it. But possession was seen as a matter of use, not a matter of eternal right. This event-centered attitude made a class of people such as thieves, grifters, speculators, or capitalists impossible – not because such activities were taboo or prohibited, but because they were impossible, given the climate of the societies. People couldn't steal something that belonged to someone else because only one person can use something at a time. The idea of dynamic, ongoing patterns of relationship were clearly understood and lived by. This basic assumption regarding the nature of time-space-action had the consequence of creating a naturally cooperative society as well as individuals within that society who intuitively thought in terms of the good of the whole – the tribe-earth-universe-self – when they thought of the self or the "part."

The Native Americans knew that the basic law of human universal consciousness was event-ual in nature, and that the event, the use, determined behavior most rationally in terms of human harmony and human development. The Europeans called them savages because they did not bow down to the idea of paper-ownership, or of personal possessiveness, or of ownership of the many by the few, and justified their genocide in these terms. Even as late as 1887, Americans justified the biggest land rip-off since the Mexican War by declaring: The one thing these people (the Cherokee) lack to make them civilized is the virtue of selfishness. So to teach Native Americans to be truly civilized, they gave individual Indians a certain amount of land for nuclear family units and said it was each family's to use or sell (mainly sell) as they chose.

THE BETTER TO EAT YOU WITH, MY DEAR

They claimed that this was in the best interest of the Cherokees, as well as of all other Native Americans affected by the Dawes Act. But forty-seven years later, the Merriam Survey revealed that Native land holdings had shrunk by two-thirds since the Allotment Act had been in effect.

The existential message of the transaction was this: Civilized people can take our inalienable rights away. It seems fairly obvious from this that a society intent on eradicating theft in all its forms must eradicate "civilization." Cooperativeness, the willingness to share goods and land, is not possible in a basically selfish framework; yet, by the words of the United States Congress, selfishness is a basic virtue of civilization. And self-possessiveness – this is mine/if you use it, you owe me money for it – automatically creates theft-systems. Yet the ability to think in terms of cooperation makes it humanly possible to effectively exert a measure of control over what happens to you. It eliminates the need to be defensive, distrustful, and paranoid, and allows for a greater interplay among humans on terms that human psyches and spirits can comprehend. When the concepts of possessiveness or proprietorship disappear as being meaningful in our lives, the haunting sense of separation from the universe will be lessened because possessiveness requires selfishness, and selfishness is separation.

IT ALMOST SEEMS AS IF THE GOVERNMENT ASSUMED THAT SOME MAGIC IN INDIVIDUAL OWNERSHIP OF PROPERTY WOULD IN ITSELF PROVE AN EDUCATIONAL, CIVILIZING FACTOR

LITERACY

Western civilization was erected on twin pillars, so to speak: possessiveness and literacy. The twin facets have allowed the phenomenon known as politics to determine most of our behavior for several thousand years. And yet, on the face of it, the idea that my literacy makes me more powerful than someone who is not literate is ludicrous. In point of fact, the ability to read does little for me, except possibly allow me to earn a living in ways that violate my best instincts and potentialities. Yet it is true that the big fish can read – even though the obverse is not true and never was, that is, that the little fish cannot. But so long as the little fish believe that reading will, in and of itself, transform them or their progeny into big fish, that the magic power of literacy will allow transformation of their relative power-situation, literacy will be a tool for the exploitation and manipulation of human beings – the same kind of tools that land ownership (possession) and domination over others have been.

The Cherokees were broken on that particular wheel; they believed what their literate teachers said about the power of literacy so they became literate, Sequoyah made public the Cherokee syllabary, and in ten years the overwhelming majority of the people were able to read and write. They printed their own newspaper, *The Phoenix*, which was bilingual; incorporated their nation on paper in a Constitution; wrote letters to each other; wrote down incantations, chants, minutes of meetings; studied the Bible assiduously; and cultivated the companionship of literate and important non-Cherokees. Many married white women, some took black people as slaves, and, by Cherokee Nation law, they divested Cherokee women of political rights. In other words, they took up all the mechanisms of power that they believed would enable them to live as a sovereign nation, a republic on this continent, ally to the United States. They read the laws of the United States, obeyed what they read, and activated all due processes in their fight to retain ownership of their homelands. Imagine their amazement to find themselves walking, destitute, sick and dying, eight hundred miles from their ancient and beloved home, in spite of their literacy and "civilization." They were called "civilized" by whites, but they were powerless to change their fate. When the big fish said, "It's time to eat you little-fish Cherokee," they were duly devoured. And all the literacy in the world was useless to save them.

2.
The Savages in the Mirror
Phantoms and Fantasies in America

I.

THE SAVAGES
As we rowed from our ships and set foot on the shore
In the still coves,
We met our images.

Our brazen images emerged from the mirrors of the world
Like yelling shadows,
So we searched our souls,

And in that hell and pit of everyman
Placed the location of their ruddy shapes.
We must be cruel to ourselves.

The first thing that they did after landing was to steal all the corn they could carry from a nearby Wampanoag village. The natives of that place had seen them coming and, having been previously treated to the visits of white men, had fled into the forest. The next day the Puritans came back; yesterday's haul had been too little, they felt, so they took what was left in the storage bins.

> They had now no friends to welcome them nor inns to entertain or refresh their weather-beaten bodies; no houses or much less towns to repair to, to seek for succor ... All things stand upon them with a weather-beaten face, and the whole country, full of woods and thickets, represented a wild and savage hue.
>
> — WILLIAM BRADFORD

There was a Wampanoag village that had been emptied by previous contact with the Europeans; the inhabitants had died of some disease the year before. These poor, "weather-beaten bodies" repaired thereto and made themselves at home. The village that succored them was one filled with houses covered by elm-bark of generous size, walled around by a "stockade" fence, which thus nicely separated from home that which they most feared: woods and thickets that, to their minds, represented a wild and savage face.

It is strange that accounts of early American experience overlook the presence of other human communities – a negligible presence, we are led to believe, all but gone right after the first Thanksgiving dinner. Despite American folklore that is all too often offered to children and adults alike as "fact," there were thousands upon thousands of people living in settled, agricultural communities along the Atlantic seaboard. And it was these societies – or, one may fairly say, this civilization – from which the colonials drew the strength, courage, and concepts upon which to base both their revolutions against England and, much later, Spain and to devise a form of nationhood that recognized the equal rights of all adult citizens, male and female, "high born" or "common," to have a voice in their own governance. And though it took them well over a century, from 1776 to 1947, eventually they recognized their founding ideals in law. "The shot heard round the world," as the American Revolution of 1776 was termed by pundits and philosophers of the eighteenth and nineteenth centuries, was fired from an Algonquin and Haudenoshonee gun.

Whoever the first Americans were, they weren't the Puritans, whose idea of social organization was to lock all citizens within the palisades, whip and chain people to stockades or to wagons or horses from which they were dragged out of town, or to banish them, alone, to the wilderness for in any way disagreeing with the "town fathers," who were the sole recognized authorities. Thus, it is strangest of all that "our images" were suitable mirrors of being, while we were and still are not allowed to be there at all.

I have sat through more hours of American History and American Literature than I care to contemplate, and seldom is the word "Indian" (even that misshapen idol) mentioned. "With all due respect, ma'am," ever the courtly professorial expert of white supremacy, "Indians never had any effect on America at all." (America's a self-made Marlborough man, ma'am).

Did you know that the Cherokee tipped the balance of Spanish power that gave the south Atlantic coast to the English?

That the Haudenoshonee ("Iroquois") dominated the power struggle among France, England, and Spain for over two hundred years?

That the Chickasaw platoons who ran missions for Andrew Jackson during the War of 1812 were the reason for the victory of the United States over England?

I didn't.

I spent twenty-two years in school, and I didn't know that.

Nor in all those years was I ever given this moving speech to memorize. Delivered by Ta-ha-yu-ta (Logan), the lone survivor of his community and family during the French and Indian War, this bit of eloquence was featured in the McGuffy Reader, used for several generations in American public schools as exemplary oratory.

> I appeal to any white man to say, if he ever entered Logan's cabin hungry, and he gave him not meat; if ever he came cold and naked, and he clothed him not. During the course of the last long and bloody war, Logan remained idle in his cabin, an advocate of peace. Such was my love for the whites, that my countrymen pointed as they passed, and I said, "Logan is the friend of white man." I had even thought to have lived with you but for the injuries of one man. Colonel Cresap, the last spring, in cold blood and unprovoked, murdered all the relations of Logan, not even sparing my women and children. There runs not a drop of my blood in the veins of any living creature. This called on me my revenge. I have sought it; I have killed many; I have fully glutted my vengeance. For my country, I rejoiced at the beams of peace. But do not harbor a thought that this is the joy of *fear*. Logan never felt fear. He will not turn on his heel to save his life. Who is there to mourn for Logan? – Not one!
>
> – TAH-HA-YU-TA [LOGAN], IROQUOIS

The French and Indian War was fought in the mid-1700s, before the founding of the Republic. The Puritans, historically deemed the nation's forefathers, had come ashore not two centuries before. But they were not the first Europeans to colonize what is now the United States. New Mexico was colonized long before Plymouth. Why was Puritan Colony designated the earliest American settlement? Why do chronological history or literature books start with the Puritans? In terms of the present boundaries of the United States, the Southwest was entered first and subdued (more or less). Then Florida. Then New England and New France. Then California, Navajoland/Apache. Then the Plains. But American history marches ever westward, from the northern Atlantic coast of the United States to California. Let us be ever mindful that that history speaks English. But that it does so is accidental. English was made the national language by one vote over German because a cart carrying two delegates to the Continental Congress meeting on the issue broke down. Those two delegates, who were prepared to cast their votes for the German language missed the meeting. These instances of historians' oversights can be explained, of course: Europeans didn't invade, conquer, and "settle" America; Yale and Harvard – with barely perceptible assists from Andover, William and Mary, Dartmouth, and Princeton – did. There is more than a grain of truth in this explanation, but there is another, more intriguing, one: America has amnesia.

The American myth, for some reason, depends on an "empty" continent for its glory, and for its meaningfulness to Americans. The Adam who names the beasts and the birds, who tends God's garden, wasn't to be beat out of his place, dethroned as "Firstborn of God" by Spaniards, Dutchmen, Frenchmen, or, heaven forbid, savages.

> President Jackson asked,
> What good man would prefer a forested country ranged with savages
> To our extensive republic studded with cities
> With all the improvements art can devise or industry execute?

The question that has haunted me for several years now is: What did they see when they saw their images emerge "from the mirrors of the world"? People don't develop amnesia for the love of forgetfulness – or do they? Certainly, there is a passion for memory loss in American thought. Thoreau speaks with indignation of the grip of history on the free growth of the (civilized) soul. "One generation abandons the enterprises of another like stranded vessels." And his construction is not unique to himself nor to Americans. He was aware of the Aztec ceremonial renewal of all possessions every fifty-two years (but probably not of its meaning as renewal). He confused history with bondage, perhaps because the history of Europeans was the history of the bondage of others as well as themselves.

> Then through the underbrush we cut our hopes
> Forest after forest to within
> The inner hush where Mississippi flows

And were in ambush as the very source,
Scalped to the cortex. Yet bought them off
It was an act of love to seek their salvation.

The mind is a curious instrument – that of a culture no less so than that of a person – and its existential messages are more profoundly illuminating than its protestations. This amazing trick of memory-loss is such a case. It might tell us why America is ambivalent at best, schizoid or schizophrenic at worst. For how can one immediately experience the present without regard to the shaping presence of the past? Yet Americans have been, at least in the expressions of their artists and scholars, profoundly present-oriented and idea- or fantasy-centered. Their past has fascinated them, in a made-up form, but the real past is denied as though it is too painful – too opposed to the fantasy, the dream, to be spoken.

Pastor Smiley inquired,
What good man would allow his sins or his neighbors'
To put on human dress and run in the wilds
To leap out on innocent occasions?

Is that what they saw – their ideal of sin personified?

It is fairly clear that the European transplants did not see "Indians." It is possible that they did, as Josephine Miles (whose poem I've been quoting) suggests, see themselves. Certainly, this connection is borne out by the curious scholarly amnesia regarding the tribes who, contrary to popular American opinion, covered this continent as "the waves of a wind-ruffled sea cover its shell-paved floor," to quote Sealth (Seattle). Until recently, American figures have estimated the entire contact population of the tribes to be around 450,000. The numbers now estimated are around ten million, and this figure is rising. Some maverick researchers have put it as high as fifty or sixty million (present in what is now the United States).

I suppose if I saw myself as murdering, one way or another, several million people and hundreds of cultures, I'd long to forget my past, too.

President Jackson asked,
What good man would prefer a forested country ranged with savages
To our extensive republic studded with cities
With all the improvements art can devise or industry execute?

"The only good Indian is dead," they said; now that the Indian is presumed dead, he gets better and better all the time. The "Indian" can be interjected into the American dream, transformed, un-humanized, a sentimentalized sentinel of America's ideal of virtue. Nobody loves a drunk Indian because a drunk Indian is real, alive, and not at all ideal. The "Indian" was one with nature, they say; and who can be more "one with nature" than a corpse?

> Miss Benedict proposed,
> The partial era of enlightenment in which we live.
> Brings Dionysus to the mesa and the cottonwood grove,
> And floats Apollo to the barrows of the civic group
> To ratify entreaties and to harp on hope.

Americans may be the world champion forgetters. Yet their story has a strange logic of its own, and that logic is solidly based on the unconscious motives that propelled the actions and the rhetoric in the first place. And America has cultural amnesia, at least with regard to the Tribes. He, "American Adam," is born innocent, purer than Christ, having neither mother nor (legitimate) father. Yet all that is born on earth has parents: why is it so important that America pretend to be different in this respect, to reject her commonality with all things? The mother, the land, is forgotten and denied, but the father, Europe, is not forgotten so much as attacked, as in a Freudian Oedipal drama, conquered over and over, a recurrent bad dream.

> The question, whether one generation of men has a right to bind another, seems never to have started on this our side of the water. Yet it is a question of such consequence as not only to merit decision, but place, also, among the fundamental principles of government.
>
> —THOMAS JEFFERSON, 1789

The mother: Indian, earth, and Nature (seen as one thing, according to Brandon in *The Last Americans*) were submerged into "the infinite pool of the unconscious," hopefully never to be recovered. Perhaps this is Oedipal also, Frank Waters tells us in *Pumpkin Seed Point*, that the Indian represents the lost unconscious that Americans must reclaim and redeem.

It was an act of love to seek their salvation.

The eternal Mother is forever forbidden to man, the story goes. The gulf between mother and son is enormous and widening. And this is the schizophrenic split: Americans are forever forbidden to love the source of their being and so, their being in itself. Since Mother can't be loved, her falsified image, a grotesque fantasy, must be forever conquered and possessed. However violent the fantasization process, violence is a necessary component of the repression: Indians won't be fantasized and erased; they endure in spite of everything. History persists as well, but the fantasy is out of control, threatened with exposure (and annihilation) by ever-present reality: another recurrent nightmare.

II.

The Americans separated themselves from their paternal heritage, or so they believed. They removed their maternal heritage from sight and embarked on the expediencies of treaty, fraud, murder, mass enslavement, duplicity, starvation, infection – deliberate as well as accidental – whipping, torture, and removal. They needed land, it is said. They were greedy, it is said.

But to my mind, neither need nor greed can explain the genocide. Neither can explain the raging destruction of the earth. Neither can explain the single-minded, horrifying assault on the tribes as tribal entities, long after Indian presence was reduced to nostalgic memory, long after Indians could possibly be a military or economic threat, so long after that even today the assault continues. What obscure drive causes this single-minded pursuit of destruction?

America, the lonely hero, sprung full-blown out of the mind of God. The moral condition. The righteous imperative. Without father or mother, alone, divided, singular, driven to destroy all that speaks of cooperation, sharing, communality. The Puritans' own communes couldn't last a single generation. I am told that "thirty years is a long time for a Utopia to last." (In America, I silently add. Other utopias have lasted millennia. But they weren't based on the idea that a single individual was more than God.) It seems that Americans, loving loneliness best of all freedoms, die from it. Perhaps the central truth of early colonial experience in New England was the enormity of their sense of isolation. Far from all that was familiar, the colonials learned, perforce, to view alienation as rugged individualism, making it their defining virtue. Isolation and self-referencing became "self-reliance," providing the basic theme for American civilization for the ensuing two centuries.

The loneliness of exploration was, and is, a compelling idea for Americans. The lone hero still wanders, determined and self-assured, however lost, across the pages of America. Ronald Reagan in the forties and Robert Redford in the seventies flicker in their autistic heroism across the projected screens of American life. The Great American Cowboy is cheered for his self-reliance; the most hated American is the one who accepts society's help through a welfare allotment. And it isn't a matter of virtue in the Protestant sense that creates this peculiarity: It is not that taking care of oneself is a virtue. It is that the hero is, above all things, lonely and happy in his estrangement from all bonds that bind and cling, depend and shape. Andrew Jackson was idolized for his singular determination to let no considerations of social need or wish, of moral or legal *noblesse oblige*, interfere with his isolated, splendid determination.

In America, law substitutes for custom. In America, society substitutes for love of family, comrade, village, or tribe. *Walden* is the self-proclaimed triumph of the isolated, superior individual. Alone with nature, not in it. Not of it. One can be with it as a scholar is with a book, but as an observer, not a creative participant.

Indians are called primitive and savage not because they commit atrocities; everyone commits atrocities one way or another. Indians are designated primitive because they place the good of the group and the good of the earth before that of the self. Mexicans are denigrated not because they speak with an accent, not because they take siestas, not because they routed American heroes at the Alamo, not because they have what Americans want – a large share of North America – but because they think *sangre* is more important than reason, that *la familia* is more important than fame. The community is the greatest threat to the American Individual Ethic; and it is the community that must be punished and destroyed. Not because Americans take much conscious notice of community, but because community is what a human being must have to be human in any sense, and community is what Americans deny themselves – in the name of progress, in the name of growth. In the name of Freedom. In the name of the Hero.

A person can't cherish glorious loneliness from within a community. So, most women, as keepers of community, are also despised: Remember

"Momism?" We are a constant reminder of the lonely male's need to belong to others so that he can belong to himself. And it was the natural and necessary belonging of the Native American that so infuriated the Americans, so that those men who are America's greatest heroes rose to commit mass murder of the tribes. The difference between Native Americans and Americans, William Brandon says (*The Last of the Americans*), is that belonging is most important to the Indians, while belongings are most important to the Whites. But what are belongings but a badge of isolation, a mountain of clutter that walls one off from those around? Thoreau revealed the most about himself (and his admirers) by saying that he felt that the name Walden was originally "walled in." He was most taken by the idea that Walden (or White) Pond had no apparent source for its water, and no outlet. Entire unto itself. A very moist desert dependent on nothing. Caused by nothing. Surrounded by smooth, regular stones. A wall to keep its pristine clarity, its perfect isolation. Secure.

It is not so strange that everyman-America hates and fears Communism. The very word strikes at the root of the American way and at the heart of the American sickness: a communist is one who must depend on others. A communist is one who must cooperate. A communist is one who must share.

And it is no wonder that the American Scholar is believed to live in an "ivory tower"; that utopians invariably take themselves off to splendid isolation from the contamination of others; that Americans are obsessed with the terror of "infectious disease"; that we are obsessed with "privacy"; that our proudest document is entitled, "The Declaration of Independence."

I have always wondered why Americans never cooperate on anything. Why even a corporation, a company of many persons, is defined as a "legal individual." I begin to see why. Strange that Dionysus is relegated to the "mesa and to the cottonwood grove" and Apollo to "the barrows of the civic group" – neither of which are considered American by rugged-individual Americans. And today, Dionysus is dying of thirst on the mesas and in the dying cottonwood grove, while Apollo is on his way to outer space. They cut off Dionysus's water supply and sent Apollo to the moon. Both are thus beyond the reach of encounter or confrontation. All that is left for America to deal with, to find itself with, are myths and mirrors and shadowy reflections that twist in on themselves and on time and space so that truth, the truth about America's past and America's identity, can never be found, never be affirmed or renewed. And in this way everything becomes relative, nothing related instead of the other way around, the only way we can remain sane.

> Reading today this manual of wisdom,
> In the still coves
> We meet our images
>
> And, in ambush at the very source,
> Would buy them off. It is an act of love
> To seek their salvation.

It is not that Americans are lonely that matters here, but that Americans cherish loneliness disguised as solitude as though it were a wife. They take her to their breasts and cleave to her with the determined clutch of catatonia. They will not let her go. They protect her with all the ferocious murderousness of a jealousy-crazed lover and will kill anything that threatens to tear their loneliness away.

It occurs to me that governments are instituted among men to keep them apart. And so is capitalism. And its fodder, money. And so are "nuclear" families – highly mobile, of course. And so is progress, the touchstone of corporationism, of the nation, and of every American's life. It occurs to me that the "melting pot" never worked because it was not intended to work and that schools and other institutions are designed to teach and reinforce the principle that group experiences are painful, anti-human, demoralizing, like the infants in Orwell's *1984* were taught through pain to fear music and flowers. Loneliness, the beloved of the American Hero, is a coiling clinging snake. It is strangling the life out of the people, the families around us, killed by the murderous creation of our own minds. Yet it is seductive, hypnotic in its murderous intent, because however fiercely loved, solitude is not really possible, in this world after all.

> . . . And when the last Red Man shall have perished and the memory of my tribe shall have become a myth among the White men, these shores will swarm with the invisible dead of my tribe, and when your children's children think themselves alone in the field, the store, the shop, upon the highway, or in the silence of the pathless woods, they will not be alone. In all the earth there is no place dedi-

cated to solitude. At night when the streets of your cities and villages are silent and you think them deserted, they will throng with the returning hosts that once filled them and still love this beautiful land. The White Man will never be alone.

— SEALTH

Why is it essential that the American be self-reliant, communityless – without a place to belong, a past to remember, a beginning in the roots of time, a heritage that would give them a meaningful place in the living circle that is life on this earth? Americans have an overwhelming, consuming need to be different. Do we cling to loneliness because nothing can be so peculiar as this monstrous love affair with isolation?

> *Professor Roy Harvey Pearce quoted,*
> *These savages are outlandish Tartars and Cain's children,*
> *Though someone reported once, "They do not withold assent*
> *From the truth set forth in a credible manner."*
> *Is it possible?*

III.

In 1974, Americans can no longer afford the masochistic love of loneliness. The problems that confront us cannot be solved by a lone hero riding into town, a "law unto himself." No *one* can save us, but we must learn how to save ourselves – all of ourselves. We cannot do it unless we have models of community; America needs to become a tribe.

In our history we have pursued a consistent policy of exterminating Indians; that guilt rests as heavy as would matricide. Along with Indians, America has relentlessly destroyed the Earth and Earth's creatures – Indians, Nature, Earth, all of these are America's mother who must be denied. The lone/lonely hero must be more than god; he must be entire unto himself, "walled-in." But the destruction wrought by individual initiative necessarily haunts us now, because everywhere we look, we see death: past, present, and future. And death is what America has fled for five hundred years.

There is something that can be done; there is a way around the destruction, but it requires giving up America's real love: loneliness. This time, America can't do it herself. She needs models for community; for a rational place for femininity in the community; for ways to integrate diverse lifestyles and ethnic values into the national community; for regaining deteriorating neighborhoods; for ways to handle "deviance" so that the deviant can be allowed to continue as a participant in the community's life, and so that most "deviance" just won't occur. America needs child-rearing models and models for communities that integrate and support families in their economic, interpersonal, and child-rearing tasks. America needs a guide to the overhauling of institutions so that they can foster persons and communities instead of dividing and destroying them. America needs to find ways to preserve identity that do not result in destruction of the community: an individual who has no home, no place, is not a human being, but a prey of every vagrant whim and demagoguery. Humans cannot exist in isolation; they go insane. America needs to learn ways to preserve the individual's sense of identity, and the nation's, in a pluralistic, culturally diverse society. America needs to resolve the "leadership" problems (crisis, say some); to learn how to live in balance and harmony with the living environment; to learn creative, participatory ways of meeting the challenges of survival and technology instead of destructive, apathetic reactions toward them.

America needs a way to understand how society and community can function harmoniously and how a person can fit meaningfully into the massive body of this century's life. Above all, America needs a tradition that is relevant to this continent and the life upon it; America needs a sense of history, a sense of America's place in eternal time, a way to use history as renewal, not as denial. To do this, America must absolve herself of the historic guilt toward her predecessors and heal the split in her soul.

> One party to the purchase
> Receipts the purchase price and hands us back
> His token of negotiation which redeems:
> We Cannibals must help these Christians.

America has a ready way to find those models so desperately needed, assuming America intends to solve them. To do this, though, American scholars and officials have to stop looking at the American Indians as "primitives" or "curios." They will have to give up the concept of Indians as mirrors of idealizations and projections of imagined sinfulness and see us instead as peoples who know how to resolve the problems all of America faces. The tribes today and throughout history provide brilliant and solid models that America could learn from and build on. Instead of treating the tribes as "problems," America should relate to us as a potentially creative force in American life.

Most Native Americans see themselves as necessarily a part of America. Red and White have been through five hundred years of experience together; whether that experience was good or bad, it has been bonding. As for the partners in an American marriage, that bond has been born of pain, fantasy, love, and shared grief as much as of horror and death, punishment and guilt. Native America has lived through every attempt at conquest and annihilation and knows that the human spirit is, in the last analysis, unconquerable. That knowledge alone, given in blood, written all over this continent in agony, can free Americans from their fear of annihilation, if Americans are willing to share the agony and redemption with Native Americans.

For thousands and thousands of years, the tribes faced the problems of community and survival, growth and freedom, and solved them; the only problem they could not solve was America's passion for isolation, that ambivalence, that destructiveness, that "craziness," those policies, and that contempt. Above all, the contempt, for, make no mistake – however benevolent America's patronage has been, it was always patronage; it is still patronage. Indians don't need that patronage, they need respect. They need to work together with greater America to resolve that last dilemma, which, cannot be resolved without cooperation.

It is easy to say *how* America can solve the cruel problems that face us, but it is impossible to say that she *will*. For ever since white men came here, they were torn. On the one hand, they loved freedom, and the Native Americans helped them in that love, supported them, taught them what freedom means. But on the other hand, the immigrants hated freedom, feared it, feared to make the adjustments and sacrifices and immolations of self that freedom requires. They thought that the isolated self was the badge of strength and glory; they didn't see that a free being is free as a member of a universe of member-beings, and they feared that perception as they feared the Devil and death. So in their terror and conflict, they tried to enslave all that was free-thinking, perhaps to compromise between that love and that fear, that attraction toward freedom and that repulsion from what it entails. But they could never enslave the Indians; they had to resort to destruction in the attempt, as they had to destroy their own emblem, Eagle, as they destroyed Buffalo, Wolf, Whale; as they are presently determined to destroy

Coyote and Mountain Lion. And failing in that destruction of Native peoples because they finally couldn't bring themselves to do it, nothing was left but to deny the Tribes' existence, meaning, and way of life.

But suppose they finally succeed; suppose all the free creatures are finally exterminated – dead or changed beyond all recognition; suppose all this Turtle Island is reduced to a wasteland of dead waters and dead plants and dead mountains. Will America have finally succeeded in realizing her dearest dream? For then America will be alone, with only death and terror for comfort and companionship.

We have finally reached that place: the seeds of destruction and the seeds of life have reached their season of harvest. Whether the one or the other is given to the people to eat depends in part on which seed grows hardiest in the soil that is America. It's reaping time; now we see how well we have sown.

3.
All the Good Indians

Yesterday, a student said something that forced me to contemplate a world without Indians. He said that the elder people knew that we were disappearing, and when something is ending, it gets smaller. He said it's like a shutter on a camera, the opening grows smaller as it closes. That is why, he said, so many of us have begun to write: to write everything down so that there will be a record.

The student is the second chief of his tribe, the Narragansett; he has been an active and involved Indian, working for his tribe and his people for well over a decade. He is at Berkeley studying Native American Studies and anthropology, readying himself to research and record everything he can about his own tribe and others accurately in terms of both perspectives.

The class let out after five o'clock. I left the U.C. Berkeley campus walking down Telegraph toward the parking lot. As I walked, I saw people going past me. I saw the shops, the goods on display in the windows. I went by restaurants and coffeehouses. Nowhere did I see an Indian, an item produced by or even reminiscent of Indians, a food or beverage for sale that was identified in my mind, or in the minds of those others around me, as Indian. Coffee is Indian, but not really. Corn, turkey, tomatoes. Pumpkin, chili, tortillas. So many things. But no Indian visible anywhere, not even me.

Less than twenty-four hours later, I still haven't begun to deal with his remark.

But walking along Telegraph, I remembered a time when I had lived in an Indianless world; I was in Oregon, attending the University in Eugene. For the first year or so I never saw or heard of an Indian. I was the only Indian I knew. That was around 1967. Sometime in 1968, a package arrived in the mail from my parents. It was a signed copy of N. Scott Momaday's *House Made of Dawn*. I believe that book saved my life.

How do you touch extinction?

How do you comprehend that the entire world is about to vanish?

Sitting Bull did that. He comprehended the totality of death. He went with Buffalo Bill's Indian circus, like the last exotic striped quagga goes with the zoo. He told the people to see to it that the children got educated in the white man's schools, and he worked to get schools opened so they could. They left the wondrous way of the Sioux. He left it. They became ranchers and farmers, Christians and bureaucrats, soldiers in the conqueror's armies, welfare recipients. Their life expectancy was as little as forty-four years in the sixties. It hasn't increased.

Crazy Horse chose to fight and to die instead. They bayoneted him when he came to the fort to talk. They bayoneted him because they couldn't shoot him. His medicine was such that he was invulnerable to bullets.

They used to dance the ghost dance. They wept. They knew what they had lost, what was gone. They tried to dance it back.

In Oregon, I didn't know the name of the disease I was suffering from. I was seeing a shrink. I didn't know that I was only grieving and lost. I thought I was mentally ill.

In Oregon I was involved. In the civil rights movement; in the peace movement. I taught and spoke and wrote. I struggled. One night at the local campus bar I was in a conversation with some people – two radical black men, a white man (my husband), and a couple of SDS-types. We were talking about why the movement was important. One black man said I couldn't know how significant it was. That I had no reason to care. He said I was a "groupie," a "voyeur." The other one said that wasn't so; I had at least the same difficulties black people had. I faced the same oppression, repression, depression. "She's a woman," he said. "For her it's even worse." Nobody said, "She's an Indian." Not my husband. Not even me.

It is 1982. I live in California. I teach at Berkeley. In Native American Studies. The Indians I see are in my classes (2 Indians out of 40 students) or in the department's offices. Out of some 30,000 students enrolled at "Cal," something like 160 are American Indian.

Out of 200.6 million people (more or less) in the United States, slightly over 1 million are American Indian.

When I think of the figures, I wonder how I could have lived 43 years thinking the world was *not* bereft of Indians.

But, I think, there are millions of us south of here. In Mexico and Central America, in South America. But just a day or so ago I read that the Guatemalan regime recently massacred 2,500 Indians. A few months ago I read that the Sandinistas massacred several hundred or a thousand Indians. A few years ago I read that they hunt Indians in Brazil with airplanes; when they spot them they bomb them, napalm them, throw nets over them, and haul them away to camps where they are raped, beaten to death, starved. Or in the time-honored fashion of the invader, they just throw down some bundles that contain poisoned food, pestilence-infected clothing and blankets. Scratch scores, hundreds, thousands, millions of Indians.

Some say that upwards of 45 million Indians lived in what is now the United States on the eve of contact. Government records put our numbers at 450,000 in the 1970 census. The population of Indians in the United States hasn't doubled in ten years; the count was just more accurate.

Some health workers say that over 25 percent of Indian women and 10 percent of Indian men in the United States have been sterilized without their knowledge or consent. Scratch several hundred thousand future Indians. Many Indians "marry out." Go to the cities and get lost. Over two-thirds of all American Indians live in cities now. Maybe more. They walk down Telegraph, or Central, or Market, or Fifth Avenue. They see themselves nowhere they look. Scratch several hundred thousand more. They say, The only good Indian is a dead Indian. There are millions of good Indians somewhere.

Do you remember the child's song, "One Little, Two Little, Three Little Indians?" The first part counts one, two, three, up to ten. The second part counts backwards: ten, nine, eight little Indians, seven, six, five little Indians, four, three, two, little Indians, one little Indian. It's on my mind right now. I learned it in the forties. I forgot it later. It comes up today.

Lens closing. So light doesn't get through. But the camera leaves a picture for posterity.

I remember the sixties. A time when American hippies discovered Indians, rediscovered Indians. A decade-long Columbus day. In the early seventies a story about that was published in Rosen's *The Man to Send Rain Clouds* anthology. It was written by Simon J. Ortiz. You should read it. It's about an old Pueblo man who goes to San Francisco looking for his granddaughter who has disappeared. He goes to the Indian Center on Valencia Street to see if anyone there has seen her. But there are no Indians there. The building is locked. He is befriended by some hippies. They are practicing to be Indians. They take him back to their pad, hoping he can turn them on to the proper Indian uses of peyote. He doesn't find his granddaughter – they don't know her. A picture, a record, left by an Indian, a Pueblo writer named Ortiz.

And *House Made of Dawn*, another picture. From which the hero, a long-hair Pueblo Indian who can't speak, disappears. The only Indian book I read in the sixties was *House Made of Dawn*. At the time, I didn't realize what the end of it meant. I thought Abel ran into life, into tradition, into strength. It was not until the late seventies, when I saw a film rendition of the book made by a group of Indian filmmakers, that I realized that in the end Abel ran into another world; that he reclaimed himself as a long-hair Pueblo Indian man by running out of this particular world-frame, this particular universe, this reality. In other words, he died. Abel was a good Indian.

When my student spoke, I thought of *House Made of Dawn*, about what it meant. I understood the record Momaday had made. The one about how the Indian vanishes, with a fine, soundless song; the one that got him the Pulitzer Prize.

And I have known for a long time that what an Indian is supposed to be is dead. But I didn't until just that instant, as my student spoke, understand that what Sitting Bull said was not a statement wrung from him by defeat in a years-long war; it was a statement about who and what Indians are in America. More than forgotten, more than oppressed, more than terminated, relocated, removed; the word for it is extinguished. Dead.

The only book by an Indian I read in the sixties was about the reality of indianness. Just as the book I began writing in 1970 and finished last spring is. Which I didn't realize until today.

I can imagine a world without Indians. It is a world that has surrounded me most of my life. I only just now recognized it – a world that will have records – pictures, foods, artifacts, heritages of Indians, all transformed into something unrecognizable to an Indian. But it won't matter, I guess. All of us who cannot live in such a world won't, and all of us will be good.

4.
American Indian Mysticism

I live, but I will not live forever.
Mysterious moon, you only remain,
Powerful sun, you alone remain,
Wonderful earth, you remain forever.

— KIOWA WARRIOR DEATH SONG[1]

American Indian spiritual traditions are as varied as the lands they live on, as varied as the tribes are from one another, and as multitudinous as the spiritual disciplines practiced by various spiritual societies within each tribe. It's not really possible to give a full account of traditions of such variety and multiplicity in a brief paper. And while numerous works have detailed the spiritual traditions of various communities or, more properly, of individuals within these communities, few scholars have written about American Indian spiritual practices within the context of world mystical traditions.

Non-Indians are most familiar with the mysticism of the Plains peoples, which presently tends to center on Sun Dance, Sweats, Pipe-holding, circularity, Peyotism, and a new being usually referred to as "The Great Spirit."[2] There is a seeming homogeneity in writings and teachings of spiritual practitioners among the Plains peoples (including Lakota, Pawnee, Kiowa, Crow, Winnebago, Cheyenne, Comanche, Tonkawa, Otoe, Kickapoo, Sac and Fox, Hunkpapa, Crow Creek, and more). However, the apparent uniformity of mystical tradition among them is more apparent than actual and tends to obscure the rich diversity of spiritual practice among individuals within these groups, as well as from group to group.

Nor do the mystical practices of the Plains people have much in common with those of tribes from other regions of North America. Pueblos have their own ways, and their ways vary from Pueblo to Pueblo. Navajos have their own ways, and while there is a certain congruence in mystical understandings among all members of the Diné (Navajo), there is variation from locale to locale in the Navajo Nation. Other Southwestern groups such as the Yaqui, Papago, Pima, Apache, Mohave, Chemahuevi, and Yuma practice traditions that are each particular to themselves; and again, within each given culture, the traditions practiced further vary among the many subgroups.

The same must be noted for the tribes of the Southeast, the Northeast, the Prairies, California, the Northwest, and the West, with each region encompassing hundreds of groups and subgroups, some large, some tiny, but each devoted to a spiritual way that can differ markedly from that of its racial kin.

Truly, to speak of "American Indian mysticism" in itself creates a seriously false impression. Particularly in matters mystical, there is no "Indian" way. There are many ways that are followed with devotion by contemporary American Indian peoples, ways that reach back into time immemorial, and that remain vital and valid even after centuries of assimilationist policies practiced by the United States and the Christian churches.

While it is necessary to say that tribal mystical practices are as varied as the tribes are, it may still be instructive to make a few generalizations about tribal mysticism as practiced by Native American people over the past several hundred years, keeping in mind that any generalization is only accurate in a limited way.

RESPECTFULNESS FOR THE POWERS

It is reasonably certain that all Native American peoples view the land as holy — as intelligent, mystically powerful, and infused with supernatural vitality. The Native concept of land includes meteorological phenomena such as wind, rain, clouds, thunder, hail, snow, ice; geophysical features such as mountain ranges, rivers, lakes, ponds, waterfalls, seas, canyons, mounds, bluffs, and rock formations; and non-humans such as birds, insects, reptiles, and mammals. The sky, sun, earth, and certain constellations (these vary from group to group) are always included as holy.

Mysticism among American Indian peoples is fundamentally based on a sense of propriety, an active respect for these Natural Powers; on a ritual comprehension of universal orderliness and balance; and on a belief that a person's every action, thought, relationship, and feeling contributes to the greater good of the Universe or its suffering. Human beings are required to live in such a way that balance is maintained and furthered, and disorder (also perceived as disease) is kept within bounds. Through active efforts in every area of private and communal life, one is responsible for maintaining equilibrium – that is, the proper activity of human beings (or "two-leggeds," as some tribal languages phrase it). Other orders of creatures have other tasks. Only if each species occupies itself with the tasks proper to its being, can the Universe function in life-enhancing ways. When any species fails to meet its obligations to the All-That-Is, everyone suffers – human, animal, plant, and non-mortal kingdoms alike.

Pretty Shield, the elderly Crow Medicine Woman (Wise One) Frank Linderman interviewed at length in the 1920s and 1930s, told him many stories about medicine animals. One story, about chickadees, was prompted by Linderman whistling the chickadees' spring song as he entered the kitchen where he and Pretty Shield met. She told Linderman that when she was very small, she had been walking with her grandmother, and they came upon some chickadees. She knew the birds had been stealing fat from the meat drying on racks in the village, and "because they were full, they were all laughing." She threw some dry buffalo chips at them. Her grandmother carried the little girl to a nearby bush where the scattered chickadees had landed. She apologized to the birds, saying the child would never throw anything at them again, and asked them to forgive her because she didn't know any better. Then her grandmother told Pretty Shield a story about how she had lost a good friend because "the woman had turned the chickadees against her."

> My grandmother's name was Seven-Star. . . . She was a Wise-One [a Medicine Woman]. She would have only a black horse; and her medicine was the chickadee.
>
> She and another woman, whose name was Buffalo-That-Walks, had built a fire among some bushes, and both were working on robes that were pegged to the ground, with the fire burning between them. . . .
>
> A chickadee flew into a bush beside Buffalo-That-Walks. "Summer's near, summer's near," he said, over and over, when he hopped about in the bush.
>
> Buffalo-That-Walks was a cross woman. "Be quiet," she said to the little

chickadee. "Don't you believe that I have eyes? I can see that the summer is near as well as you can. Go away. You are bothering me."[3]

The chickadee persisted in his conversation until the woman threw a stick at him. The bird dodged the stick and said to Buffalo-That-Walks:

"Yes, I suppose I do bother you, . . . And now I will bother you a little more. You are going to be wrapped up in that very robe you are making so soft. I came here to tell you this, and you threw a stick at me."

Then the chickadee flew to a bush that was near my grandmother. "Summer's near, summer's near," he said, as though there was nothing else he could think about. [Seven-Stars] picked up her little girl. The chickadee had made her afraid. "I threw no sticks at you," she said, starting toward her lodge with her child in her arms.[4]

Buffalo-That-Walks tried to convince Seven-Stars to stay, saying that she should ignore the chickadee because he'd say anything, but Seven-Stars told her friend not to say such things and went to her own lodge. Later Seven-Stars brought some good fat to the bush where she thought the bird would find it, and he did. According to Pretty Shield, the chickadee

. . . came while yet my grandmother was there. "Don't worry," he told her, picking at the back-fat. "You are not in this trouble. You have nothing to worry about. It's the other one."

Buffalo-That-Walks died that very night, and they wrapped her in that very robe, as the chickadee had said. Grandmother told me that as soon as Buffalo-That-Walks was put away, the village moved, and the dead woman's man did not go with the village. He stayed behind to mourn for his woman.

While he was sitting by the tree that held his woman's body, the chickadee came to him. The man smoked deer-tobacco, offering his pipe to the chickadee. "I am sorry that my woman mistreated you," he said. "I wish you would be my friend, chickadee." The little bird sat on the man's hand, and talked to him. "I am small," he said. "My strength is not great. I only run errands for the big ones, and yet I can help you. In the morning a Person will come to you. Listen to what he has to say. I must go about my own business now."[5]

As the chickadee had promised, the man was visited by a powerful Spirit bird who said he would be the man's Helper because he was sorry for what his woman had done.

The following spring another chickadee came to Seven-Stars and told her to meet her at the creek. After doing a sweat and making herself ready to speak to the chickadee, Seven-Stars met the chickadee, who told Seven-Stars her future and the importance of every creature tending to its own work every day. The chickadee flew higher and higher into the air:

> Straight up it went, growing larger and larger and larger, until it was as large as a war-eagle [mountain, or golden, eagle]. "See," it called down . . . there is great power in little things." And then [Seven-Stars] saw that the bird held a buffalo calf in each of its taloned feet. "I am a woman, as you are. Like you I have to work, and make the best of this life," said the bird. "I am your friend, and yet to help you I must first hurt you. You will have three sons, but will lose two of them. One will live to be a good man. You must never eat eggs, never. Have you listened?" asked the bird, settling down again and growing small.[6]

EVERYTHING, EVERYDAY IS SACRED

Some of the more bowdlerized accounts of American Indian mystical experiences treat them from a Western point of view, giving the impression that these states are uncommon, eerie, superlatively extraordinary, and characterized by abnormal states of unconsciousness. But tribal testaments indicate otherwise: paranormal events are accepted as part of normal experience – even expected under ritual circumstances. It is just that few of these events are recorded by white observers, largely because Western sophisticates are unprepared to accept the events, or the person who recounts them, with equanimity.

Linderman, who recounted Pretty Shield's experiences, found recording the dreams of old Indians bewildering:

> Trying to determine exactly where the dream begins and ends is precisely like looking into a case in a museum of natural history where a group of beautiful birds are mounted against a painted background blended so cunningly into reality that one cannot tell where the natural melts into the artificial.[7]

Because he believed there is a clear division between mind and material "reality," Linderman looked for a clear boundary between the dreams and waking experience. But to tribal traditionals such divisions do not exist, at least not in the sense that they do for Westerners. Nor is there a clear line between sacred and secular for tribal traditionals.

Traditionals live each day in the arms of the sacred, aware that whatever they do will have repercussions far beyond the merely psychological and personal, because everything is sacred or infused with Spirit and Mind. In a very real sense, the dream is what we live every moment. That's why Indians believe we must all do our daily work and make this life as good as we can. Holy People are more intelligently disposed toward those who meet their ordinary obligations with awareness of the extraordinary nature of mortal existence than toward those who choose to be careless and disrespectful in their daily lives, even if they meditate and pray mightily on occasion.

Alice Marriott, the anthropologist who spent much time among Kiowa and Cheyenne women, tells a wonderful story about the fine line between dreaming and reality. An elderly Kiowa woman named Spear Woman, upon hearing from her relatives that there were buffalo at Fort Lawton, said she needed to see them once again. She said that long ago she had failed in her part of a ritual, and she was the one who kept the buffalo from coming back. She had been afraid of them and had "thought them back into the hole in the ground" from which they had originally emerged. She wanted to tell them how sorry she was to keep them shut up down there. Since she was old, she needed to see them right away, saying "soon it will be too late."

Although it was during World War II and gas rationing was an ever-present consideration, her son said they had just enough gas to make the hundred-mile round trip. Spear Woman was not willing to just get in the car and go. She spent four days preparing so everything was just right. "You owe respect to the buffalo. They kept us alive," she told her granddaughter Leah when she didn't want to shampoo the car's upholstery. Finally, everything met Spear Woman's satisfaction. Dressed in her best clothes, her face painted in the old ritual way, she planted herself firmly on the good Pendleton blanket she had placed over the car seat, and gave Leah, who was driving, the signal to go. When they arrived at Fort Lawton it was midday, and the buffalo were resting, staying out of the hot noonday sun. The women had lunch and rested until the shadows were long. Finally Spear Woman told Leah it was time to go see the buffalo.

> There was a little draw ahead of them, across the bluing prairie, and there was something dark moving along it. Spear Woman saw it before Leah did. "There they are. You'd better stop. I'll call them this way."

She stood up in the car and lifted her voice out of her throat, not loud, but clear and high and true. It ran across the grass to stop the herd and turn them, and Leah understood why women always went on the hunts in the old days. It was to draw the herds to them with their voices. No man had a voice that could do that.

The buffalo had changed their course, and were moving jerkily along and up the draw. They were coming nearer, and Spear Woman called to them again. They actually began to hurry then.

Spear Woman stood in the car beside her granddaughter. Tears ran down her face, and her mouth tasted salt, but she was singing; she who had never made a song before found words in her heart and sang them aloud.

> Once we were all free on the prairies together.
> Blue and rose and yellow prairies
> We ran and chased and hunted.
> You were good to us.
> You gave us food and clothes and houses.
> Now we are all old.
> We are tied.
> But our minds are not tied.
> We can remember the old days.
>
> We can say to each other,
> Those times were good.

Something had happened to the buffalo. They were near to the fence, now, but they had stopped. The clear, high call they had obeyed; the song puzzled them. The herd broke apart, shuffling and snorting against the wire, and Spear Woman, dropped from her song, stared at them.

Then she saw. They were yearlings, little more than calves. And she had been singing to them about the old days. The tears were still on her cheeks, but she began to laugh. She laughed and laughed . . . and Leah stared at her, in wonder and fright.

"Of course, you don't understand my singing," Spear Woman said. "Of course, you don't know what it's about when I sing about the old days. You're just calves. You don't remember. You were born inside the fence, like my own grandchildren."

Then she sat down in the car and waited to be driven home.[8]

For tribal peoples, spirituality and mysticism are communitarian realities. The community and every individual within it must ever be mindful of the human obligation to spirit, balance, and the relationship (or kinship) that exists among all beings, so that all might prosper. The sick have an obligation to be well, the weak must become strong, the selfish must become able to share, the narcissistic must learn to put others' interests on a par with their own. All members of a community must live in a good way, ever mindful of the Power and Mystery that fills and surrounds them.

In the old days, most, if not all, of the members of a given tribal society were initiated in at least a few methods for achieving mystical awareness. In every tribal society, girls were trained in the mystical responsibilities that fell to every woman and were at least aware that special mystical states and responsibilities were privy to certain holy women and female ritual leaders. Similarly, every boy learned his spiritual and mystical responsibilities and was aware that certain men experienced special states.

Thus, while mysticism in the West is a kind of special experience familiar to only a few, all Native American peoples feature various disciplines and practices by which mystical power is sought, and to some extent virtually every individual is a seeker or a holy person, and in some sense many are both. Among the disciplines widely practiced – and usually considered central to spiritual seeking – were dreaming, vision-seeking, purification, fasting, praying, making offerings, dancing, singing, making and caring for sacred objects, and living a good and varied life.

THE PATH OF THE MYSTIC

In tribal cultures, ecstatic, mystical states don't so much convert into emotive personal experience as into physical experience or experience with direct effect in the physical (that is, as a consequence of entering an ecstatic state, a practitioner can do something actual). Visionary experiences, in themselves, are either a direct requirement for some ritual activity in which the individual is engaging or are a prelude to a life as a holy person.

In discussing sacred ways of knowledge, Beck and Walters say the following about "ecstatic states":

> In a state of ecstasy or altered consciousness an individual may find that he/she
> may lose the ability to think or speak in an ordinary way. Other means of per-

ception and communication take over then. . . . For example, individuals who have experienced once or many times this kind of altered consciousness find that they can, without previous experience, compose songs, see into the future, foretell events, see into a body or into an illness, and even fly.[9]

Thus, a practitioner might enter ecstatic states to locate game for the hunt, call game to the hunter, excise a disease-bearing object from a patient's body, "teleport" a lost saddle or rifle from wherever it was to the room where people have gathered for the recovering-lost-articles session, empower an object or create a talisman or amulet, create a rainstorm, or cause a wide variety of effects in the material world. In short, a tribal mystic is a person who is conversant with certain mysteries and can bring about certain effects in reality as a result.

These Native American mystics who have been categorized as shamans, singers, priests, wise ones, conjurers, or holy persons (the variety of names reflects not only local parlance but also points to distinctions among different sacred methodologies) are in consciousness and competence analogous to saints, yogis, masters, shamans, prophets, and swamis in Eastern and Middle Eastern traditions. The ability of these tribal mystics to manipulate extraordinary energies and forces, to travel to distant places (in or out of body) by means other than physical, to see and know the supernatural as well as the natural world in its multitudinous interactions are similar in effect to those attributed to sacred practitioners in the Old World.

What these mystics do cannot really be described as simply psychic, because they are manipulating laws of the universe understood to be sacred, powerful, beyond the ordinary realm of people who may otherwise be able to exercise paranormal abilities. Nor can these practitioners be compared to mediums or "channels" as presently characterized in the United States. These tribal adepts operate at a level of mystic competence and experience far beyond that of most tribal persons who are already inclined, as a group, to the mystical by genetic and cultural heritage. We're talking mega-spirituality here!

The Powers these adepts draw from reside in what I call "Mythic Space." Entering this space, which at its center or heart is "the creation," takes a certain kind of training as well as an inborn temperament. Growing up in a tribal environment is only the beginning; of course, having a secure mystical social foundation certainly makes the next stages easier to master. Practitioners learn to enter this "space" more and more deeply, to inhabit it, and to bring from it, to their work, whatever energies are needed for the good of the people.

For tribal cultures, knowledge and power are always connected, as Essie Parrish, the Pomo Dreamer, notes:

> The Creator has placed everything in a great storehouse – everything that has happened or will happen to mankind is there. All knowledge is placed there. This knowledge is let go or given to the people through the shaman in different ways, at different times and in different places. When the Creator sees there is a need for knowledge-power, the Creator provides this to the shaman for [her] people.[10]

What sort of event might cause a person to walk the path of power? The compulsion to start along the arduous sacred path can come in many forms: happenstance, a vision in which one is commanded by a Spirit Guide, affinity for such pursuits evidenced from early childhood, tradition, or heredity. To my mind, several traditional mystic pathways – seduction, stumbling into power, Spirit Seizure, and abduction – seem particularly illuminating because they stand in such stark contrast to American Christian spiritual practice. In many ways they seem to directly conflict with Christianity and Christian mysticism.

SEDUCTION AS A PATH TO POWER

Seduction is the term I use to refer to practices of *seeking* Power, and, in a nutshell, seduction is the preferred mode of seeking Power among Native Americans. Seekers use a multiplicity of seductive ploys to attract the attention of a Holy Person, as lovers might employ a variety of ploys to attract the attention of the beloved. While in Sufism, the seductive nature of the quest clearly involves passionate, unending desire (witness the plethora of tales about Majnun and Laylee), the tribal mode is more frequently represented as hunting, feeding and clothing, gift giving, and pleading, which are believed to eventually compel a response from a Power (should one be so inclined).

A seeker courts Power in the same way a hunter courts his prey. With infinite care, timely stalking, and complete disregard for personal comfort, the slow, steady quest progresses. Numerous gifts, such as pollen and turquoise, are laid in footprints of the prey; smokes and prayers are offered to coax the Power into communication with the seeker-hunter. If the seeker-hunter is lucky, she or he will eventually cajole and flatter the Power into agreement and secure her or his aim.

Mountain Wolf Woman describes one variant of this mode – the importance of being good to old people because, as she says, "The thinking powers of old people are strong and if one of them thinks good things for you, whatever he wishes for you, you will obtain that good fortune. That is what they [the traditionals, the older ones] always said."[11] She says this not only because she believes it, but also because she's courting a certain old man she respectfully calls her grandfather. Although he was actually her brother-in-law, she properly refers to him as grandfather because she sought and got sacred information from him, which implies a respectful relationship. That he think strongly of good things for her was important because he had knowledge she wanted. To get it, she had to work for it.

> I used to give things to this old man. He wore buckskin moccasins, he always wore Indian shoes. He did not like hard-soled shoes, so I used to make buckskin moccasins for him. He appreciated whatever I did for him. If I ever went to a town and there was a secondhand store, I always looked at the pants, big pants, and if a pair seemed the right size, and a shirt, I bought them. I would give them to him. "Grandfather," I used to say to him, "I brought these things for you."
>
> "Oh, granddaughter," he used to say, "you are doing a great kindness."
>
> Quite often I did things of that sort for him. I often fed him. If he were coming by on the road when it was close to mealtime, I would call to him, "Grandfather, come and eat."
>
> "Oh, good!" he would say. He would come and eat there and he would be so grateful.
>
> Sometimes if there was a coat that seemed the right size, one of those nice overcoats, if I could afford things of that sort I would buy them and give him such things.[12]

Eventually, she buys him a small stove and installs it in his "tarpaper wigwam." He is very grateful and asks her what she wants, noting that she has given him food and clothing and has treated him very well, doing many kindnesses for him. She has earned the recompense the old man has known all along she was after. He finally acknowledges that she has made sufficient payment and has shown enough determination, sensitivity, awareness, and competence to indicate that he owes her and that she will not take the Power lightly or misuse it foolishly or selfishly.

She tells him, indirectly, as is proper in the Indian way, that she likes the Indian medicines and has a need for them as well as knowledge of how they are truly useful for healing ailments. He tells her that she has asked for something valuable, that he is getting old and that, because probably no one in his family wants his knowledge, he is willing to pass it on to her. Much information, face-saving, and implication is conveyed in his, as well as her, phrasing. He continues:

> . . . A long time ago when you were a little girl this was meant to occur. Way back then you were working for it [the information and the power to use it]. When mother used to give medicines to the white people, you used to help her by being her interpreter. Since that time these medicines were going to be yours. You have been working for them since long ago. You have been working for this. Today it has come about.
>
> It is good. You will prescribe Indian medicines. I used to do this; now you will do it. The power will all be yours. You are not yet holy, but these medicines are holy. . . . These medicines are going to talk to you. If someone sets his mind on you, that is, he is going to buy medicines from you, you will know it before they come to you. And when they come to you, say to them, "You will be cured." If you put your mind to it intensely, that is where you will have your power. . . . You are going to be a medicine woman. You are going to cure sickness. This redounds to your honor, my granddaughter.[13]

SPIRIT SEIZURE AND STUMBLING INTO POWER

While those who want Power often engage in a variety of active endeavors to court the Power's attention, such activity is no guarantee of success. If the Power is uninterested, the Power does not come. Among the Lakota, *hanblecheya* ("crying for a vision") is a tradition practiced at least once upon a time by most, if not all. However, not all were granted seemingly miraculous power. The capriciousness of their situation reminds me of Stephen Crane's poem, "A Man Said to the Universe": the fact that one exists doesn't obligate the universe in any way.

While it is true that all human beings have obligations to the right working of the Universe, the Universe is in no way compelled to respond in ways humans might find felicitous, nor to respond at all. (Of course, in tribal terms, Universe is an inaccuracy – the universes, the Powers, the Multiplicities would be more accurate expressions in English.)

In some traditions, accidentally stumbling upon a group of practitioners engaged in certain mystical ritual activities means the hapless individual has been "drafted" into that sacred society. He or she will be required to learn the ways of the society and, depending upon the society, to participate in its public and private activities. Usually membership in societies such as these is secret (or as secret as anything can be in the tightly interconnected communities that characterize Native America), and the obligation to participate is mandatory.

According to the ancients, there are no accidents on the sacred path, so what appears to be happenstance (in ordinary terms) is considered to be "ordained" in mystical terms. The accidental, unwilled nature of being chosen heavily implies that an individual cannot decide to pursue a spiritual practice; that no amount of seeking, studying, praying, working, trying, begging, bargaining, or paying will get an unchosen chosen.

In fact, the spiritually powerful are chosen more often than they do the choosing – and once chosen, these individuals cannot refuse their duty without suffering severe penalty to self, loved ones, and even the entire group. There are many stories about how persons become involved in the Mythic Life of their people – pointing out the many ways one can stumble onto a mystic path from which there is no return.

A person might find her/himself walking the good road by means of a personal tragedy that catapults the individual into non-ordinary realms and gains the attention of the Spirits. Or the person might suffer from a life-threatening illness, enter a coma, be abandoned in the wilderness, be abducted by a Holy Person, or simply be commanded by a Voice "from nowhere," as it were – all examples of what might be called Spirit Seizure. The great vision stories of Sweet Medicine, Handsome Lake, Black Elk, Quanah Parker, and Wawoka all attest to the quirky nature of spiritual blessing upon hapless mortals.

Sweet Medicine, a long-ago person, killed a member of his band, and although it is said that the killing was accidental, he was banished in accordance with the laws of the Cheyenne People. One who was banished could not go to a neighboring tribe for shelter, because only perpetrators of serious crimes were banished, and others would not want such a one living among them. So Sweet Medicine, left helpless and alone in the wilderness, went to the Wichita Mountains to live out the remainder of his life. There he was taken in by Supernaturals, who instructed him in their ways. After four years of transformation, he was given the laws of a new Religion (Life Way) to take back to his people and told to instruct them in how to live in a good way.

Returning to the people, he was welcomed into the Sacred Lodge (a place of amnesty for anyone requesting it – even one who had been banished), where he told the council of his experiences and his charge. He was authorized to teach the people and lived among them for several generations – until the Teachings were firmly established. Before his death he prophesied the coming of the Whites. He warned his people that, if they lost their way and fell into bad habits foisted upon them by the newcomers, they would be extinguished as a people.

Handsome Lake was in his adulthood at the close of the American Revolution. Because the Americans falsely believed the Iroquois had been allied with the British, the Seneca were reduced to penury under the "Law of Conquest." Many Seneca succumbed to grief and severe deprivation brought on when Americans sacked their villages, salted their fields, and ran them off into the forests. Also, the white traders brought "fire water" for the purpose of reducing the natives to comatose drunkenness, so they could not defend themselves from merchantly predators, government agents, land speculators, and other scoundrels. Many Indians became alcoholic – Handsome Lake was one of these.

During one bout of drinking, Handsome Lake lay exposed in the snow for a long time and nearly lost his life, but he had a vision similar in detail and clarity to that of Sweet Medicine long before. His vision featured a Holy Person, a "blue" man, according to Handsome Lake, who prescribed new ways the people were to live under conquest. Like Sweet Medicine, he brought Sacred Laws – the Code of Handsome Lake, or Gaiwaio, as it is known to the Six Fires of the Iroquois Confederacy – to the people at the command of Holy People who had taken responsibility for their survival in the transition from the old ways to the new.

Like Handsome Lake, Nicholas Black Elk is a post-contact medicine person. His story (or, at least, pertinent parts of it) has been rendered in John G. Neidhart's account *Black Elk Speaks*. As a small boy, Black Elk suddenly fell into a comatose state for several days. During this time he was taken, in an "out-of-the-body state," to a supernatural realm where he witnessed several events. He saw these events in the Lakota way, and their significance became apparent as his life unfolded. Among other things, he saw the defeat of his people at the hands of Whites, saw the "hoop of the nation" broken. He also saw it mended and whole, operating in concert with many hoops. The vision is thought to apply to the term of his life and years beyond his lifetime. While Black Elk lamented, before Neidhart, that he had failed in his given task to bring about the mending of the hoop, many believe he did not fail. His lament was a proper one, because *heyahas* (like many Native Americans) never pray from a boastful place but from one of humility instead, where they make it clear to the Powers that they, the shamans or medicine people, are less than nothing – poor, pitiable, inadequate, without ego or accomplishment before the Holy People. It is a convention, that prayerful stance, and it's one found among mystics the world over.

As a consequence of his great vision, Black Elk possessed shamanic powers of various sorts, including Elk power, which made him virtually irresistible to women. He also had spiritual responsibilities to discharge during his life. The Plains Wars, ending with the Massacre of Black Kettle's band at Wounded Knee in 1892, broke the hearts and the backs of the People. Yet as the Supernaturals had shown Black Elk, neither their great vision nor their spirit were broken. Over the century since then they have made each of the painful descents and ascents the Holy People showed him. Some wonder if these next few years will bring about the final scene of his vision, the scene where the Nations' hoops are whole again, and the People once again live in vigor and peace.

ABDUCTION AS A PATH TO POWER

Abduction is a variation of Spirit Seizure confined to women in most traditions.[13] For reasons often left obscure, the woman is usually unmarried, an outcast, or in some sense left unprotected. The Navajo mythic account of the abductions of Snake Woman and Bear Woman, which gives rise to the major Chantway systems of Diné (the Navajo people), is a classic example of how abduction can provide the path for a woman to become a Sacred practitioner. (While this story may be about mythic Supernaturals or their charged representatives, both human and non-human, it demonstrates again the idea that the supernatural world lives next to the human, and that certain agents are empowered to move freely into the one to bring its energies to play in the other.)

During a battle two enemy warriors raid a village and abduct two maidens. Taking them to the cliffs, they lead them deep into ancient ruins, where they spend the night having intercourse with their captives. In the morning when the young women awake, they see only bones, and among them those of a bear and a snake (who come to life as Bear Man and Snake Man). Dismayed by their discovery, the young women are compelled to leave the ruins by the magical creatures, called Snake Man or Bear Man. Later they separate, Bear Man taking his captive one way, Snake Man another. Each takes his captive to his mother, where the young women are subjected to numerous tests, most of which they fail (the teaching method of the Supernaturals). Eventually, the time comes when each woman is considered to have achieved competence by her teacher, the mother of her Supernatural captor. She is then sent back to her people to give them the Chantway she has earned the right to sing and bestow. Beauty Way is the Chantway that Snake Woman transmitted, and Night Way is the Chantway Bear Woman gave.

After each woman transmits this knowledge and its attendant Power to the appropriate people, she returns to the mountains as a Holy Person. Her continued existence in the Knowledge and Power of her abductors is actually the source of the power that enables the Chantways to heal the ill.

As may be seen from these accounts, when persons engage in concourse with other realms – "countries" or "worlds," as some tribal practitioners call the various universes – they generally receive instruction composed of tests (and accompanying failures) or experiences that are seldom explained in ways Westerners would find intellectually satisfying. They are given strict rules to obey, either on certain occasions or for the rest of their life, and are usually given specific tasks to carry out among their people on return to mundane existence.

THE RESPONSIBILITY OF POWER

Among tribal people spiritual practitioners can enjoy many benefits, ranging from the people's respect (as demonstrated in their providing for the practitioner's material needs) to their fear and awe. However, it also entails certain sacrifices and numerous responsibilities that can be burdensome and even devastating. Having a Power to guide your life generally requires living differently from others in your community, and, for people who place great value in community, this demand can make life difficult if not painful. Essie Parrish comments that the Dreaming kept her awake at night. Certain foods, activities, and relationships are often eschewed for limited periods or for entire lifetimes. These restrictions are dictated by tradition, or by the Spirit People themselves, and are determined by the nature of a person's "Power" and requirements of the deity or spirit she or he serves. Pretty Shield and Mountain Wolf Woman, wise women of different tribes, both comment on certain foods they had to forego and other constraints required by their Power. However, as all practitioners attest, failure to follow prohibitions set down by the guiding Power will inevitably result in consequences suffered not only by the practitioner but also by those close to her or him – even by the entire community.

Those who are called – even those seized by Supernaturals – have choices, dictated by temperament and circumstance as much as by "free will." The actions each person takes, the decisions of the Spirits to whom they're accountable, and the exigencies of history and tradition may draw practitioners further and further along the Path of Power and Beauty, or may dump them back into "normal" life at any point. They may keep whatever Power was mastered during the sojourn into other lands, or may lose much of what was gained. The overriding factor seems to be how their practice melds into the overall gestalt (*kopishtaya*) of the hemisphere as seen from the point of view of the "folks in the next room" – the Powers of the planet and solar system.

CONCLUSION

In all the rich tapestry of native spiritual practice there lies a bewildering variety of spiritual paths that can be traveled by Native people throughout the Americas. Yet, the land, our mother, and all her children – the immortals, the non-human Persons, and all other species (animal, plant, mineral) who are also her children and our elder siblings – are primary and forever. Known as Turtle Grandmother to some, Grandmother Spider and her sacred sisters to others, Earth and her sisters, galaxy and her multitudes – it is for her we live, and by her will we make, do, pray, and seek. In recognition of this fundamental Truth, the old Kiowa sang his Death to the Powers. It is a good song, one we are fortunate to have been given. In return, we must live each day, each event, each turn of fate and happenstance, loved or disliked, comforting or painful, funny or aggravating, and everything in between, with whatever balance and immediacy we are capable of. It is our obligation to do so – and our primal right. In this way, we can also sing in the face of our own transition from here to here, "Wonderful earth, you remain forever."

5.
Haggles

"Haggle: a persuasive speaking that a hag engages in. Nagging (see Mary Daly, *Gyn/Ecology* and *Pure Lust,* for more on these terms)." In the 1980s Paula Gunn Allen delivered haggles (the definition is hers) as part of a weekly series of "gynosophic gatherings" in Oakland, California. The gatherings, held on Sunday mornings at Mama Bear's coffeehouse, were, according to Gunn Allen, a "woman's worship service celebrating the bond of womanness among ourselves and in connection with our sisters on every continent, island, sea, and in the sky."

WHERE IS ONE CIRCLE . . . ?

Last night Judy and I were talking to some people about this gynosophic gathering in terms of a "kirk," which is a church that is a "circle," interestingly enough. Anyway, we were saying that I was the "pasture" and my daughter said, "Yes, she's outstanding in her field."

It took me four hours to figure out what the joke was! Well, here I am out standing in my field and it's time for another haggle.

I want to talk about balance, complexity, murder, and things like that. The song we just sang said, "Watch our circle grow." If I were writing that song today, I would change it to "Watch our circles grow." I wanted to do an experiment today, but I don't think I will. Instead I'll just talk and you'll have to do the experiment; I want you to see with your body as well as with your eyes what this room looks like right now. *Feel* the other women in the room. All those little moonshapes everywhere . . .

Now we could do what has become a feminist thing to do, and that is to form a big circle around the room. My sense of a big circle around the room is that we have all lost each other when we do that. What happens is that I'll be too far away from most of the people, and each of us will be too far away from most of the people. But the way we are presently seated, around a number of tables, we have little clusters of folks who can chat with each other and as a consequence have a sense of each other as we go into the service. So what we have is a network of interlocking communities here, which is, of course, how life works. Because that is the kind of circle that life is. That's the sacred hoop that the Lakota talk about. It's the dynamic sphere of being, in which everything is held. But everything works in little circles like that, round and round and round . . . so there's not just one circle but many.

Those of you who have been coming every Sunday probably recognize that I am on my favorite schtick, or my favorite broomstick, as the case may be. And off I'm going, and, look, there is no such thing as *one*. I can't find a "one," and I've been trying for weeks and weeks, in fact, for years and years. I wrote a poem about this several years ago, and since I wrote it I keep thinking about it. Where is there a one? A one anything? One sun, no, there are millions of suns. One planet? No, there are lots of planets. One rain drop? No, there are lots of rain drops. I can't think of a single "one" anything.

Another thing I just noticed is that we just sang "*The* Rose." Think about that. There's *the* roses and *the* roses grow on *the* rose bush. English is a very funny language, at least as we speak it today. It gives us the impression that isolation is the normal thing, and that connection is abnormal. When we want to feel connected, we begin to exert great amounts of energy. All the energy we are exerting because we don't want to be alone *is* all about being alone, you understand. All the energy we are exerting is saying I don't want to be alone, exert energy, I don't want to be alone. And the message we are conveying is: This is all about being alone. Alone is really important. But if we were to relax and notice ourselves, not to mention this room around us, we would know that *alone* is an absurdity. We don't have to work to be connected. You do have to work at being alone. It's very hard to imagine that you are alone when all of reality around you is continually telling you, over and over, that the last thing you are is alone. You are always *with*, always *with* . . .

I had occasion to see a documentary film and write a response to it or a dialogue with it or whatever. The film was called *Wilderness Journal*. It was to be shown on PBS and then to be used in classroom work in ecology classes. The film finally came, and I went to the viewing room to see it. It was all about how precious wilderness is and how we must protect our wilderness. There were a number of interesting points in the film, but one that was immediately visible was that the only people of color in the film were some Indians. And we all know, of course, uh, that Indians *are* wilderness. Well, it had occurred to the filmmaker (who's a very good man, I'm sure, I don't mean to make fun of him) to have, among the seven or eight men, a Shoshone and a man who had a Hispanic last name and a mild, very mild (mild to my ear, which is sensitive because I was raised in New Mexico) Chicano accent.

But all of these men had the wherewithal to go to the wilderness. They were all middle-class people who thought of the mountain as some kind of park. And what the discussion was about was what kind of park this should be. Some said, "Well, it should be a park where I get to be the guide and take an occasional person with me when it's comfortable to do so, to see the park, and I shouldn't let them use toilet paper because it pollutes the wilderness. . . . " O. K. Some said, "Well, we should use it intelligently, save some, use some; some people should live on it, there should be water interests, logging interests, mining interests." Some people said, "No, no, we can't have that because wilderness is where a man goes to find his connection with the universe." Over and over they said, "It's the only place where a man can be alone."

Now that says something, and it says a number of very odd things. First, it says that being alone is some kind of a privilege; it says that only a certain very privileged few should be allowed to have this privilege. And it says that interest, public interest, should protect those few people's right to be alone. When you examine it, it begins to make a lot of sense because *alone* is not a natural state; you have to go to a great effort to get aloneness. And, in the world we live in, aloneness requires great resources. A great deal of money is what it requires.

On the other hand, the Indians of that particular tribe had recently realized that human encroachment on the wilderness areas within their reservation boundaries was really destructive to the animal balance in the area. So they went back to their ancient tribal way, and they had to name it a tribal law, violation of which would incur penalties. The old way was that, once in a person's life as a small one, a child, he or she would go out into the wilderness and spend a few days. While there, that child would receive a spirit friend and animal friend that would then be with them the rest of their lives. That journey was the only time that the person would ever encroach upon the space of those beings who actually don't like cities and farms and mines and rivers and dams and all those kinds of things.

What the Indians are saying is that they are recognizing the right of wilderness to be wilderness. Wilderness is not an extension of human need or of human justification. It is itself and it is inviolate, itself. This does not mean that, therefore, we become separated from it, because we don't. We stay connected if, *once* in our lives, we learn exactly what that connection is between our heart, our womb, our mind, and wilderness. And when each of us has her wilderness within her, we can be together in a balanced kind of way. The forever, we have that within us. Forever is when we have our guide so we also have our wilderness. But when we leave the wilderness, we leave it to be what it is. That's one thing.

Another thing is that it's the nature of wilderness not to be presbyterian. I use "presbyterian" as a metaphor for organization or over-control. The tendency is to think that somehow everything, or at least everything that I do, has to be perfect. And perfect doesn't mean moving with exhilaration, joy, and the sense of just being together. Instead, it means that anybody who judged what I am doing could not criticize my work. It also means that by trying to be perfect and presbyterian, I am singling myself out in a particular way. You remember the poem read last week of Adrienne Rich's about the musing over the artful thing that is of the woman's making, knowing all the sources of things, where the feathers and the beads and the shells and the cloth all come from. This artful musing is opposed to the "I am going to paint a picture and I am going to have my picture in the blah blah gallery and they are going to recognize my great talent." Which takes a lot of effort and a lot of money. It's a very hard thing to do. But it's a very easy thing to do to make a bit of loveliness that's a musing between yourself and your world. There's a real difference here between what's hard and what's easy.

Where I come from, I was raised with a number of Protestants of the Presbyterian variety, as well as atheists and other sorts of Christians, including Catholics, and Jews. And what I noticed about the Presbyterians was everything always had to be perfect. It had to be not only clean, but every corner had to be dug out. You not only waxed the floor, but you left not one streak, not one place where there was a little more wax than another place, because that's not perfect! You had to do it perfectly. What that does is it creates an enormous sense of isolation. And to emphasize that sense of isolation, you have picket fences around the house. Now picket fences aren't merely joy sticks stuck in the ground to keep the dogs off the lawn or to give the lawn a sense of orderliness. You know what a picket fence is – it's a very tightly organized, carefully calibrated line of little soldiers there, deftly placed around the house. And what you have to do with the picket fence is to keep it painted. And if it begins to crack and the paint begins to peel, you have to go out and sand and paint it. That's what you have to do with everything. So, of course, you, well, I don't know about you, but *I* am overburdened because I can never, never, never catch up, no matter how hard I try.

What I noticed the other day when I had twenty things to do and I was standing watching the laundry do its thing in the washer and trying to sweep the water off the floor because the plumbing leaks and I was thinking about this mountain of things I had to do to be perfect was that this is an entirely out of balance way to think. For one thing, I was imagining that I had to do it all by myself. And for another, I was imagining that *it had to be done*. And I was, of course, assuming that it could never happen, that I'm a failure and I might as well go to bed. That conclusion is rather nice.

Now, I could have started in the beginning and said, "Heck with it, I'm going to bed!" But I realized the amount of resources it takes to be a good presbyterian; it takes a lot of people in your household who are your slaves or servants and who do exactly as you say. And it takes the money to feed and clothe them. Or, alternatively, it takes a great deal of money to buy a bunch of appliances and hire service people to come in on a contract basis to do it for you. Or, perhaps if you had a large family of adolescents who were so totally brutalized that they never whined, complained, or disobeyed, you might be able to use that as an alternative to arrange this kind of thing. Now there is a kind of balance in that and it's this kind of balance: on this side you put in ten pounds of lentils and on the other side you put ten pounds of lead weights. By golly, you *know* you got ten pounds of lentils because the scale isn't tipping to either side.

And that's the kind of balance, the idea of balance, that most of us have in our heads. When we think of balance, we think everything has to be equal. We don't even think everything has to be equal; we really say everything has to be identical to the standard of measurement we are applying, in this case, ten pounds of lead weights, and nothing must ever move. If nothing ever moves, everything dies. And that is the interesting thing about extreme orderliness in the law and order sense of the word. What happens in fact in a system that demands absolute order is that you get an enormous amount of unnecessary death, a tremendous amount. So people are dying all the time, animals are dying all the time, and they are not dying in the natural course of change and transformation; they're dying in the very abnormal course of attempting to hold everything still so I won't have to wax the bloomin' floor again! That's what that kind of balance leads to: it leads to intense efforts to control everything because I'm too tired to wax the floor again. Absolute order means absolute death.

Chaos, on the other hand, means the enormous vibration of energies; so, the more wilderness, the more something is just dancing in such a way that it doesn't have a pattern that we can perceive. That's one kind of balance. The other kind is absolute death. Where our sacred hoop goes is somewhere within all of these. Order, of a balanced sort, of a sacred hoop sort, of a feminist sort, I hope, and of a Native American sort, I know, is the kind of order that expects complexity, that expects all of the particles to be whatever they are at the moment: some birthing, some dying, coming into physical manifestation, going into another kind of manifestation in the natural course of things, in the natural course of seasons and cycles. In that order, the order of the Grandmother Gods, whatever something is at a given moment in relationship to everything else makes it what it is.

The Oglala medicine man Lame Deer puts it this way. "If it weren't for that beetle there," he says, pointing to the beetle on the ground, "I would not exist." And what he means is that all orders of existence depend for their meaning on the context and identity of everything else. That's why there is no such thing as *the* rose. There is no such thing as *a* circle, and there mustn't be. Because if we attempt to make there be, we will cause the unnecessary death of ourselves and other beings.

What we must understand is that balance means equilibration of a huge number of diverse particles/wavicles of energy, stuff, folks of all the orders of the beastly kingdoms, all the orders of the non-physical kingdoms. The interplay of all of these enables us to be, and if that interplay is messed with, is halted, is organized, we die. And everything around us dies.

So maybe next time we sing that song, we will "watch our circles grow. . . . "

SOME UNDERLYING VALUES: AUTONOMY AND VULNERABILITY

In the western world, after several thousand years of underground community (a community that often seemed to be composed of only two women or even only one), and after nearly a century of a larger community, lesbians have developed a stunning array of customs, opinions, moral values, and beliefs about how the world of women in general, and the world of lesbians in particular, should conduct itself.

These prescriptions for behavior are expressed in terms that refer to political awareness of the community or to personal love relationships, as in: Don't be racist, don't be sexist, don't be classist, don't be sizist, don't be speciesist, don't be . . . what did I forget? . . . ageist. For heaven's sake, don't be ageist; because if you are, it's you you're calling names. That one gets real personal real quick. Or in love relationships: Don't steal another woman's girlfriend.

And while these rules, or rules of this sort, are explicit, they are not particularly embedded in a value matrix and so aren't easily understood or easily followed except in mechanical and often punitive, guilt-producing, blame-laden ways. White man ways. Today I want to meditate with you on some underlying values that I think must be the fundamental basis upon which a feminist, a lesbian ethic, must be based.

The Gynosophic Gathering is, as you know, devoted to the black aspect of the triple goddess Wisdom, Sophia. I went to a conference at U.C.L.A. on the dark Madonna. One of the things that one of the speakers mentioned was that the black aspect of the goddess in ancient times – in Europe, in Mesopotamia, in the Middle East, and so forth – was wisdom, wisdom itself, which is precisely what this poem you've heard gets to. Wisdom arises from experience consciously blended with knowledge, choice, and understanding. It seems to me that knowledge, understanding, and choices depend on two characteristics: autonomy and honesty. Autonomy and honesty depend on vulnerability, on fragility.

Truth, acceptance of the truth, is a shattering experience. It shatters the binding shroud of culture trance. It rips apart smugness, arrogance, superiority, and self-importance. It requires acknowledgment of responsibility for the nature and quality of each of our own lives, our own inner lives as well as the life of the world. Truth, inwardly accepted, humbling truth, makes one vulnerable. You can't be right, self-righteous, and truthful at the same time. You can't recognize the fragility of others, when you are being true, without accepting that their fragilities are your own.

An ethic based on this kind of truth is compassionate and strong. It is supportive of autonomy and of a sense of self based on affirmation of reality rather than on fantasy, because it recognizes the power of vulnerability, the power of fragility, and the danger of denial. Consciousness, which is the midwife of wisdom, the helper of Sophia, requires vulnerability. The invulnerable, the controlling, the tyrannical, the brutal are as far from consciousness as being can be. Consciousness begins in vulnerability. It grows through autonomy and its blossoms are truth, its fruit is wisdom. Externalized knowledge, projected morality, blaming, and guilting lead away from Sophia because they lead away from truth, from understanding, and from self-generated choice.

And what is vulnerability? Just this: the ability to be wrong, to be foolish, to be weak and silly, to be an idiot. It is the ability to accept one's unworthiness, to accept one's vanity for what it is. It's the ability to be whatever and whoever you are – recognizing that you, like the world, like the earth, are fragile, and that in your fragility lies all possibility of growth and of death, and that the two are one and the same.

Are you ashamed of eating? Are you ashamed of being afraid? Are you ashamed of being open to hurt or loss? Are you ashamed of being alive? Are you ashamed of rotting? Do you have to be perfect – slim and youthful and handsome and popular? Supermom. Superdyke. Superwoman. Probably you can be those things for a time, but not for long. On the other hand, if you intend to walk in the shadow of the Great Mother, you can recognize and come to terms with your inability to be god, enjoy the fragility – the fragility that alone will take you home.

6.
Father God and Rape Culture

In their letter to potential contributors to a Milkweed publication, the co-editors of *Transforming Rape Culture* comment that they "have concluded that our culture is a rape culture not only because its woman-hating aspects are conducive to violence against women but also because – as became evident in the trials of William Kennedy Smith and Mike Tyson – for many people rape is indistinguishable from consensual sexual relations."[1] I would go further and say that for many people the oppression and abuse of women is indistinguishable from fundamental Western concepts of social order. The ubiquitous concept of evolution, deriving as it does from the "civilized" belief that the strong must prevail over the weak, the superior over the inferior, the violent over the peaceful, and the order of patriarchy over all, leads inexorably to rape, "ethnic cleansing," the devastation of all who are not members of the elite ruling class that is always male, and to fascism in its subtle and glaring forms. The only way to transform rape culture is to dismember patriarchal civilization in all of its myriad forms and expressions.

It seems to me that the underpinnings of sexual dominance are simply a particular case of the systemic belief that dominance is synonymous with superiority and that superiority is a reflection of the divine. These beliefs underlie the entire apparatus of Western civilization since its infancy; I can see no easy way to avoid rape and other forms of violence against those excluded from the inner sanctums of power other than by dismantling the entire philosophical and social order that requires them as a human body requires breath.

An hour or so ago I spent some time with three English women who are actively engaged in New Age spirituality. One is a psychic healer, one a beginning Reiki practitioner, and the third teaches religious studies some-where in England. They each firmly believe that spiritual power comes from on high, that there is a single source of it, that the source is good, and that any person can "channel" that power (not a word that came up in the conversation, but the idea it represents did) to effect healing or other benefits to people in need . . . sort of a spiritual trickle-down theory, it seems.

I am not questioning the efficacy of psychic or spiritual healing, but rather the concept upon which each of these women was erecting a spiritual theory, a theory that formed the basis of her life, her thoughts, and her understanding of herself as a spiritual being. They were unalterably convinced that true power comes from above; one kept gesturing toward the ceiling when referring to the source of spiritual power. They held that the origin of that power (the ceiling, as near as I could see), testified to its essential benevolence. In other words, they firmly believed that since the source of spiritual power came from on top, it was good. They were greatly taken aback at my suggestion that perhaps it didn't come from "above," that maybe it wasn't benevolent, and that there was no place known as "on high" for any sort of power to come from. They understood me to be implying that intervention in another's distress is bad. I eventually left, feeling distressed myself and somehow wrong, as though I had caused offense and pain to women who were sincerely engaged in beneficial work.

But the issue of the origin of power is central to the question of how a rape culture can become one where violation of bodily and psychic integrity is unthinkable – not forbidden, mind you, but literally never considered. For as long as we live in a social system that defines right on the basis of group or personal above-ness, or superiority, rape must continue, as must the depredations connected with racism, destruction to the biosphere, elitism, homo- and lesbophobia, child abuse, and all the subtle and gross manifestations of trickle-down conceptualizations of the nature of the good, the real, and the wholesome.

In order to understand the nature of the difficulty facing those of us who would transform Rape culture into Nuturing culture, it is necessary to recognize the development of systematic concepts of superiority in Western political and spiritual history. In their eye-opening history of Christianity, *The Messianic Legacy*, Michael Baigent, Richard Leigh, and Henry Lincoln offer a sufficiently accurate and succinct synopsis of superiority's political etiology:

The Messiah whom Jesus's contemporaries awaited was a variant of a familiar and long established principle. He was the specifically Judaic equivalent of the sacred priest-king. The principle underlying this figure obtained throughout the ancient world – not only in the classical cultures of the Mediterranean and the Middle East, but among the Celtic and Teutonic tribes of Europe. . . . Among other things, kingship functioned as a kind of conduit through which man was linked to his does [sic – God?]. And the social hierarchy culminating in the king was intended to mirror, on the terrestrial plane, the immutable order, coherence, and stability to which the heavens seemed to bear witness.

. . . The priest king was invested with a divine status of his own, becoming a god in his own right. Thus, for example, Egyptian pharaohs were deified, regarded as avatars of Osiris, Amon, and/or Ra. In a somewhat similar fashion, Roman emperors promoted themselves to godhood, claiming lineal descent not only from demigods such as Herakles, but from none other than Zeus himself. In Judaism, of course, the prevailing monotheism of the first century A.D. precluded any deification of the Messiah. Nevertheless, he was more than just royal. He was also sacred.

The principle of sacred kingship continues well into later Western history. . . . it . . . lies behind such developments as the medieval conviction that a monarch could heal by the laying on of hands. . . .

From the Merovingians [fifth to mid-eighth centuries, c.s.] to the Hapsburgs, European dynasties regarded themselves, and were regarded by their subjects, as enjoying a unique mandate from "on high." . . . Strictly speaking, the king was nothing more than a servant, a vessel, a vehicle, through which the Divine Will manifested itself.[2] There is inherent in the concept of civilization a profound belief in superiority, in status. Deeply embedded in Western thinking is the conviction that order, harmony, goodness, propriety, and peace all stem from a hierarchical arrangement; monotheism, while not essential to this concept, certainly takes full advantage of it. And while Western "democracies" make much of the right of the people to self-government, as in the concept of elected officials as "public servants," the underlying belief is reflected in every institutional and informal social convention. Within the Western paradigm, power, authority, and social order descend upon the pubic from a higher authority, and that authority is always patriarchal, whether wielded by women (rarely) or men.

In most Western nations, that authority rests in officials putatively elected by citizens. But the candidates are in effect appointed by power-ful families and interests that are patriarchal structures: masculinist and status/superiority-oriented. They are inevitably devoted to the proposition that they are the higher minds who therefore know best how to organize economic, spiritual, and social affairs so as to gain the greatest benefit from them. In turn, they believe, the lesser beings who serve them can enjoy the benefits of social order – whatever those benefits might supposedly be.

All Western nations, following the example of Rome, and before Rome of Alexander's Greece and Xerxes' Persia, are organized bureaucratically and hierarchically. They are all structured upon the trickle-down model, as are the state religions and other institutions that uphold authority's strong-hold. Regulations are initiated at the top, then segmented and dispersed throughout the system; they are implemented and enforced by those hold-ing ever-decreasing increments of scope, information, and authority. Power increases as one goes up the "chain of command" (rises toward the ceiling), approaching its maximum at the level of prime minister, president, pope, secretary-general, or CEO. Yet the true power is held not by elected officials but by tiny networks of private interests that have formed those govern-ments and allied institutions to provide for their defense, promote their welfare, and secure the blessings of a free ride to themselves and their pos-terity. Given the structure of the system in which Western human behavior occurs, both the outward and, more importantly, the internalized, psycho-logical one, how is it possible to move off rape to consensual sex, off con-quest to negotiation, off abuse and victimization to nurturing and empow-ering others for their own sake? How can a citizenry that can tell the difference between rape and consensuality be established and politically empowered? How can such a citizenry even be identified?

DEMYSTIFYING PATRIARCHAL AUTHORITARIANISM
The question of difference must be addressed in any discussion of rape culture. The matter of difference, coupled with superiority-based values, affects not only women but all those who are pictured as inferior in a social system that, under patriarchy, divides the world into two basic classes, neither of which applies exclusively to gender. There are the mas-ters and their underlings. That's it. The master class is small, closed, and patri-think dominated, while the latter includes everyone else on the planet;

no, more – it includes the planet herself. It probably includes the entire universe, or rather the entire polyverse.

Constantine, founder of the system in which we presently live, was said to have made Christianity the official religion of the Roman Empire; in fact, he did no such thing. A devout follower of Mithras, the Sun, and an initiate of the secret society of Sol Invictus, Constantine merely borrowed the Jewish belief in monotheism, added it to his Sun religion, and promulgated it as the "new" religion of Rome. Jesus was not the divinity Constantine chose to elevate above himself, God the Father was. This patriarchal god, it can be argued, was the god of Abraham, made comprehensible throughout the non-Jewish world as the Sun Triumphant, Mithras as sole God.

Until the reign of Constantine, polytheism of a sort was common in all parts of the Old World except Israel, though with widespread hierarchical organization of authority beyond the human into the Big Gods Jupiter (or Zeus), Apollo, Dionysus, and the like, and little gods, amongst whom, of course, figured female deities as wives and/or daughters of the "higher" powers. The subjection of the feminine to the masculine had proceeded apace in the pagan world and was particularly noticeable in Babylonia,[3] Persia (remember Ahura Mazda and his prophet, Zoroaster), Sparta, and finally Rome.

Needless to say, the subjugation of the feminine had been firmly established in Israel, where it thrives as thoroughly today as in other circum Mediterranean countries.

The cult of Sol Invictus was Syrian in origin, introduced into Rome about a hundred years prior to Constantine's reign, and was essentially monotheistic. It borrowed its authority and much of its practice from the old Goddess religion, powerful in the entire Mediterranean area during the preceding three millennia, which it then quashed. Baigent, et al., have this to say about the religion of the Sun Victorious:

> In effect, it posited the sun god as the sum of all attributes of all other gods, and thus peacefully subsumed its potential rivals with no need to eradicate them. . . .
>
> [Constantine's] primary, indeed obsessive, objective was unity – unity in politics, in religion, and in territory. A state religion that included all others obviously conduced to this objective. And it was under the aegis, so to speak, of the Sol Invictus cult [sic] that Christianity proceeded to prosper.

In choosing a god for his sponsor or patron, Constantine turned – on a nominal level, at least – to the God of the Christians. He did *not*, it is important to note, turn to Jesus. The god Constantine acknowledged was God *the Father* – who, in those days prior to the Council of Nicea [*sic*], was not identical with the Son.[4]

Further clarifying the origins of patriarchal civilization in Western nations, Baigent, et al., cite Alistair Kee's telling comment: "The religion of Constantine takes us back to the context of the Old Testament. It is as if the religion of Abraham . . . is at last fulfilled not in Jesus but in Constantine."[5]

At the time of Constantine's masterful maneuver, Eusebius, Bishop of Caesarea and esteemed Doctor of the Roman church, had this to say in praise of the emperor: "He grows strong in his model of monarchic rule, which the ruler of All has given to the race of man alone of those on earth."[6]

Let us note here that the bishop uses the word "man" – or its Greek equivalent – advisedly: he does not mean to include women in his statement. It's true the translation would be clearer if it read, "white man of privilege; aristocracy" so that modern audiences could read his statement as he meant it, for only aristocratic males were, in those times and those nations, thought to be human. This becomes evident in another passage from his treatise: "Monarchy excels all other kinds of constitution and government. For rather do anarchy and civil war result from the alternative, a polyarchy based on equality. For which reason there is One god, not two or three or even more . . ."[7] making it extremely clear that monotheism is a political move upon which the conquest of all nations is premised. The writers of *The Messianic Legacy* do not record whether Eusebius or Kee make note that monarchy under a father god and an Emperor excel other kinds of government, but it is clear that at the time Eusebius wrote, the shift in power from the Feminine – coded as "anarchy, civil war" – and "polyarchy based on equality" was the outcome the Fathers of Western civilization (and its allied forms throughout Asia) desired. One must also note that while the Bishop of Caesarea does not approve of civil war, he has little difficulty with wars of conquest, to which his support for the Constantinian empire attests. It is significant that both multiplicity ("polyarchy") and egalitarianism are excoriated; empire cannot flourish where these hallmarks of gynarchy hold sway.

The woman problem, as Western thinkers are wont to characterize our very existence, is allied to other "problems" patriarchy faces in its quest to secure fatherly dominance; in the United States, the Indian Problem and the Race Relations Problem simmer alongside the Drug Problem and the Crime Problem, awaiting solution. They mix rather neatly in with another herd of problems having to do with the economy, the political system, the collapsing environment and its heretofore necessary resources, the banking industry, the market, the welfare system, the health system, the educational system, and many more. Dear me, what's a poor empire to do? A veritable polyarchy of problems beset it, and it possesses only one point of view with which to address them. After all, there's only one daddy, and so many of us problems for him to endure and rectify! The solution, it seems, is as clear today as in Eusebius's day: Unity. Oneness. If we can all be made to be, think, and act alike, the problems will disappear – and us along with them.

Constantine's work, the task he took unto himself and made actual, bears bitter fruit in our time. All over the modern world the cry for unity gains momentum: it rises from the Right and from the Left. It informs the Green and the New Age. It shapes the Market and the multiplex of European and Arab polities, as it takes over vast regions in eastern Asia and continues to stalk those nations only recently freed from its thrall. It gains momentum as it is seen as the solution to not only civil war but to planetary devastation. We are admonished at every turn – particularly by citizens of the "Aquarian conspiracy" – to recognize that "we are all one people."

In mid-August 1992, there is another of those World Days scheduled. Posters and flyers abound in Glastonbury, a town I have dubbed Berkeley East, and all the capitals, all the centers of counterculturality, make ready for a telethon via satellite, a device that makes the planet, as McLuhan sagely observed decades ago, one village. But maybe female one-worlders have less reason to celebrate this global unification and shrinking than they suppose. We must not fall into the patriarchal trap set for us millennia ago. Maybe many of us are so enmeshed in patriarchal culture that the bars have become invisible, but make no mistake: countercultural people are among the wealthiest, best educated, and most powerful class of people the planet has yet produced, and wealth and privilege are invariably self-perpetuating and unalterably self-protective.

I am an American Indian. I know that the One World called for in the "new Paradigm" of counterculture thinkers is hardly, if at all, different from the One World that figures so prominently in the Bush-Reagan-Thatcher vision. I doubt that it differs much from the one sketched by the Nazi Party, or by any other fundamentalist, centralizing political movement; they are all variants of the message promulgated and enforced by cruel and vicious policies of genocide, gynocide, and multiple forms of terror to which the Roman Empire-cum-Roman Catholic Church (both the Empire, and neither yet ended) has long devoted most of its wealth and organization for the past two millennia. The Roman Church has long depicted itself as "One, Holy, Catholic, and Apostolic," and only the last of those fails to refer to the monolithic, monopolistic, monarchical monotheism upon which the patriarchy bases its power.

SEXUAL DIFFERENCES AND POLYARCHAL AMBIGUITIES

Recently, an exciting slender volume came into my possession via Angela Miles of the University of Toronto: *Sexual Difference, a Theory of Social-Symbolic Practice*, edited by Patricia Cicogna and Teresa de Lauretis and originally titled *non credere di avere dei diritti: la generazione della liberta femminile nell'idea e nelle vicende di un gruppo di donne* in its 1987 and 1990 Italian versions. The Italian title, while unwieldy for an English-language readership, is livelier, lovelier, and much more revealing than its mind-numbing p.c. English counterpart: "Don't believe you have rights: the question of women's liberation is the idea and the practice of a women's group."[8] *Sexual Difference* details historical actions and conversations that took place in the feminist community in Milan and around Italy in the eighties; Miles summarizes it in her letter to me.

It develops an argument that feminism's concern with women's autonomy, and not just protection, must be based on the recognition of women's difference from men. Part of building our ability to do this, they argue, involves learning to comprehend the "idea of a female source of social authority" and developing "a genealogy of women who were legitimized by referring to their female origin." Since "in the social order thought up by men, there are no forms of symbolic bond between a woman and the woman greater than herself, who is her mother," women need to work with the notion of the "symbolic" or "autonomous mother," which "indicates the symbolic authority which female speech acquires when it is free from the need to be accepted and from the fear of being rejected."[9]

Essentially, the women of the Milan Women's Bookstore Collective hit on the principle that has guided American Indian, native Hawai'ian, and other indigenous de-colonization movements: the principle of self-determination, which, along with the equally important allied principle of sovereignty, gives us focus and clarity of purpose. These principles imply that we as a particular community (Laguna Pueblo, Cherokee, Pine Ridge, Kashia Pomo, Hawai'ian, Surinamese, Melanesian, Kurdish, whatever) decide how we will govern ourselves, what our laws are, who holds power and wields influence. It is the certain guide to the content, structure, and significance of all our institutions, including those impinging on our spiritual, sexual, and familial lives; how our citizenry is composed; who lives where, does what, is related to whom, marries, divorces, and has sex with whom; whether descent of children is matrilineal, patrilineal, through clan or band membership; who buys, sells, or exchanges what, and with whom; what constitutes the nature, content, aims, and standards of the education of the young; and what actions constitute criminal offenses, and what penalties will be exacted for them. In short, the community itself will in all matters make all decisions pertaining to itself, its lands, and its progeny.

Sexual Difference chronicles the history of feminist action and theory in Italy in the eighties, focusing on a number of struggles and issues such as abortion rights, rape, and the theoretical basis of Italian feminism. The issues are presented as entwined within one another, and while that entwinement creates a variety of painful snarls, its interlocking nature also clarifies the fundamental issue women everywhere must face: the fact of difference. There is no way around it, as the record makes clear: women and men are fundamentally, essentially, and eternally not the same.

The theory that the book presents is founded squarely on the fact of difference and looks to the actual experience of women for its basis. Of course, this discovery is not unique to feminists of northern Italy, though it may be more critical to their situation than to others. The depth of mistreatment suffered by Italian women is far and away more profound than that experienced by women in the United States, who have benefited mightily from the gift of high status for females that characterized Native nations at contact. This status was bequeathed to the dispossessors. Unlike in the States, in modern Italy women seldom eat out unless accompanied by men; women who are unmarried are most likely to be firmly under the control of a tyrannical father; and a married woman's life and breath are her husband's to control.

In Italy, the heavy hand of Father God (a.k.a. Father Church) is every-where in evidence, and that power, more social than ecclesiastical, more political by far than spiritual, shapes every smallest thought and gesture of Italian civilization. To my American Indian eyes, Mussolini's brand of fas-cism differed from that of his predecessors and heirs only in manner of dress: the politically "religious" fathers of Italy wore and wear dresses, while the contemporary secular ones do not. For women, government by prelate, dictator, nobility, or elected official is ever the same: men go wher-ever, however, and whenever they please, women don't. Because men are extended the privilege of status, they rule "as gods" over the women in their households, if not in their province and notion.

In *Sexual Difference*, the discussion of what the writers term "The de-bate over the law on rape" is compelling. A subsection in Chapter Two chronicles a free-wheeling debate over reproductive rights that took place at the *Umanitaria* Conference in Milan. Included are recommendations for legal changes, the law's inherent inequality with respect to women, and, most telling, the revealing question raised by a female participant: "I'm in-terested in understanding why man's law should continually be revived again and again among us, now in the specific sense of legislation."[10]

Her pointed comment was provoked by a proposed bill that would pro-hibit sexual violence, which had been laid before the Supreme Court by its feminist authors. They had failed to first consult the wider community of women because "The authors of the bill took for granted that other women would back it."[11] As it turned out, the larger community was not so easily deflected from the position that insisted on the fact of difference, in this instance, the differing needs, concerns, and situations among women, and also the glaring reality that male institutions and processes are hardly likely to serve women. Many who participated in the debate believed that to single out a particular facet of women's oppression, be it rape or repro-ductive rights, was to deny the across-the-board oppression every woman suffers.

> The proposed law, in fact, singled out only one part of women's overall experi-ence of hardship and suffering; it focused on that part only, to the detriment of other suffering, including abortion, which continued to be shrouded in indiffer-ence and silence. Now it was rape's turn to symbolize a human condition and cast a shadow of forgetfulness, almost of denial, on all the rest of women's suffering.

But what was most unacceptable was that some women, in the name of all, offered that specific suffering up to the state for its intervention and protection.[12]

The general thrust of the discussion was largely that, in our attempt to free ourselves of our internalized sense of inferiority, many of us turn to those we see as possessing our self-esteem in hopes that they will bestow it upon us, if not in fact, then by association with their superior social and political position, a kind of "status by association" that marks a mind-set created by acculturation in a dominant-submissive social system. This tendency is a disguised form of the "wife" syndrome, translated to the political, economic, and social arenas. Those suffering from an analogous phenomenon in Indian Country are termed "apples," a sobriquet for those who hope to recover their sense of self-worth by finding acceptance among whites through the adoption of white standards, mores, and beliefs.

The women at the *Umanitaria* Conference were discovering the apple-syndrome among their ranks, and eloquently resisting it. One articulate participant remarked, "Do we really want to switch from the marginality of our official quasi-nonexistence to being citizens equal to men? Or do we want to use this marginality as a starting point for changing our condition and all of society with it?"[13]

Her question is of particular moment. Is it possible, at any level, to seek our sense of self as women and as individuals, as culture-bearing adults, and as beings shaped by the historical circumstances we did not create but with which we must contend, within structures that have for centuries deemed us inferior, branded us evil, degraded us beyond all recognition, named us not-human, not possessed of wit, intelligence, reason, love, or soul? And were it possible, is it desirable? Must we endure also the humiliation of persuading our tormentors to grant us our humanity?

SCAPEGOATS OF EMPIRE AND THE EMPIRICAL VOICE

Of all the versions of the Arthurian story available to [Malory] in the fifteenth century he seems to be drawn in particular to those from the pens of Cistercian monks whose writing betrays how much they fear women.

In Malory most women are supernaturally malignant or false to their husbands. They bring about the downfall of good knights.[14]

The speaker is Morgan le Fay, protagonist of Fay Sampson's historical novel *Herself*. In it, Morgan's story is examined in its many versions, from Geoffrey of Monmouth to Marian Zimmer Bradley. As Sampson's Morgan observes, it is the thoroughgoing misogynist Thomas Malory's treatment that has taken the greatest hold on the minds and hearts of the general reading public. We should note that Malory's treatment is considered by academics to be the major source, and its use by literary and popular chroniclers, in both film and print, alerts us that a major cultural myth is thereby presented; that myth is the categorical and utter threat and evil of woman. For not only does Morgan le Fay represent evil in a particular (supernatural) form, but Morgause, Nimue, and the ill-starred Guinivere, each in her own way, faithfully symbolizes some projection of male loathing of and gynocidal impulse toward women onto the very objects of his murderous rage. Morgan continues:

> But I am the queen of evil.
>
> Who is this man who has branded his image of me so searingly on the imagination of the twentieth century?
>
> It is charged that on the fourth of January, 1450, Sir Thomas Malory . . . lay in ambush . . . for the purpose of murdering the Duke of Buckingham.
>
> That on the 25th of May of the same year he broke into the house of Hugh Smyth at Monks Kirby and raped his wife Joan.
>
> That ten weeks later he raped her again.
>
> That the following year he engaged in sweeping cattle raids and twice extorted money by threats. . . .
>
> He seems to spend the rest of his life in and out of prison. It is as a prisoner that he ends his story of Arthur with expressions of piety and hopes for release. . . .
>
> This is the man who writes the epic account of the deeds of gallant knights in shining armor. He has influenced all our imaginings.
>
> A would-be murderer. A rapist.
>
> Should you trust what he tells you about women?[15]

There is a fundamental danger in turning for help to those who hold us in contempt. There is a fundamental delusion in believing that those who profit from our subjugation and suffering will willingly end it. The fact is that neither women, Native Americans, or the Feminine have any place in the social order of the patriarchal West other than as objects, robotic as they might be, who will serve the father's interests, cater to his whims, endure his caprices with smiling amiability, and accept his rages, blows, and outrages with the sort of stoic, warm, loving equanimity he attributes to those women he has designated "saints."

As women, as Native people, we must recognize that we are now and forever outside the patriarchal social contract; we are perceived as superfluous to the workings of Civilization, civilization being a code-word for patriarchy. One man recently said, "The reason we need women is because sheep can't type." The judge in a recent court case in England opined, "Women's purpose is to serve men." I heard a raggedy black preacher on the street in Ann Arbor, Michigan, recently confide to a woman seeker, "Women can be important helpmeets for men, you see." It is in view of all this that women must take careful note of the Milan collective's pronouncement that

> . . . for a woman, the freedom earned in relating among women is her freedom, and . . . the social contract by which she freely binds herself to her fellow [*sic*] women binds her to the whole world as well. A woman . . . is responsible for the world inasmuch as she must answer for herself to other women. She has no social obligations which are not derived from the obligations to other women.[16]

If we replace the term "women" with "Native peoples," we can see the underlying rationale for self-determination movements and the source of their strength and persistence in the face of all but overwhelming societal, political, militaristic, legalistic, and economic odds.

ON THE ROAD TO THE FEMININE(S)

I write "feminine(s)" so that no one will mistake my meaning. The new paradigm must be understood as multiplicitous. The way out of the Master's House of monstrosity, monopoly, monotony, and all his other mono's – unities, onenesses that amount, in the end, to facism, to dictatorship, to tyranny, and to geno- and gynocide – is by way of a passionate, thoroughgoing, and, yes, uncompromising commitment to multiplicity, to the concept of difference. Autonomy cannot be a concept reserved for autocrats; it cannot be a right conferred only upon those who carry some goodguy's (or good-gal's) seal of approval. To have any meaning, it must be firmly grounded in those principles that the Bishop of Caesarea and all his heirs find so odious: polyarchy and equality. And it must be firmly based upon a secure, articulate, formal sense of the Feminine.

As a daughter of what the anthropologist Bronislaw Malinowski termed "the last existing Mother-right culture," Laguna Pueblo, I see the feminine as both my birthright and the best source of information upon which to base a creative response to history's contempt for women. In a similar vein, the Milan Women's Bookstore Collective writes:

> It is not the severity of their oppression that explains the failure of female free-dom, but the lack of authority, of symbolic authorization – that authorization which a woman can receive only from a female source because it is the only one which legitimates her in her difference. And which she receives only if she agrees to submit to a female measure of judgment.[17]

As it happens, modern Italian women, like their sisters over all too much of the planet, have no vital tradition to look to for sources of validation. Because of this, *Sexual Difference* argues that women must create female sources for that validation. To this end, they argue that the true source of female liberation must derive from:

a. gratitude to the largest, most powerful female in a woman's life, her mother;

b. willingness to see herself as part of a female commonality – in other words, to recognize that she is female, not androgynous, neuter, or "the same as a man"; and

c. recognize that her femininity requires she look to other women for evaluation, judgment, and approval, for only by virtue of these three can a woman experience the sense of social bonding and public validation upon which to build a solid sense of self-esteem.

In other words, they argue that "Sisterhood is Powerful" and is, indeed, the only source of a woman's strength when coupled with a profound acceptance of her daughterhood.

Laying aside the cavil that we in the feminist community in the United States have devoted some time and much paper to these ideas, it should be said that readily accessible, widespread social models for female validation presently exist and can be creatively adapted by modern non-Native women across the world.

At Laguna Pueblo, gods really are female. I should say that the major deities are female, because the traditional Laguna people aren't monotheistic or exclusivist in any way. The system was traditionally female-centered, as reflected in its matrilineal, matrilocal, and matrifocal structures (if such ungainly Westernized concepts can be said to reflect Laguna systems with any accuracy). Women enjoyed (and to an extent greater than their sisters in the larger community surrounding the Pueblo) positions of respect and authority in a variety of venues, being largely responsible for the economic, political, social, and spiritual functioning of the community as a whole.

In such a system, women receive validation for their gender, rather than in spite of it; their difference is perceived to be of great value at every level of the polity. It is from the Feminine that male power of all sorts derives, and the values upon which that civilization are founded are basically those of the feminine. They include multiplicity, nurturing, respect for all that lives, harmony, peacefulness, kinship, integrity, honor, and profound engagement with the world of the supernaturals. In our language, male leaders bear the title "mother," and membership in clan and family derives from the maternal line, as does property, right to acreage for planting or grazing, right to membership in various spiritual societies, and status in the greater community (which comes more from what you give than from what you amass). Until recent times, when Anglo law and custom had made deep inroads into Laguna life, violence, rape, theft, and abuse or abandonment of children or the aged were unheard of. Of course, Lagunas are modern people now, living on the interstate that connects the East with the Coast.

Among other things, the Laguna example demonstrates that violence of any kind is not a male trait dictated by either hormones or natural law; nor is this example exceptional. Most, if not all, Native communities exhibited little tendency toward the abuse of living things before encountering the Western patriarchal system; their communities did not single out women or children for special protection or subject them to violation because of their perceived "otherness." They didn't have to; as the rights of all beings to live free from threat of terror was a value commonly held and widely upheld until quite late in their existence (around the ninth or tenth century as centuries are counted in the West – and AFTER the arrival of visitors from Asia, Europe, and Africa, who washed up on our shores long before a perverse current threw the Nina, the Pinta, and the Santa Maria there). As a consequence of this deep value, classes of persons, human and otherwise, did not require special protective status.

Nor did they find themselves trapped in the civil war and chaos Eusebius believed would necessarily result from lack of either monarchy or monotheism. If their civilizations suffered for their feminine bias, it was only in a gentleness that protected and nurtured, shared and accepted, and valued multiplicity for its own sake, all too readily. The conquest of the Americas could not have taken place had Native peoples been more aggressive, more conflict-centered, more totalitarian, and as deeply contemptuous of the sanctity of individual freedom, of life, and of honor as their conquerors were.

Much of that system, founded in the Feminine, is no longer operative; rape is a major crime in many Native communities; child abuse is rampant; while, for all too many, the concept of honor seems to have gone the way of the Buffalo. There remains, however, a hardy presence of older, stronger values. While Native men can be maddeningly egocentric and phallocentric, and while all too many tribal governments are deaf to women's appeals for community-based action on matters pertaining to our safety and that of elder and younger members of the community, there persists among many traditional people a deeply felt respect for all that lives, coupled with a strong assumption (that goes much deeper than mere belief) that women are a central aspect of community. The fact that many heads of state in Native communities – rural and urban – are women attests to this fact of Native consciousness.

Not surprisingly, Native men who are most likely to share in patriarchal cultural norms (apple = red on the outside) are also the most likely to be active and admired in the Anglo-European world, particularly in counterculture circles. Equally unsurprising, the attitude patriarchal people hold toward all women is very similar to their attitude toward traditional Native men; their demeanor is seen as passive, feminine, and unaggressive, and as such is deemed unacceptable. One university hiring committee recently expressed grave doubts about the tenurability of a Native applicant because his students had found him unacceptable on just those grounds.

In the polity I am describing, authorization for femininity is part and parcel of the social contract; female approval and judgment is the standard of acceptance, not only for girls and women, but for boys and men as well.

But how do we, citizens of a world gone mad under patriarchal dominance, create (or re-create) a society based on the Feminine? Where most writers still refer to humanity as Man and Mankind, where there are no graceful substitutes for male pronouns, even in works largely devoted to women's experiences, what hope is there for a world in which the feminine is the basic principle upon which our lives are structured? Where violence is the norm and pacifism is seen as cause for contempt and brutality, a rape-free society might be all too utopian. At this time, we are sorely pressed to persuade most citizens to refrain from beating, neglecting, abandoning, and emotionally torturing children; we are unable to convince the majority of adults that violence against children cannot be for anyone's good, ever.

Perhaps the basic approach provided by twelve-step programs is a place to start. They convincingly demonstrate that entering into a power-struggle with an abuser is a lost cause; it is, in fact, a way of ensuring that abuse of all kinds, from emotional battery to totalitarian systems that routinely engage in mass-murder and mass terrorism, remain intact, able to slide into emotional and conceptual realms that defy language. Collusion, "enmeshment," or engagement in the abuser's paradigm has only one possible outcome: more of the same. The alcoholic doesn't quit drinking because his habit is a source of conflict, nor does the struggle over the substance improve the circumstances of the drinker's spouse, children, employers, or other near-and-dear ones. Spousal abuse ends when (and if) the abused ends the relationship and moves away. Too bad the Native nations couldn't do just that!

The solution that twelve-step programs begin to offer is the information that the abused or "co-dependent" (that is, someone who is as dependent on abuse and harassment as the abuser is) must focus on herself. She must make her needs, perceptions, values, obligations, safety, and sense of self central to her actions and concerns. By this model, we see that empowerment for women rests not in trying to change patriarchy, but rather in perceiving its superfluity to our existence. The model that the Milan Women's Bookstore Collective suggests is similar in many respects to twelve-step programs and to the Laguna Pueblo's traditional mode, and it is a viable one: if we are willing to make our membership in our common womanity the centerpiece of our lives, if we are willing to face the judgment not only of other women but of Femininity's multiplicitous dimensions; if we take women as our models and female deities as our gods; if we are willing to make the principles of the ineffable Feminine our modus vivendi and our femininity our blazing signature while taking on the causes that are of urgent concern to women worldwide; if we will accept multiplicity, diversity, difference, and celebrate them, we won't need to change patriarchy. Patriarchy is not the issue, after all. Our commitment and devotion to our feminine selves, in its collectivity and varied particularity across class, cultural, historical, and political lines is.

In a midwestern Native community we find an example that can be applied to the problem of rape. Having failed to persuade the governing body to enact and enforce regulations combatting violence against women, a number of older women banded together. When abuse of a woman occurred, the "aunties" confronted the abuser, chastized him, shamed him by making him aware that his mother, grandmothers, aunts, nieces, and daughters knew about and condemned the abuse. In other words, the women of the community took total responsibility for ending the crime that they recognized was directed against them all. They held men to the standard set by women, and by making community life woman-centered, their safety and that of the entire community was ensured. I hear that violence against women doesn't occur there anymore.

7.
The Anima of the Sacred
Empowering Women's Spirituality

I.

What is a spirituality of the feminine? Is there a separate or special spirituality for women, or is it sufficient to keep the old patriarchal religions intact and add feminine nouns and pronouns to theory and theology? Phrased thus analytically, the query eradicates much of the heated emotionality to which the fact of women's spiritual movements gives rise. And heated the discussion is. Many protest the very notion of feminine spirituality, excitedly arguing that women's spirituality excludes males or causes division and conflict where none should exist. There seems to be a feeling that women's spirituality is a subset of men's, just because humanity is generally still referred to as "Mankind," or "Man." The die-hard belief is that any concept of the sacred Feminine belies the essence of true spirituality, which, as everyone knows, is essentially monotheistic, hierarchical, and masculinist (though "androgyny" is the word most often used to camouflage the Western masculinist assumptions that underlie modern concepts of alternative spiritualities).

Under this supposedly alternative paradigm, what constitutes the spiritual is summed up on the button, available at most New Age shops, that reads "All One People," meaning all people share the same value system, attitudes, perceptions, lifestyles, and standards of living, whether they in fact do so or not. Largely because so many assumptions upon which New Age spirituality is based remain unexamined and unanalyzed for their hidden content, many people involved in New Age spirituality find the concept of gendered spirituality thoroughly frightening, thus missing the fact that gender is as basic to planetary real-life as breath, light, or any other quality more frequently referred to in New Age rhetoric.

There is nothing in pre-Christian spiritual systems that centers on the Feminine to suggest that male exclusion, gender-struggle, or even the more invidious forms of status-seeking or competitiveness are supported in either the beliefs or structures employed in pre-Christian gynecentric spiritual communities. Among the First Nations' peoples, the sacred crones, matrons, maidens, or mysteries (as the four aspects of the grandmother-god(dess)-energies are anciently perceived) all include a central and well-empowered position for sacred masculine energies (the male, like the female, is not confined to a monolithic construct). From Cahokia to Anatolia, from the Dravidian world to the world of the Keres, the varied ritual roles of males, as of females, were and are honored and employed in the life of the spirit.

Presumably, the exclusivist nature of Christian socialization runs deep; many post-Christians who define themselves as pagan, Buddhist, spiritualist, theosophist, "generic," or anything but Christian reveal in their assumptions, values, beliefs, and ideologies the Roman-based Christian patriarchal bias that informs their most profound ideas. The concept of difference evokes inarticulate fears that reveal a culture-wide sense of threat that is both pre-verbal and sociopolitical. One wonders if it is racial. Historically, exclusivist, elitist, status-centered, male-dominant values, along with cattle and subservient women, accompany Aryan peoples wherever they go.

So deep is the cultural bias toward high-status male exclusivity that the merest hint of the sacred nature of the Feminine, that radical possibility, sends otherwise reasonable seekers into a profound state of denial that is marked by invective, assault, violent fantasy, dismissal, trivialization, projection, ignorance amounting to amnesia, and allied earmarks of profound psychological distress categorized by mental health practitioners over the past century. Small wonder that this is the case; the centuries of colonization and cultural destruction have left their mark. Western nations, once deeply oriented to the feminine, have long been held under the thrall of patriarchal establishments that may have sources in Greece, Rome, Persia, the Black Sea. For all too long it has been dangerous indeed to speak of gendered spirituality, of Goddesses as Supreme Deity, of multiplicity as spiritual fact, of the *spiritual* in itself as fact, of diversity in all aspects of human and non-human life as creative, holy, and empowering, of the material as spiritual – in fact, dangerous to speak of anything at all bearing on the world of the holy in any terms patriarchy finds disturbing. Over the past five or six millennia, millions have died for their differences – be they sexual, racial, gender, or ideological – sacrificed upon the altar of the One God, the possessor of ultimate status. That god brooks no competition. He is so small-minded, vengeful, and spiritually impotent that he fears all otherness as diabolically threatening to his position and is all too willing to command humans to commit unspeakable acts to guarantee his supremacy. Evidently, he never learned the power of love!

There are many among New-Agers, of course, who vigorously affirm the feminine, as the resurgence of goddess-centered spirituality in Western nations testifies. Unfortunately, many are as yet unclear on the concept. All too often affirmation of the sacred Feminine is based on a spirit of divisiveness that proclaims goddess-spirituality to be superior to all other forms of spirituality. While they may have a point, male-bashing is at best counterproductive. It is simply another form of patriarchy, a sort of Jehovah in drag. Singing the same song, however many nouns and pronouns might be changed, cannot lead us toward the Heart of Heaven, as she is named among the Maya. A spiritual system based on dominance, status, exclusion of most members of the community, pettiness, vengefulness, or jealousy is not likely to yield the magnificent spiritual benefits that so many seek. Deepening in spirit is always and ever accompanied by a widening of consciousness and compassion on all levels of awareness. It is concurrently distinguished by a decrease in the love of status, envy, dominance-drive, and denial of what-is-so.

Unfortunately, it is too often the case that much that passes for goddess-spirituality is neither: embedded in Jungian psychology, modernist, and post-modernist concepts of myth and the sacred as merely aspects of human psychology, or in socialist constructs that deny some of the profound facts of the old goddess religions, these movements oscillate between never-never land and utopian fantasy, providing little of the very real kind of food for the soul that seekers profoundly need. The world of the spirit is not the world of human wishfulness, nor of human economics, history, or politics. It exists, in and of itself, as really and as truly as the word processor I use, as really and exactly as the universes of stars, quarks, planets, grass, red maple leaves in late fall, rain drops, and ICBMs exist. The spiritual informs the same universe as these more "material" phenomena, and, like them, it is independent of human notions concerning it. Stars and planets exist independent of our conceptualizations. So do goddesses, gods, spirits, and all varieties of supernatural and subnatural entities. It is upon the fundament of material fact and delight in both the physical and the material that Feminine spirituality is based.

Sadly, Goddess worshipers all too often fall prey to patriarchal ideas of what constitutes the holy: we are treated to the vision of a Deity All Supreme, just like God only with cunt and breasts (sometimes lots of these). She is as incapable as her jealous male counterpart of recognizing multiplicity and the sacred nature of All-That-Is. Women who seek the Feminine all too often do so from a position of self-loathing: they deny the body and its needs, dreams, desires, excesses, and frailties; they also deny the beauty and terror of life itself, seeking to evade the exigencies of death, pain, grief, loss, and the awesome mysteries that these phenomena contain in their very being. All too many I've met long only to leave the body and the planet, never to return. They believe that evil lives here and that only if they are sincerely holy can they escape its grip. And in their belief they further the designs of whatever it is that hates life, hates this lovely and beloved earth, and that hates all that is feminine, whether it is to be found in the being of male or of female human and non-human being. We create, together, the reality we are compelled to inhabit. And those who lead us into hatred of body, mind, earth, and all the simple and profound beauties and passions these wonders contain, are aware of this vital fact. They know that they must get us, human beings, to think and act in such a way that the power of our thoughts will destroy the planet that gives us life. Why they hate her, and us, so remains a mystery.

Modern seekers' suspicion and fear of women's spirituality is the tragic result of brainwashing in status-based ways of thinking when extended over countless generations and enforced by almost an infinite number of acts of cruelty perpetrated upon those who dissent either verbally or by the mere fact of their difference from the high god's notions of how everything is *supposed* to be. (His way. No others need apply for life in or of the spirit.)

The decline of the full power of spiritual life seems to have begun in Eden – at the confluence of the Tigres and Euphrates rivers, there in the marshlands presently inhabited by Muslims who are threatened by Iraqi bombs, where Jehovah first denied knowledge of the sacred to woman and man about 4004 B.C.E., or around 6,000 years ago, give or take a century or two. That was where woman became the first casualty of patriarchy's favorite pastime, the "Blame Game." One must remember, of course, that reptiles and men were also cursed, evicted, and locked out of paradise, but, as every Jewish, Christian, or Moslem child knows, the fault was woman's.

It's a little-known linguistic curiosity that the name Jehovah or Jaweh is the same name as Eve; Havva, the counterpart name in Farsi, the language spoken by the Persians, means either Jaweh or Eve. It is also worthwhile to ponder the odd fact that Western spiritual origins are not Western but Oriental; the Middle East is part of the East, or Orient. Mesopotamia is in southwest Asia. But then, Europe is also in Asia; in fact, it's on its West Coast!

At any rate, the Jehovah story and concomitant exclusivist principles spread over the entire Mediterranean region. They flowed into India, eastern Asia, and the Western regions now known as Europe, moving inexorably onward until they hurled themselves on the shores of the Americas, where at last the tidal wave of spiritual destruction began to ebb. Talk about Great Floods! The history of Western religion's rise and spread, the number of permutations it underwent along the way, raises significant questions about the nature of spirituality in all its varied forms, particularly as they recombine within the New Age spiritual movement. What if the entire idea of the life of the spirit and in the spirit as it has been received over the eons of the great Aryan migrations in all systems of Aryan descent is (a) culture-specific and (b) destructive to all living things?

The question is certainly timely; indeed, posing it now, as the entire environment faces destruction, may be rather late. Nevertheless, it is instructive to note that in every region where Aryan patriarchial elitist systems have held sway, human populations have risen far beyond the ability of the environment to sustain them. This overage has occasioned the loss of forestland, grassland, and wetland, creating severe famine, plague, war, drought, mass dislocation of human populations, and extermination of literally billions of species and at least thousands of human civilizations. The subjugation of women to the sexual whims of macho patriarchal-political goals of world conquest, which dictated that women stay home, stay in the kitchen, and stay pregnant, has caused unconscionable, irrational growth in human populations. Humans are omniverous in more ways than one, and confining them to vegetable consumption alone is no way to balance a proclivity for conquest via reproduction within the interconnected dynamics of the living web of being. The violation of the sacred, which is at the heart of the destruction of all forms of planetary life, resides in the denial of the centrality of the feminine in any and all systems that dare to claim spirituality as a primary basis of that civilization.

Angry women, indeed angry people, are waking up everywhere. We have extremely excellent reasons for that anger, even for rage. I do not mean my remarks to be construed as critical of that anger; goddess knows that our anger is not only just but necessary, if the planet we inhabit and love is to be healed. But our anger must be empowered by reason; it must feed as much on truth, beauty, delight, and freedom as it possibly can so that it will at last yield the sweet fruit of love, peace, and re-entry into the world of the Great Mysteriousness from which we were evicted by a cruel and vicious godlet all too long ago, and from which we continue to exclude ourselves by furthering the designs of murder, genocide, denial, and misuse of the power to think, to be, to comprehend, and to love. And make no mistake: we do all that when we deny or discount the central significance of the Feminine.

II.

Where I come from, God is a Woman; her name is Thinking. She is accompanied by her sister-goddesses Memory and what I will translate as Intuition, and she is an elder of the female gender. She is called Grandmother, in recognition of the spiritual significance of proper relationship and of her revered place among us, and also Spider – maybe because she both spins and lives in the fragile, inordinately strong, potentially deadly, and ever wondrous web of All-That-Is. Where I come from, society is (traditionally, though colonization and White law dictate otherwise now) matrilineal, matrilocal, and matrifocal. Here, I must note that these anthropological terms belie the truth of the Laguna paradigm where motherhood is shared among women who are siblings in clan-based schemes, which might or might not resemble the "biological" schemes that characterize Western notions of consanguinity. Where I come from, all spirituality is gender-based, and as near as historical, geological, paleontological, environmentalist, horticultural, or other measures show, the planet and the people are/were all the better for gender-based, elder-female-focused spiritual systems. No nuclear bombs, no toxic waste dumps, no chemical terrorism, no millions of lost species are our legacy. Warfare is actually prohibited, and pacifism, nurturing, healing, inclusiveness, egalitarianism among all members of the community of being, and profound spiritual and ritual awareness continue to characterize that system.

But not only is the Laguna Pueblo example pertinent to this discussion; for while I am a Laguna woman, I am also a contemporary American, accustomed to checking my assumptions, however traditional and revered, against scientific evidence. And that evidence supports the Laguna paradigm: the single cell, be it plant or animal, is seen as "mother," and when it splits, the resulting duo are referred to as daughters – just as the original Grandmother Spider "splits" and her counterparts, a duo of goddesses named Nau'sti'tsi and Ic'sti'tsi, result.

Then, too, there are interesting scientific observations concerning the femaleness of mammalian zygotes. The original zygote is marked XX, or female. Its chromosomal configuration might transform after a number of "splits" to XY, or "male," or it might retain its original identity, XX. In Indian country we say that the male is transitory (thus "active"), while the female abides forever. Maleness, it seems, is a special case, a subset, of the Feminine, just as Laguna theology, or rather, *thea*logy, holds. One has to ask how the subset became the Prime Mover? A palace coup?

Given the facts, what's the problem?

History is the problem. History, conditioning, five thousand years of warfare and terrorization of the people of the earth by whomever those alienated hierarchicalists were and are all contribute to the deep sense of unease, indeed, of barely contained fear, that surfaces when talk of goddesses, grandmothers, feminine/feminist spirituality arises. It is not easy to solve. Nor is it safe to suppose that those more vehement in their reaction against feminine spiritual empowerment are men: fear knows no gender. Many women, perhaps most women engaged in the many non-Christian varieties of spirituality that are presently available in western nations, are powerfully disconnected from the source of their identities, their spiritual empowerment, and indeed, their spiritual lives. Women engage in "alternative" spiritualities that range from Buddhism to eckankar, and include spiritualism, theosophy, sufism, santería, and most recently what I call New Age tribalism (which many confuse with Native American spiritual systems). Those who are involved in these various paths are largely unaware that they are practicing spiritual disciplines that not only deny but actively negate the practitioner's humanity and femininity. Thus, Buddhist women are invited to disrobe for the delectation of the "master" – who seems to have taken his lessons more from de Sade than from Guatama Buddha – or is there a difference? Other women busily study arcane systems that put them in touch with "ascended masters" who are believed to be superior because they are *up* there, that is, *higher*, and because they are *masters* – that is, not serfs, slaves, or women. More frightening, huge numbers of women involved in misogynist Far Eastern spiritualities, which are, after all, designed chiefly for male seekers, are eschewing the consumption of red meat, creating physiological problems that will have devastating results on them and their children (red meat is a major source of iron and many other elements that cannot be named because the entire subject is taboo). Let me remind all of us that vegetarianism inevitably accompanies misogyny, racism, tyranny, gynocide, and infanticide. It is no accident that Adolf Hitler was a vegetarian. And what were the Buddhist monks, found dressed in white and bowing, prostrate along the walkway of their master's building, doing there? They were not his victims; they were his teachers, guides, and followers. Let us also remember that Tibet was conquered by Buddhism, its native spiritual system supplanted; certainly I, a Native American-cum-Christian, perforce, cannot forget or deny it. I must ask how true, beautiful, or good a spiritual system that thrives on conquest, exclusion, and exploitation can possibly be! I also wonder if vegetarianism doesn't create a tendency toward violence as well as toward white supremacy, male dominance, and overpopulation. It is a fact that Roman soldiers ate only grain, while Celtic peoples (like natives everywhere, including India) relished their goodly portions of flesh. As far as I know (and my research along these lines is extensive), only the Celts were overly fond of warfare; native tribal-pagan people were far more likely to be either actively pacifist or simply disinclined toward battle unless their survival was threatened, and even then they were more likely to try and live with the situation than to confront it with violence, as the recent history of tribal peoples on the American continents can amply testify. The facts, historical and spiritual, suggest that patriarchal spiritual theory is based on a number of false propositions; and, as any logician knows, reasoning from false propositions is not reason but nonsense.

But the net effect of delusional beliefs about the nature of the sacred is extremely dangerous; irrationality, nonsense, kills entire races, entire species, and entire planets. Spirituality that is based on a denial that approaches the psychotic cannot heal this wounded and beloved Earth. Spirituality founded on hatred of women, denial of the physical body, hatred of the physical and of *matter*, which is, after all, the *mother* of spirit, is not spiritual in the least. The urgent necessity that faces women and men who long to encounter the greater, larger, more inclusive and therefore more Whole and balanced sacred essence that is ultimately the human and the spirit is that we heal the great sickness patriarchal thought has inflicted upon all citizens of planet Earth, human and otherwise, and return to the Feminine source of our being.

Let us begin that healing by acknowledging that if we fail to empower the feminine within and outside of ourselves, all of our attempts at righting the great destructions of the past five or six thousand years will go for naught. And if we fail to right them, to heal ourselves and our planet, all our claims to spiritual development and competency are nothing less than the most wicked of lies.

8.
"Indians," Solipsisms, and Archetypal Holocausts

The basic paradigms that underlie Native American and "other" American thought differ in a number of particulars, and these paradigmatic differences lead to endless misunderstandings of the Native world by outsiders. Native people are neither like non-Natives, nor like American popular conceptions of us, be those conceptions generated by New Age materials, films, histories, or other media. Nor can we be seen or understood in the terms by which African-Americans or other "minority" racial groups define and describe themselves. Our situation in the United States, as well as throughout the Western Hemisphere, is unique, for we are First Nations people, indigenous; we aren't so much a political minority as we are displaced persons. Further, there are federal and state laws that specifically address the legal relations between our Nations and the United States or the separate states. According to a Cherokee friend, the *Wall Street Journal* recently reported that stockbrokers carry or wear animal icons signifying their "Totem." Another Native American/Chicano graduate student tells me that one of his English professors said he didn't consider the bright, articulate young man a minority person. The remark certainly gave my friend – small, curly-haired, and dark-skinned – pause. Not content with pontificating on the student's identity, the professor mentioned another student in the class, a gifted Native American poet who comes from the reservation and speaks English with a tribal accent. "I love having her in class. It gives me a chance to see how real Indians think." Not surprisingly, my friend barely restrained himself from decking the man upon whom his grade depended. I myself have been in therapy (with a number of different people) for nearly thirty years off and on, and only one of those therapists (an extremely aware white woman) has had the wit to help me explore the degree of difference between me and white people; her most significant aid consisted in her describing to me how she, as "a privileged white woman" (her words) saw the world, "reality," and herself in relation to non-whites.

The problem would not be so urgent for mental health issues in the Native community were we not engulfed by white culture: it is the basis of our educational systems; its media surrounds us on every hand, as do its political, cultural, popular, economic, aesthetic, architectural, legal, child-rearing, and population patterns, its familial structure and bonding, and its religious norms.[1] We are hard put to find ourselves – as communities and as individuals – in this mind-destroying, endless barrage.

All but overwhelmed by ubiquitous redefinitions of ourselves and our sense of reality, one tries to write. To think. To get some kind of clarity about almost anything. One tries to function. To stay sober, to stay connected with the deeper stratum of being that is one's identity, one's tradition, one's very perception and consciousness. All too often, one gives up. Drops out of school. Flunks too many courses. Quits too many jobs. Gives in to all-pervading despair, to the murderous thoughts the white world projects daily, hourly, year after year. One gives up and lies down and dies.

Meanwhile, there seems little to do but to keep on keepin' on, as the saying goes. One writes, thinks, works, talks, hopes against hope that the horror of white-think will somehow be turned around, that white madness can be cured.[2]

White culture employs the mechanism it identifies as projection to avoid facing itself around the fact, history, and current situation of Native people and communities. Though in this instance it functions on a global scale, projection is all too clearly operative in the white world's version of Native America. In breathtakingly classic fashion, split-off fragments of the Anglo-European psyche take on an energetic life of their own, appearing to non-Indians as actual people, ideas, systems, attitudes, and values the Western collective mind dubs "indian."

As many a therapist knows, little is more frightening than being perceived as a fragment of the other's mind; interaction with someone who is fixated upon his or her disowned and misnamed fragments is devastating because it entails a loss of self at the deepest levels of the psyche. Like all projection, "white-think" is almost entirely unconscious; nameless, formless, unacknowledged, it exists as a powerful barrier to authentic communication across cultures. While it works for the survival and expansion of white culture, it also results in the spiritual and psychic murder of those who exist outside of its protection.

One example of this process in writing will have to suffice here. An article, "Digging for Medicine: Bears in Native American Healing Traditions" by David Rockwell, is almost a caricature of itself, so full is it of objectification, projection, attribution, and redefinition. Rockwell employs the past tense throughout the article, whether the practice being discussed is still in use by living Native people or not. "The Lakota considered the bear to be a curing animal. They associated their medicinal herbs with bears . . . and they *believed* . . . doctors *acquired* powers . . . they *were* not . . . Most of the tribes in North America associated bears with curing . . . and called upon [bears] . . . when they performed. . . ."[3] One is unsure whether the practices, the bears, the beliefs, or the Lakota, et al., are extinct. The subtext, of course, lets us understand that all of the above are long gone; this makes white people feel safer. If we are all dead, their genocide, terrorism, pain, and the fear stemming from their history vis-à-vis Indian America can be safely banished.

Rockwell is relentless in his recontextualization of our traditions and heritage: "The American Indian's perception of the bear as healer proceeds from a knowledge of bear behavior."[4] He is of the opinion that the eating patterns of the bear people, which, he says, are mostly vegetarian, are what held our attention. (Never mind that many a bear likes a bit of good, fresh fish now and then, and an occasional fat larvae is something of a treat.) Rockwell didn't come to his misunderstanding on his own: he is simply replicating the analytic babble that characterizes white-think. The truth of a people's past and present—whether those people are Native Americans, Muslims, Africans, or Bosnians—provides most of the scholarly material published in the past several centuries in the West. "Indians probably saw bears not as hunters or grass eaters, but as the plant gatherers of the animal world. It was a natural step from observing this behavior to associating bears with healing, especially herbal healing. As animal gatherer of herbs and roots, the bear served as guardian of the first medicines and communicator of the knowledge of healing."[5] Indeed.

The subtext of Rockwell's carefully crafted personal fantasy invites readers to draw some unwarranted conclusions: Native people are fashionably vegetarian (false—Aryans of the Hindu Brahmin class and Adolf Hitler are/were vegetarian); "Indians" are observant (a group noun that lumps all members of the race under a common rubric, eradicating our personhood); "Indians" take "natural steps" that rely on associative thinking (a projective construct characteristic of Western but not of Native thinking).[6]

By way of white observations culled from (white) literature on animal behavior, Rockwell informs us that the herbivorous bear liked (likes?) to munch on herbs, many of them possessing medicinal properties. Relying on these white, "scientific" observations, Rockwell attributes their methodology to our ancestors, defining us as white (but we "associate," implying that white researchers do a "higher" kind of analysis). His construct enables him to simultaneously use the Native world to validate white "science" and make it "environmentally friendly.[7]

This latter ploy is reinforced when we are told (via the subtext) that Bear is spiritual and wise: for is not bear defined as guardian – a New Age buzz word that signifies "Indians" and "shamanic" "spirituality" – of the first medicines? (Bear as guardian of the first medicines has a subtext: it tells us, among other things, that Bear is even better than Indian, being before us and the true guardian of human health). The net effect is eradication of Native thought and peoples: for could not any observant person, associating naturally, derive the medicines from bear behavior? Assuming, of course, that there were still herb-gathering bears around to observe!

For a wildly different view of the matter of bears, I suggest the following titles: Leslie Marmon Silko's novel *Ceremony* and poem "Story from Bear Country" (*Storyteller*), N. Scott Momaday's novels *House Made of Dawn* and *The Ancient Child*, and Gerald Vizenor's novel *Darkness in Saint Louis Bearheart*. As each of these works makes clear, logical positivism is quite opposite the situation of bears, healing, and human relations with bears in the Native world. Mr. Rockwell's piece – which I have excoriated somewhat mercilessly (though his article deserves an even deeper deconstructing) – has served merely to exemplify a common mental process, one that enjoys very high status in the modern world. It substitutes white-think for Native philosophical/spiritual thought, attributing white assumptions and thought processes to us and our ancestors – without a hint that white cultural assumptions are neither universal nor necessarily shared. Thus continues the horrifying process of colonization, only now it's New Age shamanic thought masquerading as Native American in order to annihilate the Native mind. Small wonder that far too many Native people, especially children, are suicidal. It is not that we possess a death wish, but that the huge culture around us projects its homicidal wish onto us.

One more example of white-think to demonstrate its all-pervasiveness: this one is an example of New Age cooptation and recontextualization of Native thought. In *The Mayan Oracle*, a New Age "deck," there is a passage about lucid dreaming, as the technique is (purportedly) practiced in "Tibetan dream yoga." Ignoring for a moment the obvious fact that Tibet is pretty far from Mayaland, I'll cut to the chase. The authors tell us that "[Lucid dreaming] is the practice of focusing conscious awareness on the illusory nature of reality, becoming lucid in life. It can be experienced in either the waking or the dream state – primarily through realizing that life is *all* a dream."[8]

On the face of it, given the level of American misapprehension of the actual bases of various spiritual systems, this sentence may sound perfectly lucid. However, it is exactly wrong when placed within the context of Native thought. No Native who has given much thought to tribal spiritual systems – in all their aspects and multiplicity – would agree that life is all a dream. We think that life is all real – *all* of it. The personal, the spiritual, the supernatural, the "cosmic," the political, the economic, the sacred, the profane, the tragic, the comic, the ordinary, the boring, the annoying, the infuriating. Our traditions tell us that when someone meets a supernatural on the road (or in the kitchen), that is real. And when someone meets a BIA official at a meeting, that is real. We are neither dreaming it nor making it up. Nor is the numinous (or the Great Mystery) a psychic territory peopled by split-off fragments of our unconscious, a split occasioned by repression, failure to mature in a timely fashion, or massive trauma.[9] (Now, "trauma" *does* mean dream!)

To Native thinkers, the mythic is not a trick of the human mind but a pulsating fact of existence, as real as a village, a trailer court, a horse, a spouse, and a tradition are real. Native people of the Americas are aware, as were pre-Renaissance peoples of the British Isles and on the Continent (and as are many of their modern descendants) that the numinous may be different from the "mundane," separated from it by a kind of penetrable psychic barrier, but it is no less real for all that.

Perhaps Leslie Marmon Silko is accurate in describing the white world as illusory (*Ceremony*). Perhaps that is why its writers and thinkers are so convinced that reality is, at base, an illusion. But we must remember that while white reality may indeed be a very powerful illusion (on the order of a horrible bad dream), Native reality is fact. In his novel *The Courts of Chaos*, the late Roger Zelazny (who is not Native American, but seemed pretty sane anyway) quotes writer Isak Dinesen "'. . . Few people can say of themselves that they are free of the belief that this world which they see around them is in reality the work of their own imagination. . . .'" Then he pursues the thought:

> Do we make the Shadow worlds? Or are they there, independent of us, awaiting our footfalls? Or is there an unfairly excluded middle? Is it a matter of more or less, rather than either-or? . . . Yet . . . there is a place . . . where there comes an end to Self, a place where solipsism is no longer the plausible answer to the locales we visit, the things that we find . . . here, at least, there is a difference, and if here, perhaps it runs back through our shadows, too, informing them with the not-self, moving our egos back to a smaller stage.[10]

It would be well for mental health practitioners and others interested in the system-wide development of a balanced, centered, transformational worldview to seek that place. Perhaps if such people could move their egos back to a smaller stage, find footing in a place where solipsism is no longer the plausible answer to the locales they visit, the entire country would be a healthier place. Certainly, Native people could sleep a bit easier, knowing that it is not they alone who must represent all the denied, split-off longings and unowned rages that far too many influential white writers and thinkers call "myth," "shamanism," "shadow," "archetype," and "spirituality."

For as matters stand presently, Native people are uneasy knowing that if we fail to live in accordance with the false identity foisted off on us to the satisfaction of the powerful white world, we will again be consigned to the outer darkness of poverty, disease, and hopelessness. The threat is very real, and the mindlessness, the culture-wide delusion that occasions it, is very dangerous to those of us who live in accordance with another view of the nature of reality and of the role of human consciousness within it.

Perhaps there is some consolation in being the Archetypes for an entire nation, particularly since that nation is still in the process of locating its own sense of self. But the cost of trading humanity and one's own languages, customs, and worldview for that dubious privilege is very high. For the most part Native American peoples would rather be viewed from their own perspective, a matter of respect certainly, but not easily done when that worldview is so entirely alien to one's own as the Native worldview is to white-think culture.

Which takes us to the other word in the title of this piece, "solipsism." The Second Edition of *The Random House Unabridged Dictionary* defines the term as "1. *philos.* the theory that only the self exists or can be proved to exist, and 2. extreme preoccupation with and indulgence of one's feelings, desires, etc., egotistic self-absorption." The word derives from *solus*, which is Latin for "sole" – meaning "only" or "alone." It is allied with terms such as "solitary." The root of the compound term is "soli," which is defined as "a combined form meaning 'alone,' 'solitary,' and is used in the formation of compound words. An intriguing side note that sparks all sorts of possibilities for exploration is that the next entry after "soli" is "soli^2," which is defined as "a combined form meaning 'sun' used in the formation of compound words" such as "soliform." As you can guess, it's allied to compounds such as "solarium." The Solar deity has functioned as the central archetype for all of Western pre-Christian and post-Christian civilization. Indeed, historians note that until his death Constantine, Roman emperor from 324 to 337 C.E., was a devout follower of Mithras, the ancient Persian god of light and the primary deity of the solar religion that dominated Rome and its outposts during that epoch. It was he who determined that Christianity would be the state religion, and he ordered the great center of culture, Byzantia, to be renamed Constantinople, signifying the shift. Some are of the opinion that he did not convert to Christianity on his deathbed, as Christian legend has it, but merely ordered the change in the official status of both Mithraism and Christianity in the empire. It was thus a brilliant political decision, as subsequent events over the ensuing sixteen centuries attest.

As for the first word in my title, "indian," it speaks to the fact that the indigenous peoples of this continent are not perceived as human beings or national communities by the dominating worldview. We like to joke that we're glad Columbus wasn't looking for Turkey! He thought he was in India, consequently the people he met on that Caribbean Island had to be Indians. But he wasn't, and they weren't, and we aren't "indians" except in Anglo-European discourse that ranges from history, psychology, literature, to every kind of popular culture.

A careful examination of the process by which the indigenous inhabitants of this hemisphere were dehumanized and made into Disneyesque characters, villainous or noble, will demonstrate how destructive of rational thought and consciousness stereotyping is. It is not only the target group that is distorted and dehumanized. The users of the stereotype are greatly harmed psychically as well, and they haven't any means of noticing or assessing the psychic damage done to themselves because they lack any outside reference.

It is difficult to decide which comes first: "indians," "solipsisms," or archetypes in the discourse of dehumanization that surrounds and engulfs American Indian nations and their people, but it is very clear that in combination the three lead indeed to holocausts of the mind and spirit of all who engage in or are discounted, disappeared, by them.

One day soon, Native peoples and our religions, national identities, and sovereignty can emerge from the shadows into which we have been cast by the immigrants. In the full light of day – the light we cast on ourselves, that is – we can live long and prosper. Until that time, the terrible consequences of consignation to the outer darkness of American consciousness will continue unabated. The dreadful suicide rates for both our youths and the professionals among us (the latter said to be the highest suicide rate in the nation),[11] the high rates of early death and infant mortality, endemic poverty, and the low self-esteem that must accompany a life as a stranger's shadow, might then come closer to national norms.

9.
Radiant Beings

In the great feminine mysteries of Eleusis, the event of the birth resulting from the union between Persephone and Dionysus was announced as: "Brimo given birth to Brimos!" Brimo is one form of the Goddess; her name means "the power to arouse terror . . . to rage"; she was closely associated with Pluto and Dionysus. . . . The experience of terror and chaos was understood by the initiates to be inextricably linked to the birth of a new consciousness.

— NATHAN SCHWARTZ-SALANT

I am all that has been, that is, and that will be. No mortal has yet been able to lift the veil that covers me.

— INSCRIPTION, GODDESS TEMPLE AT SAIS SAID

In 1939, the year I was born, some uranium was dug up from Laguna Pueblo land. As Gossips have it, that uranium went into the making of the Bomb, the ones exploded in New Mexico and over Hiroshima and Nagasaki. A few days before I began to write this piece, my father, E. Lee Francis, former Lieutenant Governor of New Mexico and a man who delights in personal reminiscences, mentioned that he saw the bomb blast—though whether it was Fat Man or Little Boy, I don't know. He was receiving livestock out around Zuni, and even at that distance he saw the cloud. "What did it look like?" I asked. "Like smoke," he said. "It looked like smoke."

I guess he didn't know exactly what he'd seen for some time; maybe he realized what he'd seen when Americans learned that the United States had dropped the Bombs on Japan. It must have frightened them, my father, my mother, and her family, for Bobby, my mother's then eighteen-year-old brother, was somewhere over there. On the Pacific, anyway, or at least not in Europe. His few brief letters said little about where he was. Under wartime security, citizens and soldiers alike were mushrooms. Surely local folk were unaware that the earth the strangers (they had to be Anglos, Eastern Anglos, at that) dug up and took away would be milled somewhere and transformed into radiant death.

In the 1950s we schoolchildren were subjected to frequent Bomb Alerts – one of the many acts of terrorism, euphemistically called Civil Defense – visited upon our cowed heads. In the wake of one of these, my best friend, Teresa Baca, and I talked about the Bomb. She told me that her mother, Concepción, told her the people of Cubero saw a ring around the moon a few days before the first bomb test, and they knew that something awful (awe-full) was about to occur. (A person probably gets more accurate information relying on her senses and particular tradition than from textbooks or media!) I think Concepción saw the smoke the same day my dad did. They were both very far away from Stallion Gate, where it was detonated, one up around Zuni, one in Cubero. But in New Mexico in the 1940s you could see forever. The people of Nagasaki and Hiroshima saw forever – became forever – when the sky exploded above their unsuspecting heads, a couple of months after my dad and my friend's mom saw the omen of global transformation. I think that during that awe-full summer the Earth gave forth her new self, and all that is was transformed.

Following the local Gossips' hints, my mother and I visited the area where we thought the original uranium had been dug up forty years before. We walked over the rough land, trying to locate the site of the first uranium dig. It lay somewhere near the old road that had led from Laguna to its daughter-village, Paguate, but even its traces had been obliterated when the new paved road was built to expedite hauling huge supplies of uranium ore from the mine. We both knew that the petrified body of the old giantess that my great-grandmother used to tell about marked one side of that vanished road, and her equally petrified head, flung far from the torso, marked the other; we knew that the road had opened off old Highway 66 directly across from the door to Laguna Trading Post. The lost road had begun almost at the door of the old Gunn house, where we went to eat on Feast Day at Laguna.

Mother and I figured that the giantess's remains lay close to the site we were seeking. But even knowing, we failed to find it. It was ever so much easier to find the huge tract of land overturned by Anaconda Company's vigorous mining at Jackpile mine, near Paguate. The huge rectangular heaps of flat-topped earth eerily resemble the sandstone mesas that dot the surrounding terrain, but they are not sandstone. Piled close upon one another, they are clearly human-made, and in their arrangement, they echo the image of eastern cities: towering artificial structures huddled together in fear and pain.

This year on Memorial Day, my friend Pat Smith, her friend Margaret Wimsatt, and I drove out there. I wanted to see Marquez, fabled community of my youth – my father's youth, really. I had heard his stories about it, but I had never been there. Marquez is located only a few miles from Laguna Village, just up from Paguate. It lies within the Seboyeta Land Grant, a large Mexican-American tract held by its heirs since it was granted to them by the King of Spain in the sixteenth century. When I returned to New Mexico in January of 1990, Pat and I agreed to go out to Marquez because there was mining activity out there and eerie goings-on persisted; tales of strange sightings had filtered through from there for decades.

I recall one legend in which I participated: it involved UFOs, several members of my family, a telescope, and a balmy midsummer's night in Cubero. I ran across my nephew's hastily scribbled notes, dated 6/8/75, among some papers last month. The time was between 9:15 and 11:10 P.M., the place was my parents' home on the bluff above Cubero. The notes record, "Bright object appearing very prominently in the southwest sky, conditions slightly cloudy, 63 degrees F. observed by . . . Also appeared to expel bright projectiles; colors emitted were green, red, and blue alternating flashing (unreadable) of at 1–2 second intervals. Observed a bright . . ." Here the note ends because the next page is missing. At the time we were pretty sure that the lights were circling the peak of Mt. Taylor, lying to the north of Cubero, and they seemed to head toward the other flank where uranium mining operations were underway. That side of the mountain was near Seboyeta and the fabled Marquez.

So our little band of adventurers piled – somewhat creakily – into my BMW and headed west from Albuquerque. In the heat of the early summer day we traveled on I-40. Expanding beneath the forever sky, our thoughts leaped outward to catch the echoes of *katsina*, or *yei*, the profound thrumming of mountain spirits of this land. The sky magnified our souls, and our spirits rejoiced in the huge beautiful around us; it was *hozho*, beauty. In beauty, then, we sped west, toward the legends, toward my home. Drove, minds dilated to fullest extent as when birth is imminent, we flew, aloft on the spread wings of the forever sky, gaze and hearts held safe by the brown, blue, and lavender reaches of the land. Turning off the freeway, we drove the old highway from Mesita (the easternmost Laguna village), past Laguna village to the turnoff my mother and I had taken so many years before.

This day, our band's mission was to visit the shrine at Portales, north of Seboyeta (my father's birth home), and pay our respects to the Virgin who had saved his life when he was an infant. His older sister, a three-year-old, had given her infant brother a screw to play with, and he had swallowed it. Turning blue, he all but suffocated. His frantic grandmother and mother grabbed the choking baby and set off for Portales on their knees, praying to the Virgin the whole way. They crawled a couple of miles and offered him to the Madonna, dedicating him to her. Somehow, the screw passed through his entire digestive tract and was expelled into his diaper.

The following day his parents took him to Albuquerque – at the time a very long trip on a narrow highway that wound through quite a bit of Valencia County before coming into Albuquerque by way of Bernalillo to the north. The doctor pronounced the infant well, remarking that it was a miracle that the screw had not ripped his tiny intestines on its journey. In thanks, we had a family gathering at Portales every year, praying beneath the shelter of the massive white sandstone overhang that shaded the holy spring. The last picnic was the summer after my *jide* (grandfather in Arabic) died. That would have been about twenty years ago.

I grew up in the midst of oral legends that came from Laguna, Lebanon, Germany under Hitler, and family, as well as legends of the literary kind from around the world. My mother was possessed with eclectic albeit refined aesthetic tastes, and my father was (and is) an inveterate storyteller. Mother didn't see a great deal of literary difference in Laguna traditions, stories from the Bible (only the King James version satisfied her literary judgment), Greek and Roman mythology, and a variety of materials from England. When I was very small, my sister took me on a journey to Grandma's rock garden to hunt for fairies and little people – both kinds of beings as familiar to Laguna (or so Grandma Gunn's stories indicated) as to the British Isles.

Given my background, it is natural for me to perceive otherworldly correlations between the Bomb, the mines, and the stories – correlations that reveal the transformational nature of the powers nuclear fission unleashed.

The raw ore from which uranium is milled is called yellowcake, and a supernatural female featured in much of the ritual Keres tradition is named Yellow Woman (which signifies Yellow Corn Woman). I don't think it's an accident that yellowcake is found in great abundance in the lands of Yellow Woman, where yellow corn grows in abundant sweetness. It is interesting that the Mayan word for *corn* is the same as for *dawn*, though exactly what that correspondence signifies for the Keres is unclear. It is also strangely coincidental that some naturalists see yellow corn as an antidote to poisoning by strontium 90, as many narratives in the oral tradition assert that no natural poison exists that is not closely accompanied by its antidote. And, too, the color of the feminine in the Laguna system is not pink, the color of the Sandias east of Albuquerque at sunset, but yellow, the color of sweetcorn, pollen, corn tassels, and sunrise.

There is an old story about Yellow Woman in which she is abducted by Whirlwind Man. (In other versions she is abducted by Evil Kachina, or by Sun Man.) According to the story, Yellow Woman went to the river to get water for her sisters and herself. There she was accosted by Whirlwind Man, who compelled her to go with him. She left her water jar by the river, a clue to her plight. Whirlwind Man carried her off to the other world where he remanded her to his mother's custody. There she performed the tasks that every intended wife must perform for her future in-laws. Meanwhile, her concerned sisters, Red Corn, White Corn, and Blue Corn, set about trying to find Yellow Woman, and eventually succeeded. Appropriate to Keres custom, Whirlwind Man sent Yellow Woman home laden with lavish gifts from his mother for herself and her sisters.

When Pat, Margaret, and I stopped along the road at Jackpile mine to view the strange grass growing where the company had filled one of its pits, we saw Whirlwind Man and what might have been his mother, brother, or wife, whirling in the far distance. We didn't tarry long. But the grass is brilliantly green there; it looks like the grass that grows in England and Scotland; it doesn't look like the tough grass natural to this part of New Mexico, the grass that blankets the earth all around the site except for where the mining had occurred. Fortunately, we viewed the green, green grass from the relative safety of the car. Luckily, it was hot and we were disinclined to get out and poke around on the ground, where we might have found something extremely dangerous that day.

Another story bears on the issue of nuclear fission and its effects. This one is far more central to Laguna thought than even the Yellow Woman ritual narratives, for it is at the heart of Laguna cosmogony. Naotsete, Sun Woman, was one of the original goddesses who, with her sister Icsity and Spider Woman, created the heavens, the earth, the gods, the animals, plants, the arts, the laws, and all institutions, abilities, and phenomena needed for planetary life. Eventually, she and her sister quarreled over who was the elder, and Naotsete decided to go away. She, like her sister, had a "medicine bag" (I like to picture it as a beautifully cross-stitched woven purse) that contained a number of yet-to-be born qualities or phenomena, and they discussed who would keep the various items. Naotsete took writing, or so some of the stories say, along with metal, mining, and metallurgy because her sister didn't want them. Accompanied by one of her sons (the other stayed with her sister), Naotsete went away to the east. But it was said that someday she would return; some say that she came back when the Spaniards found their way into Pueblo country, but tribal Gossips say that the Bomb's detonation marked her return.

No versions that I have heard or read suggest that the end of the world follows closely upon Naotsete's return; indeed, given the facts of the past five hundred years, I'd say that the Bomb is as likely to result in the liberation of the Native people as in their (continued) demise. Gossips hint that her return signals the end of Western colonial domination and the destruction of the patriarchy. The legend suggests that it heralds something even we can't conceptualize – something only Grandmother Spider, Thought Woman, can dream, something transformational. It is clear that the fission of the atom signals loud and bright that something sacred is going on in the universe. And it is equally clear that respect for that Great Mysteriousness – the kind of respect that Whirlwind Man and his mother show for Yellow Woman and her people – is demanded in such a sacred time. Perhaps it is because of our collective disrespect of Her awesomeness, rather than radioactive substances per se, that we sicken and die.

This is not to suggest that nuclear fission is an unmitigated blessing, but rather to reiterate a point that all ritualists know: the approach of the sacred is fraught with great danger; the liminal state, which one enters at the moment of transformation, is as likely to yield disaster as its obverse. True ritualists go through long periods of cleansing and isolation before being so bold as to approach the sacred amidst the most stringent secretiveness, all of which point to the danger of approaching sacred occasions. Modern people, of course, do not recognize the peril; raised on Walt Disney's notions of supernatural events coupled with intellectually toxic empirical (the word comes from the same source as "imperial") thought, they play with the sacred as though it were a toy, then, shocked at its devastating response, look angrily around for someone to blame for their folly. Yet what went on at Los Alamos during the making of the Bomb eerily echoes the ancient ritual practices.

In November of 1991, my Laguna mother died of cancer. Or at least, that's what they put on her death certificate. She had oat cell cancer of the lung, a kind of cancer that is unlikely to kill its host quickly, particularly when the person is elderly. But she accepted the treatment the Western doctors offered: chemotherapy and radiation. The treatment worked – they eradicated the lesions in her lung. But the cancer metastasized to her brain. More chemo, more radiation. She died, whether of the disease or of the cure, we'll never know. It is presently fashionable to attribute her illness to her lifelong smoking, and not at all fashionable to point out that lung cancer was almost unheard of until after World War II, when it became all too ordinary.

In a special report on February 28, 1993, CNN told the story of a doctor who, seeing a single case of lung cancer in 1936, called in several students. He wanted them to observe this "rare disease that [they] might never see again." It was ten years before he saw another case, the report went on, and, of course, the rate of incidence has since risen precipitously. In its report on lung cancer and smoking, CNN blamed its rise and that of other "smoking-related diseases" on the huge amounts of cigarettes the G.I.s toted in their C-ration packs! (Which were, one supposes, a kind of militaristic medicine bag.) The rationale makes little sense as the C-rations were used in Europe, Asia, and Africa, not in the United States, and given developments in realms other than tobacco use, it constitutes a trivialization of the explosive extent of the disease and its most likely causes. To wit: Not a word was said in the report about the rise in incidences' relationship to the Bomb, nuclear testing, or the horrifying proliferation of radioactive waste all over the country; for that matter, not a word was said about the proliferation of electrical apparatus-power plants, power lines, electrification of every home in the modern world or the seemingly endless variety of chemical toxins that have spread throughout the planetary biosphere, accompanied by the rise in cancer and other respiratory and immune system dysfunction-related illnesses.

In a stunning article, "Chernobyl – The Hidden Tragedy," contained in the March 15, 1993, issue of *The Nation*, Jay M. Gould cites Andrei Sakharov's contention that

> [c]onsidering only such fission products as radioactive carbon, strontium, and cesium . . . genetic damage, plus the immediate and delayed damage to immune systems, would accelerate the deaths of between 500,000 and 1 million people worldwide for every fifty megatons of nuclear explosive power.

My mother's illness began in the fifties with what was eventually diagnosed as severe allergy to "dust," "wool" (as in her precious Navajo rugs that covered all the floors of her house), and animal dander from her dog. By the eighties the allergies had progressed to lupus, complicated by diverticulitis, asthma, what might have been pericarditis, and later rheumatoid arthritis, though they may have all been lupus – a strange disease that masquerades as other illnesses, hence its name. She had quit smoking in the late seventies, when she was in her sixties. For all the good it did.

Gould clarifies some of the factors that may have been operating in the etiology of her illness in terms of Sakharov's discussion of

> "non-threshold effects," by which he meant that every radioactive particle released had a statistical probability of doing damage to either the DNA of a cell or to the immune system, by low-level internal radiation from ingesting such particles. He also predicted that radiation would accelerate the mutation of microorganisms.

During the summer of 1993, New Mexicans, particularly those living around the Crownpoint area, were terrorized by a mysterious respiratory ailment that claimed thirteen lives in a few days. The victims failed very quickly and medical experts were helpless to determine the cause of the disease. The victims were preponderantly young and in very good health, nor has smoking been mentioned in any reports on possible causes or complicating factors. One doctor was reported as saying the progress of the disease was so fast that one of his patients had died within two hours of "taking a turn for the worse." The cause of death was respiratory failure; the lungs filled with fluid.

Crownpoint-area Navajos, so far the highest risk group for contracting the mystery disease, as they live in the danger zone, are being told by their

Hataal'ii that the illness is caused by some violation of the sacred. Ernest Becenti says, "There is a hole in the sky, and bad things are pouring through it." Another Hataal'ii, Donald Jackson, is quoted as saying that the disease is "an Earth Sickness. People who still follow the old ways are not being harmed, because they know how to pray."

While "environmental" factors have been vaguely named as possibly involved in the etiology of the disease, specifics have not been given in any report that I have heard or read other than one reference to the recent dumping of toxic wastes on the Navajo reservation. Gossips repeat rumors of chemical warfare experiments at military installations near the Reservation and speculate that some experiment has gotten loose. There are also rumors of evil sorcery, skinwalking, though such remarks are heavily censored (whether by the gossips, the media, or Navajo officials, I can't say) and are, in the Indian way, somewhat vague. Indians are very inclined to talk around the edges of things, preferring indirection and similar noninvasive modes of address to the more "straight lines are the shortest" modes preferred by whites. But skinwalking and deliberate malevolence on the part of some unhappy or power-hungry ritualist are always possible, and when that possibility is coupled with the horror of seemingly more straightforward means of transformation (which is another way of saying "mutation"), the potential for disaster is truly frightening.

As far as I am aware, no U.S., state, or tribal officials have connected the ailment to the leaking of radioactivity into the soil and water in the Crownpoint area in the 1970s. Oddly, there is some kind of amnesia operating, in spite of the recent publication of the investigations Sakharov, Gould, and another Russian nuclear physicist and writer, Vladimir Chernousenko, have published. Health officials have identified Hantavirus, a virus found in Asian countries but never before in the United States, as being responsible for the disease, and believe that it enters the air around the nests of deer mice. For a time, health officials were notifying the people in the area not to clean up rodents' nests but to notify officials; officials were studying methods of eradicating the infected mice.

Given Sakharov's analysis of "non-threshold effects," and given the radioactive contamination of the soil and water in the Crownpoint area, it seems clear that the rodents have ingested radioactive particles and that those particles have resulted in the mutation of microorganisms into horrifying virulence. There is also an implication in Sakharov's analysis "that the persons with damaged immune systems would . . . succumb more easily to these new strains of infectious diseases." It isn't saying too much to point out that all of the victims, dead or somehow surviving, live in an area heavily contaminated for nearly twenty years. The median age of the victims is about twenty-five, with most being between the ages of thirteen and thirty-five.

In Belarus, the area hardest hit by radiation from the Chernobyl disaster, "there is hardly a child who is not suffering from some immune deficiency disease, either cardiovascular, lymphoid or oncological. . . . A 1989 public health survey indicated that in the three biggest provinces of Ukraine every second adult was ill." In those areas "the incidence of immune deficiency diseases has doubled or tripled since 1985 and is now spreading to all other areas that have been consuming radioactive food." Chernousenko is of the opinion that Chernobyl's "massive secondary insult to human immune systems literally sickened Soviet society," according to Gould. Gould continues to hammer the point: "It now seems clear that the atmospheric bomb tests caused sufficient harm to developing hormonal and immune systems to justify Sakharov's fear of future immune deficiency epidemics." He cites a study by radiation physicists Sternglass and Scheer that makes a clear correlation between the outbreak of AIDS and strontium 90 in human bone that two decades before the outbreak in high rainfall areas of Africa registered at "the highest levels in the world." This assessment was made after people there had received "heavy fallout from the atmospheric bomb tests." Sternglass and Scheer "conclude that fallout is a factor in the impairment of immune response that can show up when young adults encounter the newly mutated strains of sexually transmitted viruses," Gould reports ("Chernobyl – The Hidden Tragedy").

With respect to the Four Corners disease, we have seen that the greatest preponderance of victims are young and in excellent physical condition. The June 4, 1993, issue of *The Santa Fe New Mexican* reports that, according to medical investigators, "the disease may have been making people sick for years, but in isolated cases that never drew attention." They say they haven't been able to find a common factor among the victims other than the area they lived in or, in one case, had just visited. The major "common factor," high levels of radiation from the leakage at the Churchrock Mill near Crownpoint that occurred in the early seventies, seems to elude scientific thought. It seems as well to elude traditional Navajo thought, though Hataal'ii seem closer to the point: Mr. Becenti voices a traditional Navajo opinion:

Our old people ate real corn from Mother Earth. Like me, they went without running water and heat. But the white man tells our young people, "Tenderize your steak." He gives us artificial sweeteners. He gets our youngsters eating fast food that everyone knows is not of this Earth. And then he sends us TV, his form of spiritual communication. Teenagers tell themselves, "I can put a skeleton in the graveyard and get it to walk" because they see it on TV. We traditional people call that kind of thing "skinwalking." It brings you death by suggestion, and we try to prevent such bad medicine with prayer.

In 1936 my mother didn't enjoy electricity in her stone-walled Cubero home; she was raised on food from Mother Earth, an earth as yet uncontaminated by radioactive and chemical substances. But by the mid-sixties when her health began to fail in ever more frightening ways, she had enjoyed every benefit of modern technology, including the dust from the uranium mines surrounding us and the fallout from atmospheric bomb tests run in Nevada during the fifties and sixties. In 1936 there was little if any nuclear toxicity in western Valencia (now Cibola) County. By 1976, the levels of radioactivity were very high.

Gee, Ma, you shouldn't have smoked so much!

Ethel was one of those Indian people who longed to belong to the "real world." The one with nightclubs and big bands, symphonies and operas, Great Books and automobiles, beautiful clothes and refined (white) people who live in gracious settings and eat off china set on snowy white linen – and who smoke. She came by her inclinations honestly, as we say; her mother Agnes had similar dreams. How were they to know that their inner longings were virulent? My grandmother, Agnes, died several years ago of a stroke brought on by atherosclerosis, a disease my mother attributed to all the butter and high cholesterol meats and eggs with which Grandma cooked liberally over the years. But Michael Castleman, managing editor of *Medical Self Care*, notes that "fatty arterial deposits that characterize atherosclerosis also show abnormally high concentrations of alpha activity. Radiochemist Dr. Edward Martell suggests that insoluble radioactive smoke particles at the plaque sites may be directly related to the high incidence of early coronaries among cigarette smokers." While Grandma didn't die young – she was in her eighties – she did die earlier than most of her siblings, and she smoked.

According to the New Mexico Tumor Registry in 1976, Native Americans in New Mexico do not contract lung cancer; they do contract diabetes, an immune-system disability, cardiovascular diseases, pancreatic and stomach cancer. It is not a fluke that the New Mexico Cancer Control Project, for which I worked for a time, refused to deal with radiation, toxic waste, asbestos mining – all demonstrably implicated in carcinogenesis – though they were avidly engaged in an anti-smoking campaign as a major aspect of what they were pleased to call their cancer prevention program. Smoking, indeed! Not that it isn't involved, but the cessation of smoking in this country will not appreciably lessen the host of life-threatening diseases that radioactive contamination of the planet has occasioned. According to Castleman, cigarettes are radioactive partly because everything that grows is, and partly because the phosphate fertilizer commercially raised tobacco plants are treated with "contain significant quantities of radium 266 and its nine primary decay products, including lead 210 and polonium 210."

The years between 1932 and 1962 were years of terrible drought in our part of the world. During the worst of it, the fifties, the yellowcake from the open mines and the mills surrounding us blew back and forth over us; sometimes the dust was so thick we could barely see across the room, despite stuffing doors and window frames with cloth and newspapers in vain attempts to keep it out. As we watched the huge dust clouds form and sweep overhead, we used to quip, "There goes some more Enchantment!" Little did we realize the truth of our joke, though indeed we should have: one of the prime characteristics of the sacred is its wit.

The lake that gave Laguna Pueblo its name (which is actually Kawaik, or "lake") dried up. The blessed lake, rain, and cloud people had gone away, or maybe because of our great disrespect for the sacred Radiant Being who had returned, or maybe because she had some Changes in mind. When I was small, the Lagunas said that the drought came because the Anglos don't think good thoughts; that their anger, fear, hostility, isolatedness (which in the Anglo world is pridefully called "individualism" and which is institutionalized in the Constitutional right to privacy), and suspiciousness all drive away the Shiwana, the Rain People, who bring rain only when we "think good thoughts" and keep peaceful in our hearts.

Once before, when the people lived in Kush-Katret, the Rain People went away. That time they left because the men wouldn't do the right dances and prayers. They were all caught up in a new game they had learned. It seems that there was a drought – not really disastrous, just one of those that occur every few years when the biosphere is allowed to act in harmony with its own rhythms. Our Mother Iyatik^u gave the men a gambling game to occupy them, but they quickly became compulsive about it, gambling their family's possessions – which was bad enough – and refusing to perform their sacred duties, which was disastrous. Angered by the neglect, the Lake Spirits removed to another place. They refused to send the Shiwana with the rain.

The dead, our ancestors, were also indignant and wouldn't have brought the rain (which is their after-death job) anyway. As a result of the violation, the drought became very serious, and the people and animals all began to die. It seems that compulsiveness, ignoring sacred duties, and neglecting familial/clan obligations led to devastation. Which, of course, is the Hataal'ii contention. Somehow, I don't think that the solution to the Hantavirus is to eradicate rodents by poisoning the sacred Earth – and weakening the already devastated immune systems of the people further. In time immemorial the balance was eventually restored only after the people returned to their duties and agreed to live again in accordance with the dictates of the Supernaturals and their sacred code.

There are the stories about Reed Woman, who was angered by her sister Iyatik^u, or Beautiful Corn Woman, who is Mother of the people. Reed Woman believed she was being ignored – denied the proper respect belonging to her. As occurs over and over in our traditions, she left, eschewing more aggressive modes of expressing her dissatisfaction. Through the offices of a Fly, a repentant Iyatik^u acknowledged the justice of Reed Woman's complaint; Our Mother promised to see to it that Reed Woman received her proper due. Satisfied, Reed Woman agreed to come home. Her absence meant that it didn't rain; her return meant the rains came again.

In New Mexico just before it rained, the flies clustered about our porch door heavily and you could smell the sweet aroma of rain on the dusty wind. The clouds would pile thick over the sky, the temperature would drop deliciously, and amidst the magnificent panoply of Thunder and Lightning, the blessed rain would fling itself from above, a perfect and awesome benediction. After the storm, great puddles of clear water would dot the concavities in the sandstone mesas above our house. In them swam scores of tadpoles. Flies, frogs; Thunder, Lightning, Rain. Great things were afoot at such times, and everyone knew what was so.

The Cherokee have a story from the old times that also bears on our present situation. Their major deity is Sutalidihi, whose name means Six Killer. She is known as apportioner, or measurer, and she is the Spirit of the Sun, or, in white parlance, the Sun Goddess (sort of). Once a clan of magicians, the Ani Kutani, determined to kill Sutalidihi because she wasn't amenable to their will. Their disrespect infuriated her – probably because she hadn't been inculcated with the Nice Girl Code. So she raged constantly, causing everyone to burn and sicken with incurable, mysterious ailments. Their skins erupted in painful and deadly swellings, their limbs and organs developed horrible pains, their very life-fire turned on them and degenerated into growths that ran like wildfire through their bodies, leaving nothing healthy in their place. Does this sound familiar? But these symptoms were chronicled long before modern times. Radiation sickness was unknown when ethnographer James Mooney collected the myth, and its symptoms would not be reported for more than a century.

The story goes on to report that so many died that everyone knew someone who had been afflicted. The people of the Seven Districts were filled with dread, sorrow, and anger. They demanded that the Ani Kutani put a stop to the disease. They tried, but their method was to attempt the poisoning of Sutalidihi. Some of them changed into serpents whose venom, they all thought, would put an end to her. Their ploy failed, of course, but they blamed the failure on her capriciousness and on the people, who, they said, always made ugly faces when they looked up at her. The disease continued unabated, striking every household. The people began to fear that not one human being would survive, so they called again on the Ani Kutani to use their skills to bring the suffering to an end. On the theory that their first attempt was the right approach, only needing refinement, they changed two of their members into monstrous serpents, Diamondback Rattler and the Uktena.

Suffice it to say that not only did this next attempt fail, it resulted in great disaster, because the attack resulted in the death of Sutalidihi's daughter. When Sutalidihi discovered her daughter's body, she left, and the land was in darkness. Animals, plants, and humans began to sicken, and the Districts were filled with sorrow. The whole earth mourned and wouldn't bring forth life.

The Ani Kutani were told by the Yunwitsandsi, the Little People, that they must go to the Shadowlands and bring back Sutalidihi's daughter. They were to put her in a special box they were to carry, and no matter what she said or did they were not to let her out. But though they succeeded in getting her into the box, one of them could not ignore her pleas for freedom. He opened the lid just a crack, and her spirit fled. With her flight, in the form of the Redbird, the magical powers the Ani Kutani had possessed also fled. It might be that as a consequence of this loss, Sutalidihi finally relented and returned to her people. The Ani Kutani's power was broken, and the people returned to the ways of honoring the Goddesses, Gods, and spirits, and living in accordance with the laws of the Universe.

My point is that it is not the radiation, toxins, electro-magnetic overkill, or holes in the ozone that are causing planetary wipe-out. It's not about immune systems failing, TV, microwaves, or chemically treated everything. It's what they signify – the adamant inability of the white world to see the reality of the sacred, to acknowledge its living presence, and to pay homage through properly constituted ceremony. Logical-positivist modes of thinking that seek to hold on to the disease while suppressing its symptoms will not work. The radiant beings are among us. Sun Woman has come home.

> We drove to the top of the Sandia Peak out of Albuquerque that was a hundred and nine miles away from Trinity. It was raining and I could see a great plane in the sky dragging those things you take wind flow and temperature with. I could see them dragging [off the plane]. . . . Then at 5:30 a bang!
>
> I didn't hear any noise but the sky lit up at the top of the apex of the sky for about a fourth of the horizon and we just watched it and had a feeling of awe.
>
> . . . The feeling of awe I had when that light hit us was remarkable, and I don't think anyone has ever seen an explosion . . . it was either a hundred and nine or two hundred and nine [miles away], I don't remember it – the leaves of those green trees, those native trees, were kind of shining with the gold. It was different, everything changed, everything would never be the same in the world.

Those are the words of "The Woman Who Kept a Secret," as the documentary about Dorothy McKibbin, secretary to the Manhattan Project, titles her. I caught the show on PBS quite by accident last night; I was working on this article and, as usual, had the TV on. I had been watching "All Creatures Great and Small" as is my weekly wont and when it was over had returned to the keyboard when "The Woman Who Kept a Secret" came on. The spirits have a quirky sense of humor; the show began with her words, and for some reason I had stopped, mid-sentence (probably to untangle myself from a syntactical snarl) and was staring at the tube at just the right moment to hear her words: " . . . the leaves of those green trees, those native trees, were kind of shining with gold. It was different, everything changed, everything would never be the same in the world." That's what she said, and upon hearing her I jumped to turn on the VCR.

Several years ago, I noticed some characteristics that Yellow Woman and Yellow Cake shared. They are from the same land, they are the same color, and they are each radiant beings, vast intelligences whose barest acquaintances we've made. Then, there's the curious assignment of the color yellow to signify the female. I thought about these connections, and the terrifying beauty and power of the Bomb, its ritual force whereby it transforms all living things into something other than what they were before its touch. "She's coming back!" I thought, and began working on a novel that would explore this theme.

Far more devastating than radioactivity, plutonium, strontium-90, and all the rest is the kind of consciousness that leads to the destructive effects of modern life. We must end our collusion with the paradigm that neither acknowledges nor perceives the actuality of the radiant beings who inform all of life with their intelligence, their vitality, and their presence.

This is the significance of Sun Woman's return. In it, the pattern made by her existence, the legends that pertain to it, and the transformational process her return point to are clear: this is the time of the Great Transformation, the planet herself is Changing, mutating, from the profane world of patriarchal thought, to whatever lies beyond, radiant and beckoning. Transformation time is a great time indeed.

Transformation or mutation is at the heart of the sacred. The ceremonial understandings of the Native world revolve around the concept. It is the process we call "ritual," which means "to change something or someone from one state or condition to another." This is not meant in Jungian or psychological terms, but in physical ones. That is, what is referred to is actual transformation, such as we are witnessing on a worldwide scale today. Transformation is not a matter of a change of feeling from depression to excitement or enjoyment. It is not a linear process in any sense, and it does not take place in the emotions. It consists of the verifiable, dramatic shift in physical construction of a person or object from one place to another by "magical" means, or the shift in weather from a given state – say dry, with no precipitation possible given the highs and lows, barometric readings, and the like – to rain pouring from the sky from clouds that came "out of nowhere." It is a simple corn plant yielding enough ears of corn to fill a huge basket. It is a pitcher of milk endlessly filling glasses for as long as they are offered. It is water poured into cups and turning into the finest wine.

Over the past forty or so years we have watched the planet exhibit any number of changes that we attempt to explain "scientifically" and, generally, negatively. Yet we can hardly overlook the transformational nature of the changes.

A psychiatrist of my acquaintance once told me she had noticed that dreams of nuclear detonations usually meant that the dreamer was going through a period of transformation in his or her life. In my experience, that really means all sorts of loss: death of a loved one, getting fired, relationship breakup, serious illness, bankruptcy. Sometimes it takes the form of a string of "bad luck" like getting robbed, being involved in an auto accident, misplacing something precious, finding conflict breaking out all around you, getting taken on a business deal. Sometimes all these miserable events take place, and more. Usually, when the dust has settled, another life emerges from the ashes of the old one, which is evident in every aspect of the sufferer's life: she or he is changed. Sometimes the transformation is so great that it is total: the one undergoing the transformation dies. That is, she or he moves from this form to another, from the form we, here, can see to another that we can't.

In the Cherokee writer Marilou Awiakta's account of her childhood encounter with the Black goddess, we find ourselves face-to-face with the truth, ancient and arcane, contemporary and awe-full. When she was a child, Awiakta's father, who worked at the nuclear reactor in Tennessee, told her that the scientists called the reactor "the lady" and, in moments of high emotion, referred to her as "our beloved reactor. They tell me she has a seven-foot shield of concrete around a graphite core, where the atom is split." Discovering from her father that graphite is black, the child "imagined a great, black queen, standing behind her shield, holding the splitting atom in the shelter of her arms."

10.
The Woman I Love Is a Planet;
The Planet I Love Is a Tree

Our physicality – which always and everywhere includes our spirituality, mentality, emotionality, social institutions, and processes – is a microform of all physicality. Each of us reflects, in our attitudes toward our body and the bodies of other planetary creatures and plants, our inner attitude toward the planet. And, as we believe, so we act. A society that believes that the body is somehow diseased, painful, sinful, or wrong, a people that spends its time trying to deny the body's needs, aims, goals, and processes – whether these be called health or disease – is going to misunderstand the nature of its existence and of the planet's and is going to create social institutions out of those body-denying attitudes that wreak destruction not only on human, plant, and other creaturely bodies but on the body of the Earth herself.

The planet, our mother, Grandmother Earth, is *physical* and therefore a spiritual, mental, and emotional being. Planets are alive, as are all their byproducts or expressions, such as animals, vegetables, minerals, climatic, and meteorological phenomena.

Believing that our mother, the beloved Earth, is inert matter is destructive to yourself. (There's little you can do to her, believe it or not.) Such beliefs point to a dangerously diseased physicality.

Being good, holy, and/or politically responsible means being able to accept whatever life brings – and that includes just about everything you usually think of as unacceptable, like disease, death, and violence. Walking in balance, in harmony, and in a sacred manner requires staying in your body, accepting its discomforts, decayings, witherings, and blossomings and respecting them. Your body is also a planet, replete with creatures that live in and on it. Walking in balance requires knowing that living and dying are twin beings, gifts of our mother, the Earth, and honoring her ways does not mean cheating her of your flesh, your pain, your joy, your sensuality, your desires, your frustrations, your unmet and met needs, your emotions, your life. In the end you can't cheat her successfully, but in the attempt to do so you can do great harm to the delicate and subtle balance of the vital processes of planetary being.

A society based on body hate destroys itself and causes harm to all of Grandmother's grandchildren.

In the United States, where milk and honey cost little enough, where private serenity is prized above all things by the wealthy, privileged, and well-washed, where tension, intensity, passion, and the concomitant loss of self-possession are detested, the idea that your attitudes and behaviors vis-à-vis your body are your politics and your spirituality may seem strange. Moreover, when I suggest that passion – whether it be emotional, muscular, sexual, or intellectual – IS spirituality, the idea might seem even stranger. In the United States of the privileged, going to ashrams and centers to meditate on how to be in one's immediate experience, on how to be successful at serenity when the entire planet is overwrought, tense, far indeed from serene, the idea that connected spirituality consists in accepting overwroughtness, tension, yes, and violence, may seem not only strange but downright dangerous. The patriarchs have long taught the Western peoples that violence is sin, that tension is the opposite of spiritual life, that the overwrought are denied enlightenment. But we must remember that those who preached and taught serenity and peacefulness were teaching the oppressed how to act – docile slaves who deeply accept their place and do not recognize that in their anguish lies also their redemption, their liberation, are not likely to disturb the tranquility of the ruling class. Members of the ruling class are, of course, utterly tranquil. Why not? As long as those upon whose labor and pain their serenity rests don't upset the apple cart, as long as they can make the rules for human behavior – in its inner as well as its outer dimensions – they can be tranquil indeed and can focus their attention on reaching nirvanic bliss, transcendence, or divine peace and love.

And yet, the time for tranquility, if there ever was time for it, is not now. Now we have only to look, to listen to our beloved planet to see that tranquility is not the best word to describe her condition. Her volcanic passions, her hurricane storms of temper, her tremblings and shakings, her thrashings and lashings indicate that something other than serenity is going on. And after careful consideration, it must occur to the sensitive observer that congruence with self, which must be congruence with spirit, which must therefore be congruence with the planet, requires something more active than serenity, tranquility, or inner peace.

Our planet, my beloved, is in crisis; this, of course, we all know. We, many of us, think that her crisis is caused by men, or White people, or capitalism, or industrialism, or loss of spiritual vision, or social turmoil, or war, or psychic disease. For the most part, we do not recognize that the reason for her state is that she is entering upon a great initiation – she is becoming someone else. Our planet, my darling, is gone coyote, *heyoka*, and it is our great honor to attend her passage rites. She is giving birth to her new consciousness of herself and her relationship to the other vast intelligences, other holy beings in her universe. Her travail is not easy, and it occasions her intensity, her conflict, her turmoil – the turmoil, conflict, and intensity that human and other creaturely life mirror. And as she moves, growing and leaning ever closer to the sacred moment of her realization, her turmoil, intensity, agony, and conflict increase.

We are each and all a part of her, an expression of her essential being. We are each a small fragment that is not the whole but that, perforce, reflects in our inner self, our outer behavior, our expressions and relationships and institutions, her self, her behaviors, her expressions and relationships, her forms and structures. We humans and our relatives, the other creatures, are integral expressions of her thought and being. We are not her, but we take our being from her, and in her being we have being, as in her life we have life. As she is, so are we.

In this time of her emergence as one of the sacred planets in the Grandmother galaxy, we necessarily experience, each of us in our own specific way, our share of her experience, her form. As the initiation nears completion, we are caught in the throes of her wailings and contractions, her muscular, circulatory, and neurologic destabilization. We should recognize that her longing for the culmination of the initiatory process is at present nearly as intense as her longing to remain as she was before the initiation ceremony began, and our longing for a new world that the completion of the great ceremony will bring, almost as great as our longing to remain in the systems familiar to us for a very long time, correspond. Her longing for completion is great, as is ours; our longing to remain as we have been, our fear that we will not survive the transition, that we will fail to enter the new age, our terror at ourselves becoming transformed, mutated, unrecognizable to ourselves and all we have known correspond to her longing to remain as she has been, her fear that she will fail the tests as they arise for her, her terror at becoming new, unrecognizable to herself and to all she has known.

What can we do in times such as these? We can rejoice that she will soon be counted among the blessed. That we, her feathers, talons, beak, eyes, have come crying and singing, lamenting and laughing, to this vast climacteric.

I am speaking of all womankind, of all mankind. And of more. I am speaking of all our relatives, the four-leggeds, the wingeds, the crawlers; of the plants and seasons, the winds, thunders, and rains, the rivers, lakes, and streams, the pebbles, rocks, and mountains, the spirits, the holy people, and the Gods and Goddesses – of all the intelligences, all the beings. I am speaking even of the tiniest, those no one can see; and of the vastest, the planets and stars. Together you and I and they and she are moving with increasing rapidity and under ever increasing pressure toward transformation.

Now, now is the time when mother becomes grandmother, when daughter becomes mother, when the living dead are released from entombment, when the dead live again and walk once again in her ways. Together we all can rejoice, take up the tasks of attending, take up the joy of giving birth and of being born, of transforming in recognition of the awfulness of what is entailed, in recognition of what it is we together can and must and will do. I have said that this is the time of her initiation, of her new birth. I could also say it is the time of mutation, for transformation means to change form; I could also say it is the climacteric, when the beloved planet goes through menopause and takes her place among the wise women planets that dance among the stars.

At a time such as this, what indeed can we do? We can sing *Heya-hey* in honoring all that has come to pass, all that is passing. Sing, honoring, *Heya-hey* to all the beings gathering on all the planets to witness this great event. From every quadrant of the universe they are coming. They are standing gathered around, waiting for the emergence, the piercing moment when she is counted among the wise. We can sing *Heya-hey* to the familiar and the estranged, to the recognized and the disowned, to each shrub and tree, to each flower and vine, to each pebble and stone, to each mountain and hill. We can sing *Heya-hey* honoring the stars and the clouds, the winds and the rains, the seasons and the temperature. We can think with our hearts, as the old ones do, and put our brains and muscles in the service of the heart, our Mother and Grandmother Earth, who is coming into being in another way. We can sing *Heya-hey*, honoring.

What can we do, rejoicing and honoring, to show our respect? We can heal. We can cherish our bodies and honor them, sing *Heya-hey* to our flesh. We can cherish our being – our petulances and rages, our anguishes and griefs, our disabilities and strengths, our desires and passions, our pleasures and delights. We can, willingly and recognizing the fullness of her abundance, which includes scarcity and muchness, enter inside ourselves to seek and find her, who is our own dear body, our own dear flesh. For the body is not the dwelling place of the spirit – it is the spirit. It is not a tomb, it is life itself. And even as it withers and dies, it is born; even as it is renewed and reborn, it dies.

Think: How many times each day do you habitually deny and deprive her in your flesh, in your physicality? How often do you willfully prevent her from moving or resting, from eating or drinking what she requests, from eliminating wastes or taking breath? How many times do you order your body to produce enzymes and hormones to further your social image, your "identity," your emotional comfort, regardless of your actual situation and hers? How many of her gifts do your spurn, how much of her abundance do you deny? How often do you interpret disease as wrong, suffering as abnormal, physical imperatives as troublesome, cravings as failures, deprivation and denial of appetite as the right thing to do? In how many ways do you refuse to experience your vulnerability, your frailty, your mortality? How often do you refuse these expressions of the life force of the Mother in your lovers, your friends, your society? How often do you find yourself interpreting sickness, weakness, aging, fatness, physical differences as pitiful, contemptible, avoidable, a violation of social norm and spiritual accomplishment? How much of your life is devoted to avoiding any and/or all of these? How much of her life is devoted to avoiding any and all of these?

The mortal body is a tree; it is holy in whatever condition; it is truth and myth because it has so many potential conditions; because of its possibilities, it is sacred and profane; most of all, it is your most precious talisman, your own connection to her. Healing the self means honoring and recognizing the body, accepting rather than denying all the turmoil its existence brings, welcoming the woes and anguish flesh is subject to, cherishing its multitudinous forms and seasons, its unfailing ability to know and be, to grow and wither, to live and die, to mutate, to change. Healing the self means committing ourselves to a wholehearted willingness to be what and how we are – beings frail and fragile, strong and passionate, neurotic and balanced, diseased and whole, partial and complete, stingy and generous, safe and dangerous, twisted and straight, storm-tossed and quiescent, bound and free.

What can we do to be politically useful, spiritually mature attendants in this great transformation we are privileged to participate in? Find out by asking as many trees as you meet how to be a tree. Our Mother, in her form known as Sophia, was long ago said to be a tree, the great tree of life. Listen to what they wrote down from the song she gave them:

> I have grown tall as a cedar in Lebanon,
> as a cypress on Mount Hermon;
> I have grown tall as a palm in Engedi,
> as the rose bushes of Jericho;
> as a fine olive on the plain,
> as a plane tree I have grown tall.
> I have exhaled perfume like cinnamon and acacia;
> I have breathed out a scent like choice myrrh,
> like galbanum, onzcha, and stacte,
> like the smoke of incense in the tabernacle.
> I have spread my branches like a terebinth,
> and my branches are glorious and graceful.
> I am like a vine putting out graceful shoots,
> my blossoms bear the fruit of glory and wealth.
> Approach me, you who desire me,
> and take your fill of my fruits.

II.

Wyrds

orthographies

11.
Here There Be Coyote

Long ago. Haa. In a far place. Away in the north she was standing. There she stood, in the north. Born Koyukon. Born Athabascan. Daughter of salmon, granddaughter of wolverine. Sister of wolf. In that far place was she born, daughter of a Koyukon woman. Daughter of an Irish-American man.

Mary TallMountain: "Look at my face closely. It is one soon you will not see. It is a face of a people almost extinct." That's what she tells them, this elder poet, this seventy-some-year-old survivor. What is it to be an intimate of buffalo, eagle, whale, seal?

> *Once the striped quagga lived,*
> *And the tender hyrax*
> *Populous as the Bengal tiger . . .*
> *Sever the flesh from my bones.*
> *Hang them above a fireplace. . . .*
>
> *Like Ilhalmiut, Khmer, Hohokam . . .*
> *We pass through mortal change:*
> *Our features subside,*
> *Bleach, soften, dissolve . . .*
>
> *Frame the mounted head*
> *In arctic fur*
> *Or exotic plumage*

Such as is seen only in zoos or
Left captive in rapidly dwindling
Rainforests.

And recognizes the anguished kinship of extinction with a beast no more seen: quagga. Saber-toothed tiger. Mammoth. Dinosaur. And with a dying planet: rainforest, seas, lakes, stream, air. And with other races: Khmer, Armenian, "mound builder." All treading the path of disappearance, the one she sees her own ancient people on.

She lies in a hospital bed in an eerily still San Francisco. Wolf pads into her room. Looks at her, quivering eyebrows asking silent question. "Yes," she replies. "Yes. I know what they have done."

What is it to stare down extermination? Who is it?

This poet speaks directly from the precipice, looks down at the long fall, looks out at the far reaches beyond the edge of history. Poet, mystic, witness to the depredations of an age. Survivor.

Over the years I've known her, Mary has been close to death several times. She's always in the hospital, or just coming home. She's always breaking something, or repairing something. Her heart is always breaking. Her eyes are huge now, magnified into great almonds as her sight fades from looking into the misted distances for so long. She goes on and on. Like her poems, like her people, like her city, like her faith, like her earth, she continues, facing and besting unconscionable odds. She's always dying, and always keeping on.

Who is this woman, this survivor, this half-breed, this poet, this friend? If you know the land of her origins and the cadences of the People, if you recall the rhythm of Roman liturgy, the solemnity of the Mass, if you read her poetry with care, hearing the eerie, powerful silences that surround the words, you will know who she is, what extinction is, and what survival engenders.

When Mary was small, her mother gave her to the white doctor and his wife. Her mother had tuberculosis, and she knew she could not survive. She longed for her children, Mary and her brother, to live. To be educated. To have something. She wanted them to avoid the sickness that was soon to kill her. Perhaps she also wanted them to be raised with people like their father, an Irish-American. Why he didn't take them, I don't know. I know that he was not married to Mary's mother, who had been married to a much older man some years before. This man from another Koyukon village and her mother did not live together, but as they were both Catholics and had been married by the church, evidently Mary's mother could not countenance divorce. However it went, the village council decreed that while Mary could go with the Randles, her brother would remain with the people.

Mary went Outside, as they call it, with her adopted parents. A few years later her mother died, and by the time he was eighteen, so did her brother. As it happened, the doctor, her adopted father, invested his money badly and lost everything. He died when Mary was in her late teens, and her adopted mother killed herself sometime later. Bereft of her mother, her people, her education, and her adopted parents, Mary went to work. Eventually she began to drink, though finally she came to terms with her alcoholism. She began to write, to tell the story that had to be told. And while I would never say that writing is easier on one's constitution than drinking, I think it is far more survivor-oriented. Surely it is more in tune with one's spiritual needs. Just as surely it was the work she was born to do. In telling her life and the life of her far away people, she tells all our stories; she tells our lives. And in so doing not only affirms life, but re-creates it.

Coyote went out one day, and he encountered some trouble. He got himself into one of those situations, and he was killed. He fell down a cliff, and all that was left was his bones. But somebody came by, and he called to them. He talked them into giving him a bit of their fur, and trading their eyes for some flower petals. That was how he tricked them. Then he pulled himself together, the bones of his skeleton all came together and the bit of fur stretched out to become his coat. He put his eyes in and trotted off. He was always dying, Coyote. And always coming back to life.

In her way TallMountain is Coyote, and like that quintessential old survivor, she knows that if you're going to face death, and if you're going to engage the sacred, you'd better have your sense of humor intact. It had better be mature, well-formed. She plays.

Goood grease!

she intones. Conjuring images from long ago, the deep delight of gnawing a juicy, dripping hunk.

> The Old Ones clucked,
> sucking and smacking,
> sopping the juices with sourdough bread.

Grease was beautiful –
oozing,
dripping and running down our chins,
brown hands shining with grease.
We talk of it
when we see each other
far from home.

Good
Gooooood.

Imagine a poem singing the praises of grease! In a society that eschews it in all its forms. That shakes a dripping haunch at us in grave warning: grease means death where we live. Where TallMountain was born, it means life. A metaphor for the vast difference that shapes these singular lives? What is death in one is life in the other. What kills the one is what enables the other to survive. I wonder how many Koyukon can survive a low-cholesterol diet. How many tribal ways can survive the culture of Light. If the figures are any indicator, few enough.

So striped quagga and dripping chins hold hands shining with – not light but grease. There's a certain humor in juxtaposing zoos and circuses. She asks us if we "remember the marrow/sweet in the bones?" If we do, we remember the sweetness of life in the face of the kind of death that is far beyond the personal.

The death she faces in her work, as they face the hungry winter wind in life, goes beyond the death of the Koyukon, or that of wolverine, wolf, and seal. It extends to those who have erected their civilization, their cities and freeways, their pipelines and wells, their mines and dams, their power lines and recreation areas over Native lives. She writes:

The last wolf hurried toward me
through the ruined city
and I heard his baying echoes
down the steep smashed warrens
of Montgomery Street and past
the few ruby-crowned highrises
left standing
their lighted elevators useless

Passing the flicking red and green
of traffic signals
baying his way eastward . . .
through the clutter and rubble of quiet blocks . . .
and at last his low whine as he came
floor by empty floor to the room
where I sat
in my narrow bed looking west, waiting

In the quiet, empty city, in the rubble of a civilization, an Indian waits. She is looking west, in the direction the dead go. Only she and the last wolf witness. Surely this is the obverse of "Ozymandias." Similar meaning, only so much more universal, so much less about philosophic reflection and more about a simple if harrowing fact. How the mighty are fallen. How all life is banished. A vision? A dream? A poetic flight of fancy?

The poet doesn't say. Perhaps, like Coyote, even the city can reconstitute itself. Perhaps loss and grief be redeemed. May they become life once more, dripping from our chins, shining on our brown hands, glistening on our delighted, smacking mouths.

12.

Looking Back

Ethnics in the Western Formalist Situation

I had been teaching and chairing the American Indian Studies program at San Francisco State when I attended a 1976 conference. I joined the Berkeley faculty several years later, in the early 1980s.

I.

Since the late 1960s, American ethnic peoples have attempted to fit themselves, their cultures, and their structures into American academic institutions. They have succeeded only marginally, and still do not play any really active role in the development of curricula, dissemination of thought, or formation of policy. This peculiarity does not stem from the minority's unwillingness to function within the university (witness the proliferation of Ethnic Studies Programs across the country), but from the peculiarity of the American academy, which makes it particularly suited to certain kinds of understandings, methods, and concepts and particularly unsuited to others. From the Ethnic scholar's point of view, this peculiarity may appear to be due to "institutional racism," or the devastating unwillingness of the institution to accommodate itself to change, to ideas other than those promulgated since universities began in America, or to a host of other reasons. Subjectively, what it feels like is irrelevance, personal and communal irrelevance, which is far more discouraging and disorienting than overt racism could ever be.

> They have disappeared me
> as they have done to all
> my ancestors before me.
> Are you watching?

It keeps happening
when I remind you who I am
and pretty soon
you don't see me anymore –
because: I'm a left-over Primitive
and you're supposed to feel sorry
for me because

       I am poor and
       diseased and
       ignorant and
       alcoholic and
       suicidal.

You see how it happens?
What goes on in your mind
when you see any of us
wearing our ceremonial dress?

We have NOT been terminated
or exterminated.
We are all here, all around you –
but – YOU disappear US
every day!

Are YOU watching?

    – FROM *Conversations from the Nightmare* BY CAROL LEE SANCHEZ

Almost without exception, my colleagues in Black Studies, Asian-American Studies, and La Raza Studies exhibit the same sense of futility. The situation has gone beyond anger. It is simply profoundly depressing, in the classical sense of the term. And this is tragic. For the multiple perspectives of such diverse peoples as the Navajos of the American Southwest, the Blacks of the industrial states, the Japanese-Americans of San Francisco, and the Chicanos of west Texas can greatly enrich the American's experience of America and of self. The loss is all the greater when one considers the astounding talents that have been associated with the development of Ethnic Studies, both in its classroom and research aspects: people like Jan

Carew of Northwestern University; James Hirabayashi of San Francisco, N. Scott Momaday of Stanford – one could go on and on. So many people, so deeply discouraged. So completely unable, however articulate, however armed with "facts," "statistics," "logic," and even righteousness, to communicate even a minute fraction of the knowledge, the perspective, the ideals, the visions, the conceptual structures of their various peoples to the American intellectual establishment.

Why?

Tomorrow morning I intend to announce to my faculty that I am going to resign. I am somewhat surprised by my decision – I have finally gotten into a position where I have some kind of power. I have a full-time, tenure-track appointment at a large, well-known university. I chair the Department of Native American Studies. I just got a promotion. My publications look good. I speak all over the country, consult widely, meet all kinds of people. Degree in hand, I'm on my way. Or so I'm told, and so I believed. My resignation and the discouragement I see in my colleagues, their alienation from "academe," are reactions to a seemingly insoluble problem: formalism, establishmentarianism, whitism – whatever it is called, it has me beat. Depressed, overworked, hassled beyond belief, sick a large part of the time – I am simply unwilling (and probably unable) to cope with the situation, the inanity, and the downright obtuseness of the university system, the people who compose it, the research-publication Ph.D. garbage bin that I find myself in.

ITEM: Ethnic Studies faculty and the Ph.D. or its equivalent. Would anyone care to determine how many years of training as a singer, a healer, a community organizer, a tribal leader, a storyteller, and a complete conversance with traditional culture make the equivalent of one Ph.D.?

HINT: This is tricky, because it isn't the years that pertain here (we're told); there's some magical process that goes on in the conversion of one citizen into one intellectual – with papers. It's the process, not the years; the content or structure of Ph.D.'ing, that makes one peculiarly qualified to be a professor, a full-time appointment, a promotable entity.

ITEM: In order to teach Ethnic Studies in a California Junior College, you must have a credential in Ethnic Studies. Would you care to guess what the credentialing requirements are?

HINT: They do not include any of the qualifications mentioned above, except (possibly) "community organizer" – and this only if one has two years full-time experience (verifiable, paid, etc.) in the field.

Anyone care to guess who are the "qualified" teachers of Ethnic Studies?

HINT: You can bet that most of them are ex-civil servants who are not people of color.

ITEM: Salaries of all part-time people were recently cut in half at a large Junior College. Anyone care to guess how many Ethnic Studies faculty suffered a fifty percent cut in pay?

HINT: Only one member of the Ethnic Studies Division, the chairperson, is full-time.

The politics of the situation are bad. They're getting worse. It's a case of "What's your hurry? Here's your hat and coat."

But the dynamics of communication are even worse. Another poem gets at the point best, but I don't have a copy of it. It's by a Mohawk poet, who says, roughly, "I read about massacres, and someone asks me, Where'd you get that ring? I read of the chiefs, and someone asks me, What's the suicide rate for Indians?"

Or, from another poem by a Laguna poet:

> "Don't you miss your reservation, dear?"
> – FROM *Conversations from the Nightmare*

For God's sake, what's going on?

And you want to know the really awful part? I can answer that question: I know what's going on, but I don't think anyone "out there" can possibly understand it if I explain it. So I'm quitting. Turning tail, I intend to run. Far. As fast as I can. Back to Cubero, where I at least don't feel like the Emperor when he discovered that he wore NO clothes, that everyone knew it, that they were only being polite, ahh'ing and ohh'ing as he paraded nakedly by. When a mountain disappears you, it's somehow all right.

> I add my breath to your breath
> That our days may be long on the Earth
> That the days of our people may be long
> That we shall be one person
> That we may finish our roads together.
> May my Father bless you with life
> May our Life Paths be fulfilled.
> – LAGUNA PUEBLO

What does that verse mean? What Life experience does it reflect? How does it explain the Bill of Rights? Is it Classical Liberalism? Or Logical Positivism? (I forget.)

Sister Rae (Black) tells an amazing story:

> When I was a small child in school, we had one room that was called The Geography Room. There were maps of various countries of the world hung all around, on all the walls, and there was this one wall that had a huge relief map of the United States on it. Each state had little models of their primary resource on it. For example, Texas had tiny oil derricks. California had tiny oil derricks and orange groves – as did Florida. Each state had some object representing their main source of wealth. The Southern states had tiny Black people picking cotton. *People!* They were PEOPLE! Everywhere the wealth was represented by something, but we were the only *people* on that map.
>
> To this day, I have no concept of geography, or sense of direction, even. There are people I've directed somewhere, who have asked me for directions, who are still lost.
>
> I was so traumatized. I couldn't go into that room.
>
> — RAE ROBINSON

The concept is Racism. The fact is horror. What caused either one? One can pile up the facts until there is no reasoning left. I have taught Native American history and I can honestly say there can be no reasoning in the face of millions of dead. (The concept is Genocide.)

ANOTHER LONG WALK
But what is the truth
to be quantified? And why?
Counted or named?
Idea
logue
rhythm
dia
valuing the stones (logue) the night you say
stars are not purple roses no one
sees them that way so there are
limits
like limbs am-

putated still sing a lifesong
a deathsong occurs not randomly
all over
the plains we could
quantify if we knew how / many warriors died
singing their most important
name
count
which no one saw
in the limits
of their times.

   ii

Quantify the myths
symbolic utterance of the Grandfather (Lenape)
count / years on the Red Score
which does not
count for history
(qualifiers)
(quality)
What mode allows me to understand
ten or sixty million dead (records fail us)
purple blood in rivers
burned villages seven hundred or a thousand in flames who knows in the
particular time the sequence undefined, time answered, held in by the stockade
wall, the Puritan army, the Narragansett allies: no one to escape fire or sword.
How does documentation change genocide into grace?

   iii

Dramatistic?
Ritual of a blood-crazed sun?
Primitive life relieved of its burdened
existence?
Whether these records impale
the body of America on the sword of time
all of them are dead

and illiterate (non) the
primary rose
purple in no one's sight
points northward in the cold
unheeding.

Do you know how many Native peoples were killed in the conquest of the Americas?

Do you know how the Spanish conquest differed from the Anglo-American conquest?

Do you know that the Great League was similar in constitution to the form of government the Americans chose?

Do you know what the earliest policy decisions made by the new American government were?

Do you know where the concept of democracy originated *on this continent*?

Do you know the origins of the Tammany Society (later to be Tammany Hall)?

Do you know what formalism is – at least, as it works out in the practical experience of millions of people?

Do you know how a Navajo, an Iroquois, a Cheyenne, a Pueblo perceive the world?

Do you know about the African Diaspora?

Do you know the roots of the consciousness of La Raza?

Do you know how a Japanese-American sees "reality"?

A Chinese American?

A Vietnamese?

An Igbo?

Do you consider how these points of view, these perceptual-experience-ideation complexes, have affected American society?

What is it to know Zionism – not to know *about* it, but to know the world in terms of it?

"Laguna?" says the provost. "Never heard of it. It must be one of those little, insignificant tribes."

How about some kind of sociological survey: How many Lagunas are there? What are their median ages? Their longevity? Their eating and drinking habits? How many toilets with plumbing are on the Laguna Reservation? What is the suicide rate? What is the alcoholism rate? What is the median income? What form of tribal government do they have? How many tribes are there? How many Native people are there? What have they ever done? What contributions have they made to civilizations? Where is *there*? Where *how many* are?

I am very tired. I just want to go home, write books, talk to the horse, forget the whole thing.

The thing about formalism is that it excludes me. It excludes human beings. The thing about the University (bastion, God knows, of formalism, even in its most permissive era) is that it is a place where I am irrelevant. (Is irrelevant a concept?) The other thing about formalism is that it is so boring. And so very terribly depressing. The more I dabble in formalism, the more like a corpse I become. Physically. Emotionally. Intellectually. Like the trees at the end of the world that Rolling Thunder talked about, I am dying from the top. So is the university. And that's really too bad.

So tomorrow I begin my long walk back from the edge of the grave. And not a moment too soon.

II.

The varieties of American experience did not only begin in Greece. I do not have the faintest idea what John Locke did to synthesize Classical Liberalism. I was taught it, several times. I never learned it. I didn't care much about it then, and I care not at all about it now. Nor do I care why the Pilgrims had it in for the Puritans, or why the Puritans couldn't get along with the Anglicans. I do care why the Europeans couldn't get along with the Indians. I do care that European arrogance led to the slaughter of millions of Indians; the enslavement and torture of millions of Blacks; the destruction of many Chinese, Japanese, and Filipinos; the psychological estrangement of the Natives from their own home. I would like very much to know what concepts the European-Americans held that led to these occurrences. I care to know what presently held concepts result in the discouragement and chaos in Ethnic Studies and Ethnic Communities; result in the lack of sufficient funding for Ethnic Programs; result in the fact that Ethnic Studies courses are nowhere required, though multicultural studies are required by law in the state of California; why American History courses can devote a few words in a year's lectures and a few paragraphs in required readings to Native America.

I would like to know why Sitting Bull said it was all over – what he was thinking, what concepts he based his conclusions on. I would like to know why the great "Indian Fighters" inevitably became Presidents, even after 1890 when the Indians became the "Flips" and the "Gooks." (They all remain Red.)

I am not opposed to structure in academic life: in curriculum, in organization, in research and publication. I am seriously concerned that structure means oppression, ignorance, and perpetuation of ideas and attitudes that have historically resulted in the extinction or near extinction of countless cultures and civilizations. I am afraid that this will be the case because it has always been the case. Because "structure" in this context can only mean "Western structures," because "concepts" in this context can only mean "Western concepts," and the famous forty books are all books that are not mine. They are set in a time, a place, and in intellectual matrix that makes little sense to me, the study and assimilation of which can only result in painful cognitive dissonance, alienation from my self, discouragement, and profound feelings of futility, isolation, and pointlessness. I don't mind reading John Locke. I do mind being stuck with the idea that Locke, Marx, et al., came to their ideas totally within a Western framework, when I know better. I resent the idea that non-Western peoples had no influence on Western civilizations, when I know differently. I resent the inference that Mankind means Western Man, who somehow found himself (never herself) surrounded by non-Westerners who never had two ideas to rub together.

Concepts? There are more than enough of them. Too many.

And one wonders why concepts are central to Western ideational experience: Are concepts central to the life of the intellect? Many philosophers of America and Asia would specifically deny this assumption. Is it important to know which in a chain of events was causative? Is the causative factor the Ultimate Concept? Native American systems are not conceptual in any usual sense of the word. Can they be understood on a conceptual basis, then? Is it necessarily true that concepts ("ideological totalities") impel action, are the causes of events? Is the causal model the only satisfactory one? Can scholars be developed who are not of the cause-and-effect persuasion? Is experience necessarily and always concept-based?

I raise these questions as questions. Surely, I am not certain of my own answers to them, much less of any absolute answer to them. But I question the very assumptions that prompt the belief that understanding concepts will result in changed systems. I have never met a human being who changed behavior or belief by virtue of understanding the historical roots, the concept, that explained that behavior or belief, though I have seen many already-existent behaviors justified and perpetuated by concepts developed after the fact or "discovered" for that purpose.

Still, suppose that we agree that a conceptually oriented system or method is reasonable to base American Studies courses on. Suppose, for example, we try to understand "the full genesis of the Bill of Rights." We can talk about the Enlightenment, about Locke, Rousseau, Voltaire, and Jefferson. There are concepts aplenty, but the inevitable question arises: Where did these concepts originate? Then we can go back to Greece, to the supposed Democracy that Greece theoretically enjoyed, and be back in the same round-robin game. We might even mention the White Roots of Peace. We might talk about indigenous democracies that existed and flourished in America long before there was America. We can discuss the concept of cooperation, belonging, harmony (though we probably won't). We can consider the "social contract" notion of Hobbes, the "primitive" systems that underlie modern democratic theory (though we've all been there before, and real understanding of democracy, even of the Bill of Rights, continues to elude us).

Alternatively, let us suppose that concepts do not underlie American values and behavior, but that values underlie behavior, and that concepts arise when behavior and values do not exactly coincide. "Cognitive dissonance" and other types of personal and social discomfort arise, and the need to maintain values or to explain behavior that is no longer self-evident gives rise to the development of concept systems.

When one believes one thing and acts out another, one has some explaining to do. This is especially true of deep-beliefs or unconsciously held assumptions about how one – and others – should behave. When one's assumptions about reality and one's experience of reality (either from within or without) do not coincide, thoughts that justify (in the bookkeeping sense) the difference arise. The more frequently the difference between the two arises, or the more such differences there are, the more complicated and intense will be the attempt to make a reconciliation between the two. Balance is, after all, a basic need of all systems; the balance between behavior and unconscious assumptions must be maintained. When experience itself maintains this balance, no one *thinks about* what's going on – either in their society or in themselves. But when things get out of balance, thoughts, rationalizations, and mental complexes or systems arise.

I think of concepts as being abstractions. They are the distillations of long series of thoughts. This process of abstracting becomes necessary when the thoughts are so complicated, so diverse, so contradictory, and so far removed from actual experience and vitality, as to make them in themselves inoperable for the purpose of self-defense. And it is self-defense that is the point of conceptualization (in its cause-and-effect, why's-the-sky-blue, why-was-I-created, and so forth, phase) anyway. This self-defense is a matter of maintaining a sense of integrity, of coherence, of sanity (balance). The conceptualizer is seldom (if ever) engaged in her/his own life. When we conceptualize, in fact, we are furthest away from experiencing either ourselves or others as being *here, now*. When we are present in our own life, directly experiencing it (for better or worse), we do not conceptualize. The classic example here might be thinking about the causative factors in orgasm when in the throes of one, or in thinking about the causes of brutality in humankind when one is being tortured to death. Ah, but, you say, experience is seldom that vivid, that intense. Well, maybe it was meant to be.

Take democracy as a more complex example: democracy is not a concept, though it is generally treated as one. It is a series of postures, expressions of values, assumptions, and behaviors that are coherent. These imbue all social activities with a certain essence. It is a matter of the way persons go about being in the world – both interiorly and exteriorly – and a matter of social and institutional interactions that *cannot but mirror* this way of being. These behaviors are characterized by a sense of harmony, respect (or reverence), balance, and kinship (relationship) – which qualities are the basic values that govern (underlie) democratic life. They are expressed by individuals in ways characterized by the lack of a sense of personal superiority over others; a lack of the sense that some are more valuable (or relevant, or desirable) than others; a sense that everything that is in phenomenal existence belongs there, is there for good reason; and that each aspect of reality/experience is as valuable as the next. As the Lakota medicine man Lame Deer puts it (in *Lame Deer, Seeker of Visions*), "If it weren't for that beetle [pointing], you wouldn't exist."

On the other hand, egalitarianism is a concept, a recall of this sense of things I am describing. We say "egalitarianism" as though we were describing a far-off, special island. Then, because it is not directly experienced, "egalitarianism" as a concept needs to be "understood." This takes the form of analyzing its etymological background, or exploring its historic roots (sociologically), or unearthing and transcribing discourses (intellectual history) from Plato's time, or Pharaoh's time, or Peking Man's time, to the present. In the living present, one becomes more and more distanced from "being equal" – feeling neither inferior nor superior, but comfortably equal to his/her peers. One feels valuable because one's being is satisfying, self-validating on many levels.

I know what freedom is, when I am free. I know what democracy is, when I am in a democratic situation, being/behaving democratically. I know, directly, what the Bill of Rights is, when I am free, self-directed, capable of getting satisfaction and nourishment from my self, my friends and family, my work, my Earth.

So what of universities? What of the LIFE OF THE MIND? The Joys of the Intellect? I think these are natural phases or parts of experiencing. But thoughts in a nourishing situation do not have the character of "thinking about" the situation or oneself in it. There is no distance between action, perception, and ideation. Instead, thoughts are there: real, whole, intensely liberating, powerful, and full of meaning. Thought of this kind gives life to people. It does not rip them off, leaving them half-dead on the beaches of *should* and *moreover* and *however, consequently, therefore*. It vitalizes and supports the body-emotion parts of their perceiving, enhancing them.

In this kind of university, perhaps we could function in pride and confidence, and submit papers for multicultural conferences that reflect our unique point of view on American culture, that are capable of being understood as relevant by our audience. Then, maybe we wouldn't have to disappear.

So then, what kinds of courses could be offered in American Studies? Perhaps the specific courses could be left to the program to decide on the basis of where it is located, what its environmental and university resources are, and what kinds of American phenomena its students are actively and personally interested in exploring. Yet a model that shaped that exploration should be available, for all exploration needs some kind of focus, preferably one that is necessarily related to the quest rather than one that is mechanically assigned to it.

We might offer courses in comparative value systems.

And in comparative conceptual systems.

And require that students read whatever they are reading with an eye to discovering the underlying concepts and values that motivate the assertions and conclusions of the author.

This construct would allow Ethnic Studies to begin to have a fighting chance to survive, on OUR terms, within the structure of the University. If our perspectives were taken as valid in themselves, and as pertinent to an understanding of modern American society, then perhaps we would not be inadequately funded, perhaps our courses would form a meaningful part of the American intellectual establishment as they have formed a meaningful part of American society, and perhaps our courses would be respectably required, along with English, History, and Science. Wouldn't that be nice?

Such a supposition might allow us to get a grasp on the Bill of Rights that has eluded us for too long. This method would have the advantage of being applicable to non-Western systems as well as to Western ones. It would not demand the systematic exclusion of concepts that do not appear to give rise to the Bill of Rights or the Wage and Hour Law. It would allow us to examine the various aspects of American consciousness, aspects that, after all, have been shaped by many peoples, perspectives, many value systems, many concepts, and an almost infinite number of behaviors. It would also have the advantage of making it possible to use a variety of methodologies to illuminate a specific issue without requiring that either the issue, the facts, or the method be warped out of shape.

13.
Who's Telling This Story, Anyway?

My father likes to tell stories and my mother likes to research family history and write memories down. Sometimes he gets to telling a story one way, but she remembers it another way. Recently my father was telling me a tale about their youth, something about a night of dining and dancing at Billy Mearns's Casa Mañana in Albuquerque years ago. He was warming to his tale, eyes focused on that middle distance where stories unreel before a storyteller's eyes. He had hit his stride, pauses taut with drama, gestures, expression, posture all bespeaking their share of the tale. During a rush of words, my mother interrupted—"Wasn't it Billy Mearns who came over to the table just then? Billy, not Max, wasn't it?" she interjected. "No," he said, irritation creeping into his voice. "No. It was Max." "Well, I thought it was Billy," she said. "It was Max," he replied. "Who's telling this story, anyway, you or me?" he demanded. "Well, you, of course," she admitted.

But I would have liked to hear her story, too. Hers and his together on simulcast. And Billy Mearns's story, and Max's as well. I like Casa Mañana stories and was delighted to read some in Martin Cruz Smith's novel *Stallion Gate*. Reading about the old supper club in a mega-seller book made the club real, more real than my own excursions to the place after it was sold and became the Sunset Inn, after Billy Mearns and Max had gone to the twilight land where all our cronies finally go.

So many stories; so many voices telling one huge, complex, multitudinous story, a story so long no single novel can encompass it, a story so vast only the concept of cycle begins to hint at its dimension, a story so complex that only the greatest variety of devices, techniques, points of view, styles, and stances can justly reflect its infinite glittering facets, plumb its mysterious multitude of tunnels and hidden corridors – so many stories a teacher of American Literature is hard put to know where to begin or how to proceed in the face of such vastness. But, as the oracle advises, one must enter vast-ness – so let us begin.

But where?

Perhaps at this juncture we should recognize that critical discourse is de-fined by boundaries set not by writers but by critics, and not by critics sim-ply, but by elite white men in positions powerful enough to make them culture-brokers. We need to realize that we are not usually discussing litera-ture when we engage in literary discourse, but rather critical standards set by predecessors whose thought may have been pertinent at one time or to one conversation, but which are manifestly inadequate given the nature of the task we are faced with as the twentieth century moves to its close. That task is discovering the nature of American Literature, and it is a daunting one.

In "The Philosophical Bases of Feminist Literary Criticisms" (*Gender & Theory, Dialogues on Feminist Criticism*), Ellen Messer-Davidow argues that feminist criticism cannot become useful until feminist critics recognize that using the tools of criticism bequeathed us by traditional literary schol-ars necessarily results in pointless arguments about irrelevancies, among other things. She suggests a way of "reconstituting knowledge that evolves from feminist perspectives" through the method of devising "a framework that places traditional and feminist literary criticisms on a single plane of analysis." Her framework is inclusive of a variety of theories and practices because it seeks their philosophical bases, "their *subject, subject matters, methods of reasoning,* and *epistemology*" (Messer-Davidow, pp. 64–65). She continues:

> Explicitly, then, discussions of literature, whether theoretical or practical, are determined by the *subject matter selected* and the *methods of reasoning exerted upon it.* . . .
>
> The subject matters and methods are constitutive elements of the predomi-nant research tradition in Western literary study. A research tradition binds the-oretical and practical work by specifying an epistemology, which, to quote the philosopher Larry Laudan, provides "*a set of general assumptions about the en-tities and processes in a domain of study, and about the appropriate methods to be used for investigating the problems and constructing the theories in that domain.*"

The beginning issue, then, is not one of whether we can adequately discuss all the literature written in the United States since the beginning of the century (or the beginning of the nation), because, given our existing critical tools and the epistemology that gave rise to those tools, we cannot. The issue is rather to discover a critically sound apparatus that will let our studies be inclusive rather than exclusive while still providing us with a means for distinguishing aesthetically profound works from paler imitations. What we must devise, then, are critical strategies that do not descend only from Anglo-European criticism, for example, the Western Masculinist Aristocratic Tradition, for that tradition of necessity speaks only to and from itself, excluding many American works that are not based within it. To paraphrase Messer-Davidow, "when we adopt traditional perspectives, the consequences to us are the marginalization, negation, objectification, and alienation" of our American selves in the service of a far more narrow critical self.

She suggests that since it is we who are delineating the boundaries, it is we who can reset them, and I heartily concur, though I would do so beyond the somewhat restricted parameters of feminist theory, which is so intent on its relationship to the male tradition it usually overlooks the otherwise noticeable fact that the male tradition is more white than male and more elitist than masculinist. Their argument is more about whether women who differ from the established norms get to play literature, than whether or not all perspectives and experience-bases get to be part of the literary game.

Personally, I would prefer a literary participatory democracy, a new vision and practice that would enable us as critics and teachers to illuminate the great panoply of literature that American writers produce yearly. With me, it's congenital.

What would be of use to us as we begin to build a criticism that will work for the whole of American Literature would be to devise a relevant epistemology, one that articulates a set of assumptions about the entities and processes in our domain of study that does not marginalize American writers because they seem to occupy a subset of a set of constricted assumptions; we need a critical system sufficiently broad and accurate to allow the development of investigative and theoretical tools that will centralize the diverse communities and multiple voices presently marginalized.

As June Jordan wrote in her 1981 essay "For the Sake of People's Poetry:

Walt Whitman and the Rest of Us," in which she wonders why Walt Whitman, surely a white man, "some kind of father to American literature," is excluded from the canon:

> A democratic state does not, after all, exist for the few, but for the many. A democratic state is not proven by the welfare of the strong but by the welfare of the weak. And unless that many, that manifold constitution of diverse peoples can be seen as integral to the national art/the national consciousness, you might as well mean only Czechoslovakia when you talk about the U.S.A., or only Ireland, or merely France, or exclusively white men.

In the twentieth century, the American literary establishment has been engaged in essaying (albeit with much resistance) the transition from the absolutism to the relativism of the millennium to come. Writers are making that passage with a great deal more alacrity than critics, it seems, perhaps because it is in the nature of art to move just a bit ahead of the stream, to anticipate the direction the general society will take, to step along the path (or barrel along the interstate) in the vanguard.

The movement of the nation is reflected in the major works of this century, in their dominant preoccupation with maturation as a theme, the utilization of numerous voices and points of view to structure their work, the variety of styles and tonalities they select, the often fragmented, even fractured impact they effect. In essence, by their thematic, stylistic, and structural choices, American writers join Jordan in echoing Whitman, saying: "By God! I will accept nothing which all cannot have their counterpart of on the same terms."

During the same period, literary scholarship has as painfully and quite a bit more haltingly begun to grapple with the fact of *American* literature being a kind of literature that is distinct from the literature of England and Western Europe. Some of us are aware that American literature is New World Literature, as much non-Western as it is Western. We recognize that it shares as many features with African, Indian, Japanese, Chinese, or Arab literature as with the literature of its professed (but not actual) parents. Some of us are aware, as Jordan puts it, that "New World does not mean New England. New World means non-European; it means new; it means big; it means heterogeneous; it means unknown; it means free; it means an end to feudalism, caste, privilege, and the violence of power. It means *wild* in the sense that a tree growing away from the earth enacts a wild event. . . . " and that the United States is part of the New World. We are aware that we have entered another world, not solely for geocultural reasons but for profoundly intellectual and terribly physical ones. The twentieth century is the century in which America has come of age, and our writers have been busily engaged in detailing a nation's maturation. This new adult will not greatly resemble its forebears, for we achieved maturity in a way that was new indeed, bringing to our initiation a new paradigm, a new way to think about ourselves and our realities. It is an event whose implications for every aspect of our lives has barely begun to be explored, but I submit that a philosophy of literature that does not utilize the Theory of Relativity will soon find itself in the special heap reserved for whatever is disconnected from the solid ground of social reality.

It is in the New World of the twentieth century that the Old World's yearning for enlightenment blasted itself into blazing actuality: Los Alamos. Alamagordo-Stallion Gate. Nagasaki. Hiroshima. Nevada. The Marshall Islands.

White men of privilege had decreed God dead a couple hundred years before, over time replacing the absolutist determinism of Protestant Calvinism with the more desirable but equally absolutist secular determinism of Darwin, of Marx, and, eventually, of Freud. They had their reasons: fear of chaos, of loss of status, of loss of the position of authority they could only lay claim to under an absolutist paradigm. Odd, isn't it? The very class that engineered the bomb and gave credence to the brilliant if almost incomprehensible mutterings of an old Jewish genius stood to lose the most in the fallout. Put otherwise, for the rest of us it's like the poet said: "When you got nothing, you got nothin to lose."

We are here, forty-five years after the bomb, fifty-five years after Einstein showed us what frame of reference we were inhabiting. The twentieth century has seen the dawn of the Age of Relativity, and, as Vine Deloria, Jr., has it, the Age of Relatives. We need to apply its strictures to our endeavors in the hope that we will gain a broader perspective on our literature and, through it, on our own lives.

What is this bomb, this theory that wiped out our innocence and illuminated our organic relatedness in its blinding light?

According to Random House's *1966 Unabridged Dictionary*, the Theory of Relativity holds "that all motion must be defined relative to a frame of reference and that space and time are relative, rather than absolute concepts." For literary purposes, this theory can be revised to hold that "all significance must be defined relative to a frame of reference, and form and content are relative, rather than absolute concepts." But in order to generate a critical system that facilitates the study and teaching of American literature – all of it – we must let go of our childhood belief in ultimate authority bestowed from on high in a universe as devoid of change and movement as a styrofoam charnel house filled with non-biodegradable corpses. We must recognize that determinism as a useful idea is defunct; that the idea of freedom, like its companion idea democracy, entails loosening the strictures that bind us and redefining cultural boundaries along lines that reflect the actual entities and procedures in our domain. As critics and teachers we need to recognize that where we are is not where we have been. Einstein's theory and America's bomb put us on notice: the universe is a multiverse. Truth is forever moving on to the next town, forever changing shape, size, color, demeanor, class, gender, and lifestyle. The universal verities – whatever one tiny group of humans or another might have determined them to be – are far greater and more diversified than any single epistemological system of the past could have articulated, and the discipline of literary studies must perforce recognize our reality and admit that the center cannot hold because there never was one center only, but a myriad of centers in constant flux. In this century the ideal of the unitary gives way to the realization of the multiple; the belief in the fixed and absolute crumbles in the recognition of motion as the fundamental law of the multiverse.

So how do we come to terms with this mind-blowing concept, this relativity? How do we experience non-linearity, multiplicity, multiveracity? How do we apply the theoretical to the intractably practical, locate frames of reference that will enable us to accurately define the aesthetic motion that informs and enlivens every true work of art?

In "Stalking the Billion-Footed Beast" (*Harper's Magazine*, November 1989, vol. 279, no. 1674, pp. 45–56), Tom Wolfe considers the condition of American fiction in the late twentieth century and writes,

> American society today is no more or less chaotic or absurd than Russian society or French society or British society a hundred years ago. . . . It is merely more varied and complicated and harder to define. In the prologue to *The Bonfire of the Vanities* [Wolfe's 1987 novel about New York City], the mayor of New York delivers a soliloquy in a stream of consciousness as he is being routed from a stage in Harlem by a group of demonstrators. He thinks of all the rich white New Yorkers who will be watching this on television from within the in-

sulation of their cooperative apartments. "Do you really think this is *your* city any longer? Open your eyes! The greatest city of the twentieth century! Do you think *money* will keep it yours? Come down from your swell co-ops, you general partners and merger lawyers! It's the Third World down there! Puerto Ricans, West Indians, Haitians, Dominicans, Cubans, Colombians, Hondurans, Koreans, Chinese, Thais, Vietnamese, Ecuadorians, Panamanians, Filipinos, Albanians, Senegalese, and Afro-Americans! Go visit the frontiers, you gutless wonders! Morningside Heights, St. Nicholas Park, Washington Heights, Fort Tryon – *por qué pagar más!* The Bronx – the Bronx is finished for you!" and on he goes, New York and practically every other large city in the United States are undergoing a profound change. The fourth great wave of immigrants – this one from Asia, North Africa, Latin America, and the Caribbean – is now pouring in. Within ten years political power in most major American cities will have passed to the nonwhite majorities. Does that render these cities incomprehensible, fragmented beyond the grasp of all logic, absurd, meaningless to gaze upon in a literary sense? Not in my opinion. It merely makes the task of the writer more difficult if he [sic] wants to know what truly presses upon the heart of the individual, white or nonwhite, living in the metropolis in the last decade of the twentieth century.

Wolfe might have added, though he didn't, that by the turn of the millennium literary power in the United States will have largely passed into the hands of the writers now designated "marginal" by our present literary establishment. He might have mentioned that a literature that reflects the experience of this emerging America is the literature that will find its way into the canon in the coming century, and that being the case, it behooves critics and teachers to begin equipping ourselves and our students with a literary background that will enable us to understand and teach all varieties of American literature as a coherent body of work. To do that, we must publish intelligent critiques and teach works that reflect America's diverse consciousness and her multitudinous experience.

You know, America is not England. Recently visiting there, I discovered a number of things, among them the droll information that I speak English as a second language and the tiny-ness of a nation that I had been taught to see as towering over the colonies in intellectual stature. Until I went there and traveled the country myself, I had no idea that English literature is the literature of the small, while ours is the literature of the vast. How can it be otherwise? There they are blessed by a seemingly homogeneous population, while here are we, heterogeneous in the extreme. There they are writing out of a nation the size of a single largish American state. Here we are, in a nation as big as a world. Of course, our literatures will exhibit marked differences. It is our job as American scholars to recognize the obvious and deal with our literatures accordingly.

In his article Wolfe details the white literary scene of this era – the sixties through the eighties – and argues that realism is by far the most useful technique for novelists because American readers are riveted by reportage, making nonfiction outsell fiction by billions. He demonstrates through a few well-chosen examples the documentary approach of journalistic narrative that yields the astonishing phenomena of life imitating art. His examples include Elmer Gantry and Jim Bakker. "It was through this process, documentation," he writes, "that Lewis happened to scoop the Jim Bakker story by sixty years – and to render it totally plausible, historically and psychologically, in fiction."

Marshall McLuhan would know that Wolfe's anticipating the New York elections by a few years was not so strange. After all, hadn't he written that artists see where we are and where we are going while everyone else sees where we have been. We might paraphrase Gogol in this regard, saying, "Where are we going, America?" And to discover the answer, we should better examine the literature of the twentieth century from the writers' points of view rather than from those of our critical colleagues, who can only tell us how it was when we were where we used to be.

In "The Race for Theory" (*Gender & Theory, Dialogues on Feminist Criticism*, p. 225), Barbara Christian serves notice on a critical establishment that looks to itself to determine which works should be sainted, and hints at the destructiveness of that approach, echoing Wolfe but turning her sights on critics rather than on elite novelists.

> I have seized this occasion to break the silence among those of us, critics, as we are now called, who have been intimidated, devalued by what I call the race for theory. I have become convinced that there has been a take-over in the literary world by Western philosophers from the old literary elite, the neutral humanists. Philosophers have been able to effect such a take-over because so much of the literature of the West has become pallid, laden with despair, self-indulgent, and disconnected. The New Philosophers, eager to understand a world that is today fast escaping their political control, have redefined literature so that the distinctions implied by that term, that is, the distinctions between everything

written and those things written to evoke feeling as well as to express thought, have been blurred. They have changed literary critical language to suit their own purposes as philosophers, and they have re-invented the meaning of theory.

... Critics are no longer concerned with literature, but with other critics' texts, for the critic yearning for attention has displaced the writer and has conceived of himself as the center.

In the narcissistic enterprise of contemporary criticism, we have lost sight of the purpose of criticism; Christian quotes a Buddhist aphorism aptly: "The finger pointing at the moon is not the moon," underlining a fact that we can all too easily ignore in the press of our professional exigencies. I am a writer, and I recall back in '86 when I was a graduate student in the Creative Writing Program at Oregon, making the same plaint. Why is it, my fellow-writers and I moaned, that we don't study works in our courses, but only those of the critics? We took it personally, then, though even then we were also aware that a criticism that finds its own ponderings of far greater interest than poetry, drama, and fiction was largely irrelevant to our endeavors and to mundane life on planet Earth.

Confusing the menu with the meal is an occupational hazard for intellectuals, and maintaining colonial boundaries through the agency of intellectual domination is not an appropriate endeavor for professionals who would bear the title of Humanist meaningfully. Philosophical apartheid is more vicious than its political child precisely because the latter takes its shape and rationale from the former. It does little good to demonstrate for divestment in South Africa while at home intensely supporting and reinforcing an epistemology that gives to apartheid its strength and power.

But how do we maintain a coherence of discourse, continue to function as critics, maintain intellectual respectability, and, most of all, promote the understanding of great literature if we give up the standards and methods we presently utilize? I suggest that we must change the frame of reference from that of Western philosophy alone to something more nearly eclectic, redefine the entities we identify as subject and subject matters, and devise methods of reasoning we choose to exert upon them that reflect the literary processes actual American writers utilize. Should we dare to explore alternative sets of general assumptions about the entities and processes in a domain of study, as well as the methods we deem appropriate for investigating the problems and constructing the theories in that domain, we might find ourselves engaged in an endeavor that reconnects American critical studies to American literature. Should this endeavor bear fruit, we might find our-selves able to distinguish the finger from the moon, to put down the menu and eat fruit salad.

American literature is not only Western in origin and execution. It takes its shape and meaning from Native American, Asian, and Arab thought and epistemology, and the texts, like the processes of conveying the mean-ing they utilize, draw from the Native American oral tradition, Buddhist and Hindu traditions, Islam, Torah and Talmud, and oral traditions of the Celts and other "Western" societies that do not derive from the Christian Bible or Aristotelian thought. And American literature of the twentieth century takes its meaning as well from the American oral tradition, from American media, and from the particular worldview that a nation as di-verse and far-flung as America necessarily develops. In addition to all of the above, America is a nation without much of a past and is thus unlike all of its progenitors.

Lest you are wondering whether there is a text in this piece, let us briefly consider Hemingway's "Nick Adams" stories and N. Scott Momaday's *House Made of Dawn* within the context of the theory of relativity. It is within such a frame that texts can converse, not only one-sidedly as in Hem-ingway informing Momaday because he precedes Momaday, but as in Momaday and Hemingway informing each other, the texts informing each other because they and we, readers, exist concurrently. Hemingway's cycle was written in the pre-Relativity, post–World War I early 1920s, while *House Made of Dawn* was written post–World War II, more than twenty years after the Bomb, more than thirty after Einstein's theory was pub-lished. But in spite of what should be, and in many ways is, a vast disconti-nuity, they possess a certain sameness: Both employ multiple points of view to advance the narrative and generate meaning, Hemingway more daringly but perhaps less efficaciously than Momaday. They each use the respective conflicts to inform their narrative. Both authors focus on young men (Nick and Abel, respectively) who participated in these global conflicts, por-traying their protagonists as alienated, isolated figures divorced from their community. Both employ images of their protagonists' early childhood and youth to explore the roots of that conflict of which the wars are amplifica-tions, generating a view of war as a symbolic echo of inner dis-ease. In both works women are shadowy figures – absent or obscured – though they fig-ure more directly in *House Made of Dawn*, where one of the major voices,

Milly, is Abel's social worker and lover. It is through her narrative, the reflections of another of his lovers, Angela St. John, and those of other characters as much as through his own thoughts and actions that we discover who Abel is. In the structure of *House Made of Dawn*, the protagonist, a full-blood from Jémez Pueblo, is even more shadowy than the women, passive, elusive, seen more through others' eyes than through his own.

Similarly, Nick Adams is elusive, a fish who hides in treacherously deep pools and along the overhanging banks of the Big Two-Hearted River. We learn more about him through the journalistic and compelling stories and vignettes that frame each sequence than through his own perceptions of himself. Nick's fiancée, Marjorie, and his mother, confined to the dark of her room, are the only women he's directly involved with, and he rejects each of them, while a stranger, an American Indian woman who is in labor, attended by Nick's father, a viciously uncaring and racist Doctor, affects him deeply. In the story the Doctor takes his young son with him to the Indian camp, and the scene of horror that follows, told in Hemingway's flat, unemotional tone, sets the direction of the cycle; in it and its companion piece "The Doctor and the Doctor's Wife" we see that the war has gone on a long, long time, and we discover something of the sources of the centuries-long global conflict.

Exactly how long that war has continued is made clear in Momaday's account of a man torn between two worlds, unable to find a place in either – not because of the Second World War in which he served, but because of the centuries-long Indian–White war into which he and his ancestors for nearly five hundred years had been born. He is a survivor, kin to the pitifully small handful of Pecos Pueblo people who had fled the destruction of their home and found sanctuary to the south among the Walatowa, the Jémez as they are called by Spanish and Anglo-Americans.

The style, voice, and narrative stance each writer chooses differ widely. Hemingway is – particularly in the first ten chapters – his minimalist self, while Momaday waxes almost baroque, packing layers of meaning into each paragraph. Hemingway's sequence is chronological while Momaday veers wildly from past to present, blurring time into infinity as he contemplates the enduring nature of space. It is in this respect, the matters of style and of structure, that these pieces most clearly exhibit the impact of Relativity. It can be argued that Momaday, Indian to the core, is necessarily going to focus on relationships, that being a fundamental concept in Indian thought, but he carries his treatment of relationship beyond the social and the metaphysical, structurally placing it squarely in the midst of an Einsteinian universe where the particle is a wave, the wave is an object, and all motion is a function of context.

Indians have long recognized the principle of relativity, though they did not articulate it in a recognizably Western scientific framework but within the ritual framework that is the ground and sky of their being. The novel is framed in the figure of a man running a sacred race, a ritual that is enjoined by men of every Pueblo. The story begins with the run, and it ends with it, and in the course of the tale we discover the nature of motion in its relationship to community, and the boundaries of that community, which include eternity and infinity in its conceptualization. But while the concept is firmly embedded in traditional Indian life and thought, it remained for Momaday to transfer it whole into a Western literary work. Writers before him had made stabs at it, unsuccessful for the most part, or had bypassed it entirely. The net effect of the latter ploy was to lock the work, and the protagonist, into a tragic scenario where the process of conquest and colonization led inexorably to Indian extinction. But all the preceeding works had been written prior to the 1940s, and the novel itself had not yet made its pact with the new world of mathematics in any widely recognized and thus readily accessible fashion. The impact of Momaday's wedding of the ancient tribal with the avant-garde modern was the development of a protagonist who is neither hero nor anti-hero but is one in a number of elements that define and delineate the field within which they move. The duality of background and foreground disappears and they become integers of one another.

Yet we can see that Hemingway, writing in the 1920s, is groping toward this solution to the problem of novelistic decay in his time. By then all the "great novels" had been written, and his nearly peripheral membership in Gertrude Stein's group must have acquainted him with the exciting new mathmatical and painterly concepts that were sweeping Paris in this period; she delighted in bringing painters, philosophers, mathematicians, and writers together, and the conversation was undoubtedly heady, filled with ideas about breaking absolutist barriers in every arena. One of those who impacted on this group was Alfred North Whitehead, whose philosophical works pushed back heretofore perceived boundaries of thought and reframed Western epistemology.

Until this time Western thought had tended toward the heroic paradigm in which a singular hero prevails against fate, nature, love, the gods, or whatever came his way to triumph against. It was a tradition that gave rise to the American hero who, singular in his canniness, profundity, and capability, fights Indians and aristocrats, functions easily in nature like the one and rules others unconcernedly like the other, but who does both from an individualistic, isolated position. He is a man without a community, without relationships of more than a transitory nature, isolated and alienated.

In "On Olson, His Melville" (*An Olson-Melville Source-book, I: The New Found Land, North America,* ed. Richard Grossinger, Vermont: North Atlantic Books, 1976, p.6) Robert Bertholf writes: "In separation a hero is one who most successfully asserts his will over reality. . . . The imperative of 'the Lordship over nature' widens the estrangement between man and his environment, isolating him from the roots of his existence, and necessitating the manufactory of catalogues and systems of thought and analysis to replace the natural, multiphasic environment, now neglected."

It is just such a hero that Hemingway does not create as Nick Adams, though Nick is as isolated as Deerslayer and though it might be tempting to read the Big Two-Hearted River stories as if they were about man triumphing against nature. And it is true that in the final story of the sequence, "L'Envoi," Hemingway creates another character, Manolo, who could be seen as prevailing over nature in the figure of the bull he finally manages to kill, but that would misread the text. It is Manolo who is felled, and his hollow triumph rests in his blind determinism that would gainsay age and time, though finally he can deny the inroads of neither time nor poison gas.

But Nick triumphs not at all. By the time he reaches the end of the war, he is beyond the concept of triumph, willing to settle for an uneasy peace, momentarily camped between the hopeless swamp and the blackened forest. He is aware of the tragic swamp, which he does not yet wish to enter; he is aware of the return to life of the scorched forest behind him; he is aware that silence and isolation are his chosen companions, along with the fish in the mysterious stream where he can heal a little before he goes on.

> He did not feel like going on into the swamp. He looked down the river. A big cedar slanted all the way across the stream. Beyond that the river went into the swamp.
>
> Nick did not want to go in there now. He felt a reaction against deep wading with the water deepening up under his armpits, to hook big trout in places impossible to land them. In the swamp the banks were bare, the big cedars came to-

gether overhead, the sun did not come through, except in patches; in the fast deep water, in the half light, the fishing would be tragic. In the swamp fishing was a tragic adventure. Nick did not want it. . . .

– "BIG TWO-HEARTED RIVER: PART II, " P. 231

It is not Adams as hero, lord, and master who imposes his will over beings he perceives as lesser; it is not Adams as Adam, who names and therefore rules that Hemingway depicts. No, it is Adams as wounded survivor, neither victim nor victimizer but observer, a detached, nearly speechless participant in a world he never made, much less ever ruled.

It is as though in the sixteen stories that compose the set, Hemingway is struggling toward the vision that Momaday recorded in *House Made of Dawn* (p. 170), "A long time ago it was dark, and you looked in the fire and listened, and he was going on about all he knew, and he knew everything and there was no end to the stories and the songs." As Nick stands in the stream where there is no end to fishing or the swirl and pull of the current and contemplates the tragic swamp where the Indians lived in his youth, the sixteen stories in the cycle swirl their way swampward; but for Hemingway the darkness is not a sign of endless motion but the mark of absolute ending. Adams, the tragic protagonist, ends divided from his people, a pawn of conquest, a victim of white men's endless war, he ends as he begins, in the stream but not of it. He is not so much mature as hopeless, not balanced precariously amid ambiguities but locked into isolation.

Yet there is life around him – the black grasshoppers; Bugs, the caring Negro man who has befriended the blood-thirsty, crazed white fighter in a bizarre distortion of master-slave relations; but Bugs remains connected while his charge, Ad, suffers from the extreme of disconnection that plagues the other owners in the cycle; Marjorie, who unlike Nick thinks love is fun; Dick Boulton, Eddy and Billy Tabeshaw, the three Ojibway men who remain connected to honor and pride; the laboring Indian woman's husband, who kills himself in the face of the cesarean the Doctor performs on his wife without benefit of anesthetic; Peduzzi, who tries to hustle some life into gentility; Manolo's tall, red-skinned picador, Zurito.

And there is death: not the clean death of the two fish Nick catches, nor of the bull who is finally slaughtered in the ring, but the horrifying death of zombies that march through the cycle like monstrous parodies of human beings: Mr. Elliot, who was a virgin poet at twenty-five, and Mrs. Elliot, older than her husband and in love with her girlfriend; George, whose over-protected wife wants long hair, a dining room, and a cat; the young gentleman and his wife, who fail to live despite Peduzzi's urgings; the Doctor and the Doctor's wife; Renata and the uncaring mechanical crowd at the bullfight.

But it is in the struggle toward multiplicity, multiveracity, that Hemingway in this cycle approaches and anticipates the thought revolution just beginning to pulse through the West. The sixteen stories of the set move to change the framework of white men's literature; they seek to link the consciousness of the passive protagonist to other consciousnesses and thereby to create a multiplicity of points of view, a field of consciousness from whose many-faceted sides the reality he is seeking can be glimpsed.

I'm not certain that he succeeds, but neither am I convinced that he fails. The attempt is what intrigues me, the attempt to redefine the constituent elements of consciousness, the attempt to reach beyond the boundaries of received wisdom, the knowledge that death and life interplay like light and shadow on the moving water, the attempt to convey that knowledge in fiction. His attempt to portray a character as both particle and wave, moving always indeterminately across a forever moving field among other equally indefinable wavicles, part of the whole in a way that is simultaneously fragmented and complete, makes the cycle of compelling interest. Read as a groping effort toward an articulation of the theory of relativity in a literary mode, it poses questions that demand exploration.

In 1938 Alfred North Whitehead wrote (in *Modes of Thought*, 1938, NY: The Free Press, 1966, pp. 6–7) that "the notion of existence involves the notion of an environment of existence and of types of existences. Any one existence involves the notion of other existences, connected with it and yet beyond it," a formulation that might be taken as a description of what Hemingway essayed in the cycle I have been discussing. As well, it can be read as speaking to Momaday's achievement in *House Made of Dawn*.

Abel, Adam's descendant, continues the journey Nick began, moving from isolation to community. He is able to do so because by the 1960s, when Momaday was writing, the fatalistic paradigm of determinism had been largely replaced by the open-ended paradigm of relativity. Because we could now assume that all motion must be defined relative to a frame of reference, because we could agree that space and time are relative rather than absolute concepts, we could begin to acknowledge that absolutes must give way before context, and universal realities could only be discerned within a framework that could be replaced by another that would by its nature and the nature of relationship change them. It is the dawning realization in the fact of motion that opens out literature for writers in this century and makes possible the interconnecting of Western genre with non-Western consciousness; in this way the West joins the rest of humanity in the complex level of consciousness that its clinging to a childhood need for authority had heretofore denied it. Now it is possible for a novel to exist that utilizes the structure of a Navajo Chantway, that disregards chronology and temporality, that posits its coherence on the sort of random motion from which the meanings of the universe derive.

Momaday begins with the running. Francisco, Abel's grandfather, running small in the vastness of the land, running perfectly, in harmony with all that is. Because his existence is so fitting, he wins the race and, in drumming at the ensuing dance, tells the beat perfectly – no easy feat, given the structure of Pueblo music – and then goes on to heal a child later that day. He is in harmony, his individual being placed within its context so that all elements dance among all elements, making miracles reasonable and effortless.

And at the story's end, after Abel has faced madness and rage, after he has steeped himself in speechlessness and murder, after he has not only rejected all hands held out to him but has broken all customs and laws of his people, Abel, orphan child of a Walotowa woman and her stranger husband, sole survivor of his family, save his grandfather – a man who has paid for his dalliance with a witch woman, Porcingula, by the deaths of his daughter and other grandson and the withering of his leg – Abel regains himself as he watches at his grandfather's deathbed. After preparing the old man for burial in the Indian way, Abel at last takes up his place as a Runner-After-Evil. He has learned that Evil cannot be confronted or conquered, but must be accepted as a necessary part of all that is, much as his predecessor Adams has learned. Running into the dawn just after his grandfather's death, Abel performs his own act of perfect balance, and in motion discovers the meaning of the stories, of the songs:

> He was alone and running on. All of his being was concentrated in the sheer motion of running on, and he was past caring about the pain. Pure exhaustion laid hold of his mind, and he could see at last without having to think. . . . He was running, and under his breath he began to sing. There was no sound, and he had no voice; he had only the words of a song. And he went running on the rise of the song. *House made of pollen, house made of dawn.*

* * *

Which works should be sanctified and which should remain in the bin of unremarked fiction depends largely on the critical standards we apply. As I would like to understand the critical process, texts can be perceived as a multiplicity of phenomena interrelating in a dynamic field. They are neither singly nor in combination fixed or static, nor do they exist outside of social reality. As movement is the fundamental nature of all phenomena in existence, and as cultural artifacts are phenomenal, texts move. They move in their inner conversations – subject with subject, theme with style, structure with symbol, character with plot, dialogue with setting, each and every one of these with all and any within the cultural and historical field within which each rests and in the critical field within which they are framed. They move. Flow, jerk, dance, connect, disconnect, reconnect in ever new arrangements of meaning, one among the others. Text amplifies and illumines text, the whole changing shape and order with the intrusion and extrusion of each new text. Literature composes a living field. And within that field critical texts play an intrinsic part, and perhaps should be perceived as another literary genre rather than a phenomenon that is divorced, somehow, by some odd quirk separate forever from the whole of being like the old American hero they appear to emulate.

Literature is wild; a tree, a part of the ever-flowing deep and whitewater turbulence of thought, a river-like motion, a reflection of the tree of life. We must see it that way, so that the American story can be heard, illumined, explored in its multiple voices, its ceaseless telling.

For all their differences, Hemingway and Momaday – chosen as representatives of diversity for the purposes of this discussion, rather than as icons of achievement – are telling the same story, the story of modern men's alienation and despair, the story of war without cessation, the story of the hideousness of detached passionlessness. And in both, the vitality of existence moves most powerfully in the land itself, which becomes a force in itself – a psychic force, a spiritual force, the matrix from which Nick Adams and Abel have been torn. In each, the protagonist is restored to life, achieves some understanding of the ambivalent and ambiguous character of existence by turning to the spiritual presence embodied in the land. Each figure, speechless, still – Adams, the objective observer, the individuated, self-reliant symbol of white men's values; Abel, the dumb, raging wooden Indian of white stereotype – are each finally framed in movement. And it is in the fact of motion that each reaches his self-consciousness and his definition as finally human. In these works we see that who tells the story defines its parameters and its significance. In Hemingway's cycle the meaning becomes the single man surrounded by nature, resting in maturity, hopeless in the long run and nevertheless content. In Momaday's work the meaning becomes the person surrounded by life on every level, running in maturity, able to take his proper place in his community's life. What happens to Hemingway's work when viewed through the lenses of Native American critical vision? What happens to Momaday when examined in the frame of the critical vision of the West? Do the final meanings change? Are the structures more or less comprehensible?

As I struggle to describe how good fences make poor neighbors, I remember young Germans swarming the Berlin wall, seeking with hammer and chisel to tear down the structure that divided German from German, kin from kin, for almost thirty years – most of my adult life, all of my daughter's life.

An African-American was elected mayor of New York, and another African-American was elected governor of that bastion of American gentility, Virginia. In South Africa the dreadful psychic and political walls of apartheid are crumbling, and Hungary has engaged in dismantling the barriers between its borders and those of Austria.

Can we, as scholars and teachers facing the twenty-first century, fail to realize that "something there is that does not love a wall"? Can we in all good conscience persist in walling off the mainstream of American literature for a tiny group of writers, and *from* the great majority of writers in this century? Isn't it time we realized the absurdity of calling a tiny brook a mainstream, consigning the great river to marginality? It certainly makes the margins the center of the action – an odd way for margins to act! Surely in this time we can cease to behave as though Thoreau's Walden Pond requires we keep literature forever enclosed. Even Henry David came out of prison in time! Let's join him. Let's open ourselves to multiplicity, and let the winds of change and of life blow freely through our conversations.

14.
Thus Spake Pocahontas

In his exhaustive opus Irenaeus [Bishop of Lyons] catalogued all deviations from the coalescing orthodoxy and vehemently condemned them. Deploring diversity, he maintained there could be only one valid Church, outside which there could be no salvation. Whoever challenged this assertion, Irenaeus declared to be a heretic—to be expelled and, if possible, destroyed. . . . In opposition to personal experience and gnosis, Irenaeus recognized the need for a definitive canon—a fixed list of authoritative writings. . . .

— MICHAEL BAIGENT, RICHARD LEIGH, AND HENRY LINCOLN,
Holy Blood, Holy Grail

Not only has little changed since I entered the profession in the 1970s, nothing much has changed since the time of Irenaeus, nearly two thousand years ago. They're still pontificating, excluding, and power-tripping, while we're still resisting, dissenting, deconstructing, and subverting. Heresies spring up all around only to die, only to recur persistently like wildflowers, like crabgrass. We still match personal experience and gnosis with canonicity, and those who tenaciously cling to the rotting pillars of Rome dismiss us—or order us purged. It seems that as long as we remain locked into oppositional structures, nothing but "same ol', same ol'" can occur. As long as we avoid the creative, we are condemned to reaction.

The profession when I entered it was much the same as it is today, "Still crazy after all these years," as the song goes. Though I had marched, pamphleted, and taught for peace and social justice, for civil, women's, and lesbian and gay rights, and briefly served as faculty advisor for the Young Socialist Alliance; though I had been writing and publishing for several years; though the poets I published with and read with in coffeehouses and bars, on the streets, and at rallies were fairly frequently not white and on occasion not white men – as far as the academy was, and is, concerned, there was, and is, no literature other than that produced by a Eurocentric formalist elite.

Nearly twenty weary years later, the cops beating African-American men is a media sound bite, and the merciless destruction of Native people is largely ignored by all factions in the brawling American polity. Many are glad that "the war has ended," but I am compelled to object: it has not ended; it goes on and on. In the academy we hold rallies, sign resolutions, declare moratoriums, and demand divesture and withdrawal of American involvement in foreign lands, while the mutilation of people of color at home evokes barely a sigh.

I came of age in the 1960s and by the 1970s was seriously burned out. By 1972 I understood several things: If an issue concerned Native people or women, men, and queers of color, neither the academy nor the intelligentsia at large would have a word to say. We are *las disappearadas* (and *desperadas*). We are for the most part invisible, labeled "marginal," the "poor," the "victims," or we are seen as exotica. Our "allies" adamantly cast us in the role of helpless, hopeless, inadequate, incompetent, much in need of white champions and saviors, dependent upon an uncaring state for every shred of personal and community dignity we might hope to enjoy. Right, left, and center see us as their shadows, the part they disown, reject, repress, or romanticize.

Even our few solid backers in academe perceive us as extensions of the great white way; they fail to perceive us as artists, writers, and human beings-in-*communitas* in our own right. And while some of the despised are recognized, most are not seen as other than a pitiable, amorphous blob. Our capacities as creative, self-directing, self-comprehending human beings are lost in the shuffle of ideology and taxonomy; the contributions of our peoples to the literatures, philosophies, sciences, and religions of the world are ignored. Our proper place in the view of the defining others is that of servant; they have consigned us to their margins, and there we must stay.

In the mid-1960s when I was in graduate school, I was not assigned the work of one woman poet or writer. And although assigned reading included the work of a number of homosexuals, their sexuality was, and largely still is, hidden to the eyes of the self-avowed heterosexual professoriat. In the late 1980s, I envied graduate students in the Ethnic Studies Department at the University of California in Berkeley, where I then taught, who enjoyed the privilege of studying women's literature from every period, every nation, including that of the U.S. of Color, and I sometimes cast envious glances at young colleagues who enjoy a growing body of scholarship and works by lesbians and gay men. It is not true that nothing has changed; there have been some shifts in academic offerings, though for the most part these offerings are not in traditional departments or are included only at the patronizing, cynical sufferance of the academic elite.

Despite the good intentions and hard work of individuals, the establishment itself, particularly in literary fields, is unrepentantly proud of its constricted intelligence. Even worse is the willful institutional starvation of our students, accomplished by a narrowness of intellect and an insatiable desire for status and prestige. As academics, perhaps we all should concern ourselves with the consequences of institutional mind abuse.

I spent about ten years on the front of a civil war that has raged for centuries and an additional ten years reconnoitering. During that time, I came to understand that the position of power for a true Warrior is the Void. It is from the Void that all arises and into that Void that all returns. The most profoundly creative literature of the twentieth century, the most profoundly *literary* literature, is, as it always has been, the literature of the desperadoes (and, in this case, *desperadas*). It is we who are creating the shape of the new world from the strokes of our pens, typewriter keys, and computer keyboards.

This body of work, literature that rides the borders of a variety of literary, cultural, and ideological realms, has not been adequately addressed by either mainstream feminist scholarship or the preponderance of "ethnic" or "minority" scholarship. However, in the past decade a new field of study has emerged that resists definition by other critics, that seems determined to define itself. This new field raises questions that mainstream feminist and "ethnic" or "minority" approaches fail to address and simultaneously begins to open before us new possibilities for inquiry.

The process of living on the border, of crossing and recrossing boundaries of consciousness, is most clearly delineated in work by writers who are citizens of more than one community, whose experiences and languages require that they live within worlds that are as markedly different from one another as Chinatown, Los Angeles, and Malibu; El Paso and Manhattan's arts' and intellectuals' districts; Laguna Pueblo in New Mexico and literary London's Hampstead Heath. It is not merely biculturality that forms the foundation of our lives and work in their multiplicity, aesthetic largeness, and wide-ranging potential; rather, it is multiculturality, multilinguality, and dizzying class-crossing from the fields to the salons, from the factories to the academy, or from galleries and the groves of academe to the neighborhoods and reservations. The new field of study moves beyond the critical boundary set in Western academic circles and demands that the canonical massive walls be thinned and studded with openings so that criticism, like literary production itself, reflects the great variety of writerly lives and thought, particularly those in the American community. For it is not that writers themselves, of whatever color, class, gender, or sexual orientation, have been bound by ideological barriers a mile thick and two miles high but that academics have found the doctrine of exclusion and Eurocentric elitism a necessary tool in the furtherance of Western cultural goals and their own careers.

The work of women of color arises out of the creative void in a multitude of voices, a complex of modes, and most of these women are quite aware of their connection to the dark grandmother of human wisdom. Thus in *The Salt Eaters* the African-American writer Toni Cade Bambara draws Velma back from the edge of daylight and heals her through the shadowy presences of Sophia, the dark spirit of wisdom, and the *loas*, the spirits. Toni Morrison produces a body of work that draws us ever more enticingly toward the great mysteriousness from which human life and significance always arise and to which they inevitably return. Similarly, in *Love Medicine, The Beet Queen*, and *Tracks*, the American Indian writer Louise Erdrich seduces us into the forest of Ojibway women's magic, winding us ever more deeply into the shadows of ancient trees. She leaves not so much as a crumb to draw us back into the light of patriarchal day. Leslie Marmon Silko reaches into unexplored realms, the gloom of what is long forgotten but that continues to nourish our love and our terror, while Maxine Hong Kingston moves into the deeps of Han myth and memory, who is myth's beloved sister and supernal twin. The Chicana writer Gloria Anzaldúa tells it plainly: The woman in the shadows is drawn again into the world of womankind, and her name is innocence, exuberance, discovery, and passion; her name is our invisible bond.

Women return from the spirit lands to the crossroads over and over; we question, we circle around the center of the fire where the darkest, hottest coals lie. We know it is there—the nothing that bears all signifying, all tropes, all love medicine, all stories, all constructions and deconstructions.

We know this: in the void reside the keepers of wisdom. Women of color are willing and well-equipped to approach the still, dark center of the heart of the gynocosmos where nothing at all exists and whence, paradoxically, all must emerge. Other writers, strangers to the source of meaning, have talked about that mysterious, foreboding place, the dark heart of creation, but it is we – perhaps because we are nothing ourselves – who stalk the void and dance the dervish of significance that is born through our parted lips and legs. Other writers have entered the shadow, but they have named it evil, negation, woman. They have fled, running pell-mell away from her living bounty. They call us woman, other, mother, hooker, maid and believe themselves securely superior, safe from the mournful meaninglessness of our lot. Ah, but our lot is passion, grief, rage, and delight. Our lot is life, however that comes, in whatever guise it takes. We are alive, the living among the dead. Too bad those who see us as shadow, as void, as negation miss it all; so sad they haven't the wit to grieve their loss.

The dark woman has long been perceived as the dumb, the speechless, mother. And while the angrier among us protest that perception, we who are wise welcome and celebrate it. One of our sisters – albeit white and Calvinist but marginalized, closeted, all but disappeared – commented on the humor of the situation, writing:

> I'm nobody! Who are you?
> . . . .
> How dreary – to be – Somebody

Only the disappeared can enter the Void and, like Grandmother Spider, emerge with a small but vital pot, a design that signifies the power of meaning and of life, and a glowing ember that gives great light. We who are nobody are the alive – and no one knows we're here. We are the invisible – and no one cares. Silly them. They are all at the public banquet hobnobbing with the known, the recognized, the acclaimed. And, as in the history of art in our Western world, they missed the god when she passed by, the god that the ignored and dismissed white bisexual crazy lady *imagiste* poet HD once so accurately described.

The issue I am addressing here is not simply a matter of gender: It is fundamentally a matter of the essential experience of non-Western modes of consciousness. For the most part my sisters of the white persuasion are as culture-bound as their more highly prestiged brothers. In the West it is now held that gender (or sex) is a metaphor, a social construct. Further, it is held that since a metaphor cannot be used to analyze a metaphorical system, meaning is largely a trick of the mind.

But in other systems – systems not so bound in a self-referencing, nearly psychotic death dance – meaning is derived and ascribed along different lines. This interpretive mode, non-Western to its core, is explored in *The Signifying Monkey*, by Henry Louis Gates, Jr. That work, though Afrocentric in itself, suggests a way out of the Morton Salt box conundrum of Eurocentric patriarchal self-preoccupation. Gates tells us that the meaning of a Black text derives from the system of significance revealed and shaped by Ifa. The critical task is to render the text comprehensible and by that act assess its quality, by interpreting it through Ifa. According to Gates, that task belongs to Esu, the trickster, who is male and female, many-tongued, changeable, changing, and who contains all the meanings possible within her or his consciousness. Thus, a text that is malformed or incomprehensible when held up to Ifa as template is a work that has failed. Ifa, Gates writes, "consists of the sacred texts of the Yoruba people, as does the Bible for Christians, but it also contains the commentaries on these fixed texts, as does the *Midrash*" (p. 10). Esu (or Esu-Elegbara or, in these parts, Papa Legba) is, in Gates's terms, "the dynamic of process," similar to the process of critical interpretation, who "interrelates all the different and multiple parts which compose the system" (p. 38):

> Esu speaks through Ifa, because it is his *ase* that reveals – or conceals – the roadways or pathways through the text to its potential and possible meanings. Whereas Ifa is truth, Esu rules understanding of truth, a relationship that yields an individual's meaning. . . . Esu is the process of interpretation.

Similarly, by way of the ceremonial tradition as template, a given work by a Native artist can be assessed. In both instances the canon becomes "the sacred," the world of the unseen (but not unheard or unknown), and its primary texts are the myths and ceremonies that compress and convey all the meaning systems a particular cultural consciousness holds. This is not to confuse a relationship to the mysteriousness that underlies and sources the phenomenological with essentialism or absolutism. There is little that is one, holy, catholic, and apostolic in the actual world that lies beyond and within the mundane. Indeed, the true world of the mysteries is more multiplex, polyglot, and free-flowing than any churchman, whether of Christian, Jewish, Muslim, Buddhist, or revolutionary persuasion, can imagine. Its very multitudinousness certainly threatens, even terrifies, the apostles of monotony.

Hortense J. Spillers comments (in Gates, *Reading Black*, p. 244) that "the literary text *does* point outside itself – in the primary interest of leading the reader back inside the universe of the apparently self-contained artifact." That is, no cultural artifact can be seen as existing outside its particular matrix; no document, however profoundly aesthetic, can be comprehended outside its frame of reference – a frame that extends all the way into the depths of the consciousness that marks a culture, differentiating it from another. Because Western societies are fundamentally the same – they all arise from the same essential cultural base – Eurocentric critics think that culture is a unified field. French, English, German, Italian, Swiss, Danish, Dutch, Swedish, Russian, and Spanish worldviews are, at their deepest levels, part of the same cultural matrix: they all have the same mother, and that they are governed by members of the same extended family is but one mark of this profound sameness. But though these "cultures" are much alike, others are not of the same configuration, springing in no way from a similar root.

That difference is understood by many who essay to critique literary artifacts, but most assume, wrongly, that the cultural matrix from which all literature derives its meaning is the one described by French critics and other Continental intellectuals. But, to paraphrase Alice Duer Miller, other nations breed other women. Western minds have supposed (wrongly) for some time that language is culture and that without a separate language a culture is defunct. Thus, some feminist critics search endlessly for women's language and, failing to discover it, wax wroth. But maybe the idea that language defines ideational identity of a distinct sort is off the mark. Maybe – as many writers have suggested – the use of a language and its syntax, structure, tropes, and conjunctions defines identity in its communitarian and individual dimensions. In this rubric, the external system that a given work points to and articulates and that renders the work significant takes on major importance.

The worlds of experience, knowledge, and understanding, to which the works of women of color point and from which they derive, can clarify the meaning of our texts. At this juncture the critic is faced with a difficult task: the world embodied in Kingston's *Woman Warrior* is hardly the world that gives rise to Morrison's *Song of Solomon*. It is of little use to study critical works concerned with Erdrich's *Love Medicine* if one wishes to explore the significance of Aurora L. Morales and Rosario Morales's *Getting Home Alive*.

To be sure, it may seem that elements of Western literary practice are discernible in work by women of color. But the similarities are likely to be more apparent than actual. The novel itself saw its earliest development in Japan of the eleventh century in *The Tale of Genji* by Lady Murasaki Shikibu. It did not appear in Europe until a few centuries later. Nor is poetry a genre confined to Western literature, though a certain shape has unfolded in recent times that marks it as a modern vehicle. But these modern forms, whether in Middle Eastern, Far Eastern, Native American, African and African-American, or Latina communities worldwide, can be shown to derive from preexisting poetic forms in those nations that go back hundreds, even thousands, of years.

Western literary thought is a strong feature of much of the academic criticism produced by scholars of color. The critics who address the work of women writers of color are tightly enmeshed in the training they received in Western-biased universities.

Women of color writing in the United States share the experiences of trivialization, invisibility, and supposed incomprehensibility, but these features characterize the treatment of the critic-less more than that of writers blessed with a critical network that addresses their work within an established critical context. Thus, the work of African-American women is far more likely to receive appropriate critical treatment than the works of Denise Chávez or Kim Ronyoung are. It seems evident that without a critical apparatus that enables a variety of literatures to be explored within their relevant contexts, the works of *las disappearadas* are doomed to obscurity. Yet, given the prevailing ethnocentric cultural climate, devising such a system and finding it applied by a great number of critics seems a hopeless task. And if we fail to locate a system that is not ethnically skewed toward the bourgeois male European, the use of which does not obviate the insatiable status needs of literary types who fear loss of promotion and recognition by that same ethnic establishment, separatism seems the only solution.

Nor is the issue simply one of reconstructing the canon or throwing out the concept of canon, literary quality, or aesthetic norms. The recent move toward excising the discussion of these fundamental dimensions of criticism, indeed of thought itself, is hardly a useful response to the conundrum, though one is hard put to imagine creative alternatives to the situation when stuck in Western modes of thought. Perhaps the best course is to begin anew, to examine the literary output of American writers of whatever stripe and derive critical principles based on what is actually being rendered by the true experts, the writers themselves. While we're at it, we might take a look at the real America that most of us inhabit – the one seldom approached by denizens of the hallowed (or is it the hollow?) groves of academe – so that we can discover what is being referenced beyond abstractions familiar to establishment types but foreign to those who live in real time. I am suggesting a critical system that is founded on the principle of inclusion rather than on that of exclusion, on actual human society and relationships rather than on textual relations alone, a system that is soundly based on aesthetics that pertain to the literatures we wish to examine.

A text exists in relation to other texts – particularly, as Gates has demonstrated, to mother texts, that is, the sacred stories that energize and shape human consciousness – rather than in splendid autocratic, narcissistic, and motherless isolation; as should be fairly obvious, texts are cultural artifacts and thus necessarily derive from, pertain to, and reveal oft hidden assumptions and values. Given that the experience of women as rendered in literature is a societally shaped and conditioned trope, how are we to accurately interpret or illuminate texts written by women of color? Do we see them as arising out of some sort of universalist "woman's world"? Do we look to the social world the writer and text inhabit to locate significance? Do we identify women writers of color in terms of their racial or cultural groups, which in turn are identified in terms of our Eurocentric ideologies? Because such categorizations tend to define colored writers – including those who are women – as "marginal" writers outside the boundaries of "real" literature and thus as writers whose struggles and wishes are of interest only when they serve the goals and fit the preconceptions of those defining us; such an approach can only serve to oppress, distort, and silence. Should we step outside the boundaries placed on us by alien preconceptions of our lot, we are dismissed as crazy.

This is the problem posed by the work of social critics who subscribe to Karl Marx's dictate that the critical act exists as "the self-clarification of the struggles and wishes of the age" (Fraser, p. 253). Nancy Fraser comments that Marx's critical theory "frames its research in the light of contemporary social movements with which it has a partisan though not uncritical identification." She fails to notice that such a narrowly prescriptive (and proscriptive) approach in its narrowness virtually excludes the reality of the voice, text, and human meaning in the work of Third World women. Even the very concept of aesthetics, such a social-movement approach insists, is politically taboo because it is hopelessly engaged in furtherance of the white male supremacist paradigm.

This view might well be valid – but the rendering of beauty as human artifact is hardly an activity exclusive to white males, Western patriarchs, or the bourgeois. In Anna Lee Walters's short story "The Warriors" (p. 12), Uncle Ralph, a homeless alcoholic Pawnee warrior of the old school, counsels his nieces: "For beauty is why we live, . . . [but] we die for it, too." In Navajoland, the concept of *hojo* ("it beautiful is moving") is central to the ideal of human life, while in the Pueblos we are instructed to "walk in beauty" (it goes this way, *iyañi*). So far as I know, no human society is bereft of devotion to aesthetic principles, though Marxist, bureaucratic, and industrial societies come close.

But though our work draws up the moon from the creative void, signifying our cunning crafting, the critical studies concerning our work remain stranded on the far shores of patriarchal positivism. In the world of the patriarchs everything is about politics; for much of the rest of the world, politics occupies little of any part of our preoccupations. Native Americans are entirely concerned with relations to and among the physical and nonphysical and various planetary energy-intelligences of numerous sorts. The idea of expending life force in oppression and resistance strikes most Indians, even today, as distinctly weird. Like Indians, Gnostics the world over, valuing multiplicity, personal experience, community, and simultaneous autonomy, avoid the schizoid dictates of canon-anticanon binary oppositional systems or fixed lists of what is "correct" thought, action, and insight, when the fixing is outside the realm of what is personally known.

For the most part, women of color write from a profound state of gnosis and personal experience, though we refine these in the crucible of community and relationship. But many major feminist critics wish our experience to be otherwise. They deterministically compel it into a mold of their own making, dismissing any work or experience that does not tell the tale they want told. Unhappily, far too many women of color fall into the honeyed trap; having been defined by strangers, many of us accept their definitions and write from the position they have marked out for us. All too unaware, we serve their aim and maintain their comfort – a righteous task for the maid.

In "Marginality and Subversion: Julia Kristeva," Toril Moi suggests that materiality is the point, marginality the key, and subversion the function of the invisibles. Moi praises Kristeva for her outlandishness, her willingness to go to the revolutionary heart of the matter, the mutter, but in extolling the rhetorical pose of the progressive Eurocentric intellectual, Moi reveals her Eurocentric and phallocentric bias. As Moi describes Kristeva's early works, Kristeva wanders hopelessly lost in the master's intellectual house of mirrors, asking and answering her own fantastic ghosts. And while the style of her meanderings is fetching, its self-negating entrancement with patriarchal paradigms is dangerous to writers from the deeps. No patriarch can tell us who we are, nor can any describe the worlds, inner and outer, that we inhabit. Freud, Marx, and Nietzsche – the triumvirate at whose altar Moi and the early Kristeva pay homage – can hardly provide models of intellectual competence that describe and illuminate colored women's works. What they can and do provide are the means whereby gynocosmic energies are bound up in patriarchal structures and thus rendered unusable to ourselves. This situation is well suited to the position of servant we thus occupy. From the confines thus established, there is no loophole of retreat; indeed, there is no sense that anything should be retreated from or that there is anywhere to go beyond the servants' quarters.

Interestingly, as Kristeva moves toward consciousness based on some kind of connection to the real, as she goes from the absurdist position of comparing one body of words with another body of words with nary a whiff of human-experienced reality between, Moi rejects her, convinced that "the struggle" is all-important. While Moi admits that women's struggle is unique in its various dimensions and is not to be confused with class struggles, she remains wedded to the correct dialectic: We are only to be perceived and authorized when we cast ourselves as marginal, subversive, and dissident, which she characterizes as Kristeva's fundamental theory, though it is more Moi's than Kristeva's. Moi supports a criticism that furthers neopatriarchalism, though, as she sees it, neopatriarchalism includes feminist struggles carefully interpreted through the lens of the fathers Marx, Nietzsche, and Freud (Moi, p. 164).

To my Indian eyes it is plain that subversion cannot be the purpose or goal for women of color who write, though it likely is a side effect of our creating, our transforming, our rite. For to subvert, to turn under, is only the first step in the generation of something yet unborn; no, even less: it is the last step in the process of death. A truly beautiful clay pot from Acoma or

San Juan Pueblo signifies on the emptiness it surrounds; Moi is accurate in her appreciation of Kristeva's unwillingness to dissect emptiness when the approach to somethingness will more than suffice. But what she fails to recognize is that the principles of self-determination and communitarian or autonomous creativity provide the true loophole of escape. Like Moi, one might very entertainingly mistake the menu for the meal and starve thereby, a mistake that for the most part shapes elite criticism and allied fields.

It is au courant to criticize, to interpret and analyze, as if no living processes occur – well enough for those who do not buy, earn, prepare, and serve the meal but who have servants and wives to deal with the tiresome mundanities of life. But our art is not, alas, privy to such alienation from human processes, and thus it must issue from the position of creativity rather than from that of reactivity. Subversion, dissidence, and acceptance of self as marginal are processes that maim our art and deflect us from our purpose. They are enterprises that support and maintain the master, feeding his household on our energy, our attention, and our strength.

In their introduction to *The Feminist Reader*, Catherine Belsey and Jane Moore characterize feminist readers as agents of change, asserting that "specific ways of reading inevitably militate for or against [that] process," thus situating the presumed problem of women squarely in the midst of the oppositional mode (p. 1). Later (p. 10), they comment:

> In poststructuralist theory meanings are cultural and learned. . . . They are in consequence a matter for political debate. Culture itself is the limit of our knowledge: there is no available truth outside culture with which we can challenge injustice.

Odd that the concept of adversariness, deeply embedded in patriarchal structures of both the political and the literary kind, requires the aesthetic concerns of literary women to be defined in terms of the culture that oppresses and disappears us. Given that thought, one must say, with Audre Lorde, "The master's tools will never dismantle the master's house."

It is even more peculiar, albeit depressingly common among Western people, that Belsey and Moore cavalierly assume that culture is itself monolithic, worldwide, universal, and impermeable, echoing Irenaeus of eighteen hundred years ago. As a Native woman I am passionately aware that there are a number of available truths outside Eurocentric culture that enable us not only to challenge injustice but to live in a way that enhances the true justice of creating and nurturing life. And as a Native woman I must protest the arrogance of any critical assumption that human society is European in origin and that all power of whatever sort resides within it.

Artists of color can best do something other than engage in adversarial politics, knowing that since we did not cause patriarchy, we can neither control nor cure it. As recovering codependents of the abusive system under which too many have lived for far too long, we need to invest our energies in our vision, our significances, and our ways of signifyin'. We realize that we are something quite other than Anglo-European critics' definitions of us and that it is at our grave peril that we accept their culture-induced attributions rather than make, shape, and live within our own.

To be sure, women have, as actors, creators, and perceivers, been absented from patriarchal literature – but perhaps that is all to the good. Nor are persons of the female persuasion alone in that exclusion; we belong to a truly massive community of "strangers," one that includes virtually all literary artists on the planet for the past several thousand years. Perhaps, rather than bemoaning our "sorry state" as one of marginality, we might take another look at the actual situation; perhaps, in doing so, we will discover that neither "mainstream" nor "center" are where patriarchal sorts have claimed them to be. In all likelihood, we will discover readily enough that our very exclusion from the old boys' club works to our advantage: having never lived in the master's house, we can all the more enthusiastically build a far more suitable dwelling of our own.

When I was growing up, I would often go to my mother with some mournful tale of injustice. My plaints were inevitably centered on what the perpetrator had done to me. Sometimes my tale was a wonder of intellectual intricacy. Sometimes it was little more than a virtuoso emotional performance. But my clear-eyed (and intensely aggravating) mother would listen a bit and then pronounce sentence: "Yes, but what were you doing?" Or "You just worry about you." Or "Go do something else, then. If you can't get along with them, go find something else to do."

In this way, she taught me something Native people have long known and American humorists have recently discovered: the way to liberation from oppression and injustice is to focus on one's own interest, creativity, concerns, and community. Perhaps we literary sorts can put the wisdom of the ancients to good use. It is no concern of ours what "they" say, write, think, or do. Our concern is what we are saying, writing, thinking, and doing. In short, we must "get a life!"

In contemporary feminist circles, a debate rages concerning language: whether men own it; whether it is a fixed, immutable force that is reality; or whether it is merely a process that signifies nothing but through which we are all entertained nonetheless. Some feminist critics debate whether we take our meaning and sense of self from language and in that process become phallocentric ourselves, or if there is a use of language that is, or can be, feminine. Some, like myself, think that language is itself neither male nor female; it is creatively expansive enough to be of use to those who have the wit and art to wrest from it their own significances. Even the dread patriarchs have not found a way to "own" language any more than they have found a way to "own" earth (though many seem to believe that both are possible). However, perusing feminist criticism, I re-realize that patriarchs do own *critical* language, and, sadly, far too many feminist critics sling it as though it had meaning beyond the walls of the literary boys' club.

A literary text can be characterized as a "loophole of retreat," the term Valerie Smith uses in her discussion of Harriet Jacobs's trope. "Jacobs' tale is not the classic story of the triumph of the individual will," she writes; "rather it is more a story of the triumphant self-in-relation" (in Gates, *Reading Black*, p. 217).

Self-in-relation, rather than the bildungsroman model of self in isolated splendor that drives American civilization, is a primary characteristic of human cultures. I am aware that in the progressive evolution-as-fact paradigm, a main characteristic said to prove elite white male supremacy is precisely the individualistic hero metaphor. But although quite a few enterprises – literary and otherwise – are founded on the concept of individual superiority over relationship, individual heroics characterize but a small portion of literary work and represent an even smaller portion of art in general. As Smith writes (on p. 212):

> The loophole of retreat possesses an ambiguity of meaning that extends to the literal loophole as well. For if a loophole signifies for Jacobs a place of withdrawal, it signifies in common parlance an avenue of escape. Likewise, the garret . . . renders the narrator spiritually independent of her master, and makes possible her ultimate escape to freedom.

In Smith's discussion we see another new critical direction emerging, like Jacobs's, from the constriction of belief in ownership. No one can own the sublime and no one can confine the beautiful, the living, or the moving to the tiny regions too many critics reserve for Indians and other "marginalized" peoples. However, we who are seen as borderline writers can erect a criticism that speaks to the kind of spiritual independence Jacobs found in hiding, the kind that must lead to freedom from domination. We can do so by attending to the actual texts being created, their source, their source texts, the texts to which they stand in relation, and the otherness that they both embody and delineate.

The aesthetically profound story for Third World women writers is necessarily concerned with human relationships: family, community, and that which transcends and underlies human meaning systems. Without benefit of Ifa and Esu, without possession of metatext, without presence of divine interpreter (that tricky familiar of the mysteries), reader and critic are doomed to read the same book over and over, regardless of who wrote it, why they did so, or the circumstances in which the work was embedded and from which it takes its meaning.

The concept in relation or, more "nativistically," the understanding that the individualized – as distinct from individualistic – sense of self accrues only within the context of community, which includes the nonvisible world of ancestors, spirits, and gods, provides a secure grounding for a criticism that can reach beyond the politicized, deterministic confines of progressive approaches, as well as beyond the neurotic diminishment of self-reflexiveness. To read women's texts with accuracy, we need a theory that places the twin concepts of I and thou securely within the interconnected matrix of all and everything, one that uses the presence of absence to define the manifest and that uses the manifest to locate and describe the invisible. When such a criticism is forged, the significance of the passive, the receptive, the absent, the dark, the void, and the power that inheres to it will be seen as central to the process of the construction of meaning and the reading of aesthetic texts. Like many women of color who write, Anzaldúa tells us of the habitation and the power of the unseen and its relation to the reality we inhabit. In so describing, she also suggests the direction a new criticism of inclusion can take:

> Where before there'd only been empty space
> She's always been there
> occupying the same room.
> It was only when I looked
> at the edges of things

my eyes going wide watering,
objects blurring.
Where before there'd only been empty space
I sensed layers and layers,
felt the air in the room thicken.
Behind my eyelids a white flash
a thin noise.
That's when I could see her.

          – *Borderlands/La Frontera: The New Mestiza*

III.

La Frontera

na[rra]tivities

15.
The Autobiography of a Confluence

When I was very little, two of my favorite songs were "Pistol-Packing Mama" and, a couple of years later, "Don't Fence Me In." Both appropriate, given that I grew up in cowboy and Indian country, descendant of cowboys and Indians, among other ancestors. "Pistol-packin' mama, lay that pistol down." I liked the idea of a mama who carried a gun. I was about four when I learned the whole song by heart. "Don't Fence Me In," of Bing Crosby fame, must have been popular a few years later, maybe during the Second World War, maybe when I was six or seven.

But I liked it because it was about a world I understood, one that had horses and cattle and unlimited vistas, and where fences were signs of an unwanted civilization. I liked it because I knew that riding along forever, not bound, not held in, was my life, and that the comfort of fences, forever denied me, should not be a source of unease. I remember my sense of that song, its defiance, its aura of loss. For to me it had such an aura; underlying its rebelliousness was resignation and reconciliation to that loss. As if, given the situation, it was best to choose what was inevitable anyway. "Let me ride through the wide open country that I love; don't fence me in." I knew the cottonwoods, the ridges, the mountain, the stars, and the moon in the song. I knew the urge to go, somewhere, anywhere, into the forever boundless openings of the West. I knew that good fences make strange neighbors and good possessors, and that burgher order might be fine in its place, but its place wasn't the sort I wanted or recognized.

My life was more chaos than order in any ordinary American, Native American, Mexican-American, Lebanese-American, German-American, any heathen, Catholic, Protestant, Jewish, atheistic sense. Fences would have been hard to place without leaving something out, and my senses were already lost, maybe to the moon.

Of course, I always knew I was Indian. I was never told to forget it, to deny it. Indians were common in the family, at least on my mother's side. In fact, unlike many people I meet who are claiming they're "Indian" or reluctantly revealing it, far from being denied, my relationship to the Pueblo down the line was reinforced in a number of ways. I was told over and over, "Never forget that you're Indian." My mother said it. Nor did she say, "Remember you are part Indian."

I grew up on the Cubero Land Grant, in New Mexico. I grew up with wilderness just up the road, with civilization much farther away. I grew up in the hollow of the land, a hollow that was filled with grass and flowers, à la the white eyes, planted and nurtured by my halfbreed grandmother, a hollow that was heavy with trees.

My life is history, politics, geography. It is religion and metaphysics. It is music and language. For me the language is an odd brand of English, mostly local, mostly half-breed spoken by the people around me, filled with elegance and vulgarity side by side, small jokes that are language jokes and family jokes and area jokes, certain expressions that are peculiar to that meeting of peoples who speak a familiar (to me) laconic language filled with question and comment embedded in a turn of phrase, a skewing of diction, a punning, cunning language that implies connections in diversity of syntax and perception, the oddness of how each of us seems and sees. It is the Southwest, the confluence of cultures, the headwaters of Mexico. It is multiethnic cowboy, with a strong rope of liturgy and classics tied to the pommel, a bedroll of dreams tied up behind, and a straight-shooting pistol packed along. It's no happenstance that the Gunn in my name has been good fortune, or that the Indians I knew growing up were cowboys. As most of the cowboys I knew were Indians – the others were Chicanos, Nativos, and a few Anglos, though their idea of cowboy was mostly a big hat and Western clothes (long before they found fashion in New York). Rednecks – Redskins: an odd thing, a dichotomy to Americans who go to movies and believe what they see, a continuum to others who take their history straight from life.

The triculture state, as New Mexico is often called, is more than three-cultured, as it works itself out in my life. It is Pueblo, Navajo and Apache, Chicano, Spanish, Spanish-American, Mexican-American; it is Anglo, and that includes everything that is not Indian or Hispanic – in my case, Lebanese and Lebanese-American, German-Jewish, Italian-Catholic, German-Lutheran, Scotch-Irish-American Presbyterian, halfbreed (that is, people raised white-and-Indian), and Irish-Catholic; there are more, though these are the main ones that influenced me in childhood, and their influence was literary and aesthetic as well as social and personal. The land, the family, the road – three themes that haunt my mind and form my muse, these and the music: popular, country and western, Native American, Arabic, Mexican, classical like operas and symphonies, especially Mozart, the Mass. The sounds I grew up with, the sounds of the voices, the instruments, the rhythms, the sounds of the land and the creatures. These are my sources, and these are my home.

STORIES ARE ROADS, STORIES ARE FENCES

North of the house I grew up in was the mountain. East of it were the tall rock mesas we called "the hills." In a southerly direction, parallel to the line the hills made, ran a paved road, old Old Highway 66. It meandered slowly past our house and my grandmother's house next door, which was separated from ours by two lawns, bordered on one side by a dirt area where we played, the huge galvanized metal barrels where we burned trash of various sorts, the coal shed, and the clothesline; on the other by a couple of flower beds. Just past my grandmother's front door the road curved sharply and crossed the Old Arroyo, climbed the hill, and ran northwest for a mile or so until it turned a left-hand corner at the cattle guard and, a few yards farther on, joined up with Highway 66, next to my mother's uncle's wife's world-renowned cafe.

To the south of Grandma's, the road traveled alongside the Arroyo, a deep cavernous slit in the earth. Hand in hand they moved then, past the store that was next to my grandparents' house, down the way past Mrs. Rice's house, past Macano Valley that held the old Cubero graveyard in its fingers, on down almost truly south to where it connected to Highway 66 (since bypassed by I-40) and thence to Laguna (lake, home, and land-grant/reservation of the Keres Pueblo tribe named Laguna Pueblo).

At that juncture the road and the Arroyo parted. The Arroyo somewhere down the line joined the San Jose River that borders Old Laguna Village on its eastern edge. It eventually meets the Rio Puerco, which, in its turn, joins the Rio Grande in its southward journey to Mexico and the Gulf. The road, transformed into the highway, crosses each in turn on its way east to the Sandias.

Some miles past Laguna proper, but still on the Laguna reservation, you pass a road going off to the north. It crosses Laguna land and links the Cañoncito Navajo Reservation/Land-Grant to the highway. Farther along is Correo ("mail"), which I always remember, when I pass by that way at the distance that I-40 now runs from there, as the home of some Texans named Harrington whom I went to school with in Albuquerque: the daughter I was best friends with; the son I had a crush on when I was ten, for which I got in a passel of trouble when the nuns at the convent school caught me passing love notes to him over the back fence at their convent in Albuquerque. That was the same Harrington family, the father's older brother, who was the second husband of my Laguna halfbreed aunt Jessie, my grandmother's older sister. He died of a heart attack that struck him as he was riding horseback across a cattle pond before I was born.

From Correo the highway goes through Rio Puerco (Pork River), where Jido, *abuelo*, grandfather – my father's father – beat his car to death once or twice because it got stuck in the quicksandy bottom when he tried to cross from the Cañoncito/Seboyeta side; where my mother's brother went over the side when he fell asleep at the wheel and nearly died; where you're two-thirds of the way to Albuquerque, an important point when you're small and get carsick.

Before my time, old Old 66 went from Correo around in a southerly direction to Los Lunas (the moons, but really the Luna family who homesteaded there or something) and then to Albuquerque. It must have been a long trip, but pretty. You'd have come into the city (then really a very small town) along the Bosque, curving and winding along the cottonwood-crowded banks of the Rio Grande. But the way we came in was fine, too: you'd get to the top of the dreaded Nine Mile Hill and gaze across the wide valley at the strong towering hugeness of the Sandias and down at the river – the Bosque – and the trees and lawns and houses and business buildings of "town," as it was referred to by everyone I knew, so welcome to eyes drained of energy by the semidesert starkness, the huge layered distances, the forever sky that had shaped the long road there.

Or it would be night, and from the height of the west mesa you'd look down at the necklace of light nestled comfortingly on the velvet darkness of the valley. It matched wondrously the deep night sky, brilliant with its stole of stars.

The west mesa was then the Atrisco Land-Grant, since sold by the heirs for development. Snow Heights, now, and snowy with neo-Spanish and pretend California ranch-style homes that the rising middle class of the city affect.

From Albuquerque, the road leads right smack into the towering ridges of the Sandias ("watermelons") that rise five thousand feet off the valley floor; and next to them, softer, the Manzanos ("apples") bound the eastern rim of Albuquerque. The highway barely makes it through the canyon, Tijeras Canyon ("scissors" – affectionately known to some of us as tiger-ass). Beyond the mountain lies Texas (and how it lies!), Oklahoma, and the Plains, and somewhere beyond them (maybe in Ohio, because my mother's family, whose paterfamilias came from there, always called it Back East), is THE EAST. (Surely you've heard the joke, "Poor New Mexico, so far from heaven, so close to Texas," a joking sigh attributed to Governor Armijo, or was it Governor Larrazolo?)

THE HIGHWAY IS FOREVER

If you go right on the old highway out of Cubero, from the cattle guard southwest of the village, you will pass King Cafe and Bar, where the wife shot the husband a few years ago and got out on ten thousand dollars bail; next comes Budville, once owned by the infamous Bud, who was shot in a robbery. The main robber-murderer later married Bud's widow. They were living happily ever after, the last I heard, and it served old Bud right. Or so most people around there believed, at least in the privacy of their own thoughts. You pass Dixie Tavern, owned, last I heard, by a mixed-race couple I grew up with, the man Polish – no, Scandinavian. He taught me to *schottische* when I was a young teenager at a party at my aunt and uncle's on my mother's side. His wife is a Spanish/Chicano woman, one of the prettiest of our generation of Cubero women, and I used to flirt with her covertly. She never noticed (small wonder). They bought Dixie Tavern after Lawrence lost his hand in a mining accident.

Then you go by a small bar that was owned by a Cubero Mexican/Spanish-American family, then the Villa (pronounced "vee-ah" except by Granddaddy, who said "sa wee-ah"), which consisted of a cafe, motel, and general store built by my grandfather on my mother's side, run by her uncle and his wife for the greater part of their working lives.

It's, of course, closed now. Has been most of the time since they retired a passel of years ago, though my brother and his wife ran it under the new name of Country Villa for a time in the seventies. They served crepes, carnitas, and mother's fresh-baked bread, had art shows of local artists' work, and showcased entertainment from the area on weekends. Contrary to some more soured predictions, it was successful, which cost so much they had to close it down.

From the Villa, you pass Bibo's, a store and whatnot along the highway (now called Los Cerrillos, the hills – famous to me when I was small because Vivian Vance, the actress, had a house there), then San Fidel, where I went to the mission school for a couple of years and where I used to hang out at a cafe when I was in high school and listen to the jukebox playing "Born to Lose" and "I Walk the Line."

I went there on a couple of dates with a Mormon kid (dead long ago in an industrial fire) who made me feel like a fallen woman because I drank Coca-Cola (a stimulant) and smoked cigarettes. He was a nice boy, in spite of his shock at my wicked ways.

Just west of San Fidel are McCartys and Acomita. There's a gas station and cafe near the highway, announced garishly by a bright yellow sign. My great-great-uncle Beecher lived there. I think he was clan uncle when he died. Or was it his brother? He's the one who used to scold Grandma Gunn, my mother says. She remembers when she was little and living with Grandma, who she thought was her mother, and Uncle Beecher would come to their house in New Laguna (that's in the other direction from McCartys) and scold, and Grandma would cry. My mother doesn't know what he said. She was very small, and he talked in Indian so she didn't understand.

From McCartys, the *malpais* (bad country). It's a beautiful stretch of lava flow that has a clear stream and fish and grass and my German grandfather's ranch that was named El Rancho Gallito (the Little Rooster Ranch) – aptly enough. It is bordered by the Acoma Reservation, and Acomita and McCartys are Acoma villages. Their lives and ours are intertwined, whether any of us likes it or not, woven together like those of the fish, water, and plant life, the livestock and railroad, the mesas that climb slowly toward the mountain's vastness.

If you follow the stream, you will cross the railroad. You will come to Horse Springs. You will come to the foothills of the mountain. If you follow the highway, west, you will come to Grants, Anglo town. Uranium Capital of the World. Before Ambrosia Lake and Paddy Martinez, when I was young, it was the Carrot Capital of the World. Before that, before I was born and when I was very small, it was the Pumice Capital of the World. When I lived there in the late fifties and very early sixties, I called it the Paranoid Capital of the World.

More or less connected to Grants (which began as a house where people driving cattle or sheep from one pasturing place to another would stop and get fed or drink coffee, and which was owned by a family whose last name was Grant) is Milan, named for my uncle's wife's (the couple who ran the Villa) brother. Their family came from Spain via Mexico, where he and his sister – my uncle's wife – were born, I think – or was it she was born in Mexico and he, the youngest, was born in Gallup, U.S.A. (sort of)? Their other siblings were born in Spain, and one of their relatives married my mother's cousin, the daughter of the aunt who had married the Harrington – though the daughter was by my great-aunt's first husband, a Jew, emigrated from Germany early in the twentieth century.

My mother's cousin and her husband took over the store at Laguna (the one that had been my great-grandfather's, the one that was managed by my father and Uncle Johnnie, the Indian one) and ran it until their deaths – his from an accidental gunshot, hers from emphysema caused by too much smoking and not enough crying, perhaps, or was it by force of proximity to Jackpile Mine? ¿Quién sabe? as they would say at Cubero. Who knows?

Going west from Grants and Milan you pass Anaconda, the housing development and mill where people who work for Anaconda Company in their uranium mines live; where my oldest sister lived for a time when her husband, the Italian-American chemist, worked at the mill; where my next older sister lived for a very long time while her husband, a metallurgist, worked his way up from the Jackpile Mine at Laguna to the mill and then to California and then to Gallup – which is miles down the road from Anaconda.

Just west of Anaconda is or was, last time I looked, Bluewater Inn, a dancing place and restaurant where we used to go. It's where I went the first time I got drunk. I was dating the then editor of the Grants *Beacon* (believe me, Grants is a strange place to place a beacon!) and dreaming about being a writer. For a few months I wrote a column for the paper I called "Cubero Quotes." Bluewater Inn. Where the editor taught me to jitterbug to his whispered renditions of "Alexander's Ragtime Band." He called me his "Lebanesian Slave Girl" because I wore silver bracelets on my arm, given me by my grandmother (the halfbreed Laguna one). We didn't get married, though the thought crossed his mind. Me, I was going for a career. I thought I would marry, if ever, in my late twenties.

East of Grants and the Bluewater Inn is the top of the world. The Continental Divide. That's at Top of the World, near Thoreau (pronounced "threw" or "through") and Prewitt. Off to the south lies Zuni, tucked into the endless march of mesas that glimmer in the blue distance from the top of the world.

Then comes Gallup, Indian Capital of the World and Home of the Gallup Ceremonials, or so the garish Chamber of Commerce signs proclaim it. It's a colonial town, a frontier town, blasted and despairing. A white-owned town carved out of the Navajo Nation on its east side, fittingly enough.

West beyond Gallup is the endless stretch of highway that runs through Arizona and, blessedly, crosses the Colorado River and the Sierras, whence it descends into paradise. That's where dwell all good things like movie stars and farmers' markets and fresh fruit stands and Disneyland and housing developments by the square mile – orange groves, oil derricks, and the rich white people who aren't Anglos or Texans but just people, just Americans (not like our white people who aren't people anymore than the Indians or the Chicanos are people but rather Anglos, Tejanos, Indians, La Raza, Nativos, whatever). You know, PEOPLE, like are in the magazines and on the radio. You know, like in the surveys and the polls. As in "People do this and that" or "People think such and such." People, like those who live in America and who all the American stuff is developed for and said about and sold to and by. As in "People won't buy frozen food. It's too expensive, or too hard to transport, or dangerous." Or "People won't vote for this or that." As in almost everything said by Americans and supposed by them to be about the human race.

I always knew that those sentences didn't mean us, we who lived in confluence. It meant somebody else, those who lived in California. Or the East.

My life is the pause. The space between. The not this, not that, not the other. The place that the others go around. Or around about. It's more a Möbius strip than a line.

THE ROAD IS STORIES, IS DREAMS

The last time I dreamed about the Road, as we called the tiny dirt road that ran past our house to connect in one direction with the highway and in the other with the mountain on one side, the hidden Laguna village of Encinal on the other, was late summer of 1984. In the dream my mother, my sisters, and I were in our old house in Cubero. The old one built of stone, plastered with adobe mud. The one that had huge beams, not the cool kind that the rich buy for their trendy Southwest houses but hand-hewn ones made at great effort by whoever had, long before I was born, made the original structure. The beams weren't round; they were square. The walls weren't adobe brick; they were stone.

The interior was calcimined once a year when I was small (how I love the clean smell and taste of it still) and heated by coal stoves; later we had white folks' paint and butane.

My folks put in a bathroom and indoor plumbing just as I was born. My mother heated my bottle (and my sisters' before me) on a wood-stove fire, one she had to light for middle-of-the-night feedings. The house had wooden floors – pine, not hardwood, and they were shellacked, linoleumed, or painted with what was supposed to be wood-colored paint but was a sort of sick orange.

In that dream, my sisters and I were gathered, and my cousin – the one who died over twenty years ago of Hodgkin's disease, the one who was the eldest son of my uncle the halfbreed and his wife who ran the Villa – came in; and we visited for a while and talked about moving back, how we would share the space, what mother wanted for us, what had been her plans. My cousin said he had to go and went out the back door, down the slate stone path. He crossed the narrow packed-dirt path edged by sandstone rocks set upright in the ground that divided our yard and lawn from Grandma's, past her lawn, past the poplar tree and down the cement walk that fronts her house, and out to the road. He was returning to where he lived, somewhere in the Arroyo, somewhere beyond the store and the lumberyard, beyond the old barn-warehouse that belonged to my father's store, Cubero Trading Company.

My sisters and I went to my grandmother's front yard and there took the arms of an unknown woman who had died. She was why we were there. We took her arms and walked her through our house to our front yard. We laid her in a white stone coffin, and put on the heavy stone lid. Cenotaph, maybe, not coffin. Not exactly tomb. She walked there, in the dream, though she was not really conscious. She walked with our guidance and our help. When I woke up, I knew somebody was about to die, because my cousin lived in the Arroyo – not in the physical one, but in another one that is in about the same place but that occupies another space. He goes from the physical Big Arroyo to the metaphysical one, the one where the dead live, the place the Lagunas and Acomas call Shipap. He comes sometimes to tell me when somebody is about to die.

A little over two months later my brother called to tell me that my grandmother, the halfbreed Laguna one, had had a serious stroke. She remained comatose for two months, entombed in the coffin of her body. Not conscious, not dead. Just caught in between. When she died in January of 1985 she was buried next to Granddaddy, in the Jewish part of the cemetery.

If they came to colonize, those non-Indians in my family, they didn't succeed. The dead still walk Cubero, as they walk this entire land. Capitalism, imperialism, racial hatred, and racial strife notwithstanding. Perhaps Mr. Bibo, Mr. Gottlieb, Mr. Francis né Hassen did not come here to steal Indian land. Perhaps they came to keep the dead alive.

Another time I dreamed about the Road (these are not dreams, though they often occur while I am asleep), Uncle Johnnie showed up. He took me from the Road across the Little Arroyo (as we called it). It is the one that comes down from the mountain and brings irrigation water from the mountain dam into our front yard; just beyond our house and grandma's it crosses under the old highway and empties into the Big Arroyo.

We went into my parents' house, the one I grew up in. This was years after the house no longer belonged to us, you see, but there we were, in the Cubero house, at a party. There were a lot of people there, all family. A lot of noise. You get a houseful of Lebneni/Chicanos, a houseful of halfbreeds, a houseful of folk from every imaginable background and food style and noise style, and you get a lot of noise, a lot of party.

I was standing at one end of the living room and looked up to see my granddaddy and my grandmother entering. And as I looked at him (this was years after he had died) his skin color began to change, to glow with a golden pink radiance that I have since learned goes with the sort of love that is life itself, and he looked at me, in that light, and shrugged. The people in the room were almost shadows, so radiant, so vibrant had he become. They were people in a dream; he was not dreamed but seen. And what passed between us was lengthy, but it boiled down to this. He understood that he had been seriously misunderstood for his life, in his life. What the nature of the misunderstanding had been. Had seriously misunderstood what others saw when they looked at him, when he spoke to them. He came from Germany, remember. (How was he to know the variant signal-systems of those around him, from such different systems, such different thought streams?)

He looked at me, and shrugged, vulnerable, small. Just a simple man who only tried to get by. To do as he was taught. To live a decent life. He told me that in his posture, his gaze, his shrug. Perhaps in his thought. For we didn't speak, only exchanged a long long look. But I understood. Not only Granddaddy, but all of us. We are simply all trying to get by. But some of us are sure, until we die, maybe, about who we are and what is right and who is deciding these things; some of us, like Granddaddy, believe we know for sure the difference between what is good and what is not.

And some of us are forever denied that sureness. We live on the road that the dead walk down. We ride it out of town and back. By its meanders we discover what is there, what is not. By its power we are drawn into a confluence of minds, of beings, of perceptions, of styles. It is a singularly powerful place, the road that runs across the middle of the lands, the roads that run, everywhere, bordering the Big Arroyo that leads to the other place, that connects us to it and them to us. It's that road that is the center of my life; it goes to the mountain, the one called Mt. Taylor, Old Baldy, Ts'pin-a (Woman Veiled in Clouds), Kawesh-tima (Woman Who Comes from the North). The names of the mountain refer to the people who see her. She knows her real name and that she belongs only to her own self, and her dreams and memories, like her plans, are hers, not ours, to judge. And the road that goes to her also goes to town; it goes to the East and to the West; it goes to California, America, and it stays forever home.

ON THE ROAD

The events of my own life (as distinct from my community and family life, if such distinctions are possible) are fairly simple. Some of their connections are elegant, like a good mathematical proof; others are not yet jointed, joined. Throughout, the social and personal events are mirrored or reinforced by those that are more properly literary, that have a definite effect on my work.

Essentially, my life, like my work, is a journey-in-between, a road. The forty years since I left Cubero for convent school have been filled with events – adventures on the road – all of which find their way into my work, one way or another. In my mind, as in my dreams, every road I have traveled, every street I have lived on, has been connected in some primal way to The Road, as we called it, like Plato in our innocence. That Road has many dimensions; it exists on many planes; and on every plane it leads to the wilderness, the mountain, as on every plane it leads to the city, to the village, and to the place beneath where Iyatik" waits, where the four rivers meet, where I am going, where I am from.

16.
Yo Cruzo Siete Mares

He came out of somewhere to here. It is difficult to discover where it was he had been, though they tell us the name of the village where he was born and raised: Rumé, Lebanon. No one knows exactly when, or how old he was when he got here. He went back to the Old Country once and left again later; tables, chairs, and all, taking his wife and young son with him on that second journey. And he came to Albuquerque at last, stayed for a time, went on to Seboyeta, and stayed there forever. Or until he died. They like to remember him tapping his teeth and saying, "¡Mira! Yo cruzo siete mares, y ¿qué me dice?" Arabic-speaking, he learned English. But after he moved to Seboyeta, refused to speak it again. His Spanish was colored by his first tongue. "I crossed seven seas. And you're telling me?"

I would like to know him. Grandpa Francis. Don Francisco. Elias bu-Hassen. Poet. Farmer. Peddler. Merchant. Magician. Traveler. Singer to Emirs. Trader to the Druse. Owner of a sliver of the True Cross. Prophet.

So I have begun to track him through old family tales and long questionings and my own remembered journeys to his fields and orchards, his store and house. He is my father's father's father – bint Elias, ibn Nasif, ibn Elias, buHassen – and I should know him. My father tells me, reminiscing:

Back in 1882–83, my Grandfather was in Rumé . . . this is where he was born. His family had always been in the trading business – his father before him and his father before him. He used to travel to Turkey, he'd go to Egypt, to Palestine. He traded for wheat or cattle, cotton, silk. Silk was quite an industry there. I remember, when I was small, he imported some silk worms so we could see how they made the silk.

Anyway, he got into financial difficulties there in Lebanon at that time, and borrowed some money from his uncle. His uncle said when he loaned him the money that he'd take a mortgage on his home. Well, Grandpa went ahead and just signed the papers. He didn't read them because he had all the trust in the world in this uncle of his. Many days later they were having some festivities in the village. They were dancing around the fire, drinking and enjoying themselves, and someone came over to my grandfather and said to him, "By the way, Elias, I understand you sold your property to your uncle." And Grandpa said, "No, I didn't sell him the property, I mortgaged it to him."

"No, you sold it to him."

"No, I don't think I sold it to him."

Grandpa went to his uncle and he said, "By the way, Gele, that piece of paper I signed – it was a mortgage, wasn't it?"

"No, it was a deed. You sold me your property."

Grandpa said, "No, I didn't sell it to you. I just signed a mortgage."

So his uncle went into his home and brought the paper to show it to my grandfather. So Grandpa found out that he erred; instead of mortgaging the property, he'd sold it! All these people were around this fire outside there, my Grandpa used to tell me, and he'd say, "I didn't know what to do. If I would tear it up, he'd stop me. If I threw it in the fire, he'd also get it in time." So he decided to start talking real fast, you know, and as he talked he folded up this piece of paper and he kept folding it up until he got it into this small ball. Then he stuck it in his mouth and he swallowed it.

That night, Grandpa had to leave town in a hurry.

Well, he got into Beirut, and there was a fellow then that resembled him very much. He had a ticket and a passport to America, but he had gotten scared of going. In those days it took many months of travel by sea to get to the new country – to America. And if a person got sick during the journey, they'd throw him overboard. Now, Grandpa had no money. And since this fellow had backed away, he let my grandfather have his passport. So Grandpa left Lebanon that day. He took a sister of his with him. My grandmother stayed at home, as my father was just a baby. They got on a French ship. In those days there was a great fear of smallpox. In the event any person got sick, they would throw them overboard. Grandpa made friends with the French sailors, and they became buddy-buddies during their travels. Sure enough. He contracted smallpox. So these sailors hid him, and his sister looked after him, and he survived the ordeal and came into America. The smallpox left his arms crippled – he could never stretch them out full length.

When he got into New York City, he looked around for something to do, and with the little bit of money he had, he purchased some trinkets and things *and started traveling on west. He peddled these wares. He'd go on back to New York to stock up, and he'd continue.*

In the meanwhile, he'd keep sending money back to his brother to pay back his uncle. He finally got his uncle paid off. Then he continued a few years in his travels, and eventually went back to Lebanon a rich man.

But while he was in America before he returned to Lebanon, he always traveled by train. He never felt that he should pay for his hotel room, so he always slept in the depot. He had his suitcases where he carried all his wares for sale, so he'd use them for a pillow. This one time he hit this station in Kansas, so he used to tell me, on a very cold night. But the agent didn't want any bums hanging around the depot. He told Grandpa he had to get out. Grandpa told me he didn't know what to do. He had to go to the hotel. So he decided that as long as he was going to go to the hotel, he might as well go to the nicest one. In those days, Grandpa used to say, a room was about a dollar and a half for the night.

He got up to his room, and started to figure: "How am I going to get back this dollar and a half that I'm spending?"

He carried in his suitcases some Arab costumes, so he put on the tarboosh (the fez that everyone in America knows so well) and all the robes, and hung a bunch of rosary beads and trinkets around his neck. Then he went downstairs to eat supper. As he started down the stairs, a bunch of people in the lobby thought he was the Messiah. So he got into the restaurant, and they kept coming from all over. They thought he was a holy man. So, he said, the proprietor of the hotel wouldn't take any money for the room, he got a free meal, and he sold everything he had.

From that time on he always traveled first class and stayed in the best hotels when he was traveling.

"How old do you suppose he was?"

When he first came here, he was about twenty – in his twenties, maybe twenty-one, twenty-two, a young fellow, you know.

Finally Grandpa went back to the Old Country. But after some time there, he decided to come back to America. With his wife and small son, he began the trek again – to Clifton, Arizona, this time.

He never got to California as he dreamed. It took too many years to fuel up for another adventure. Or maybe he did. Maybe that's how I find myself from time to time perched on the western edge of the continent contemplating the Pacific and what's beyond. Maybe that's why I always think "the ocean" means the western one. But in this earth-phase, he'd planned a trip that summer. He was going to take

Yo Cruzo Siete Mares ※ ※ ※ 195

my father, a young man then. But he died in March. (A more pressing journey intervened.)

In Clifton, perhaps ready to settle down, one of those quirks came up that seem to have given much of its shape to his life. My great-grandmother (Houla Hanosh) took sick. Leaving his son Nasif (my grandfather, Jido, seven or eight years old then) to watch the store, Grandpa brought her back to Albuquerque. The doctor said the mining dust in Clifton (copper?) would kill her. Grandpa went back to Clifton to collect Jido and the merchandise.

But the merchandise had all been sold.

> *He'd been gone about a month, and when he returned my father, your Jido, had sold everything. He was just a young boy, and (I guess) everybody felt sorry for him. They purchased all the goods.*
>
> *Armed with his son and his stake, Grandpa Francis returned to Albuquerque and opened a store (where the First National Bank on Central is, that's where they lived, we have a picture some place, of the little house they lived in . . .). And, in the old-world way, he thought of his family. Little by little, he brought relatives over to America, set them up in business, and kept on with his life.*

The lines are interesting . . . circling, recircling on themselves. We talk all day. We record. Grandpa, Jido, Daddy, round and round, on and on. The sheep, the farms, the cattle, the good times, the blizzards, the history, the snow. Mother turns on the lights, puts supper on the table, Daddy talks on, lost in the lost places of their lives, and the vision of strong men and tough ladies, mountains and distances, the forever sky. I wonder if the clouds then were like those now. To think that in the mountains around Seboyeta they raised so many sheep, so much wool, thousands of pounds each year shipped east to come back to my great-grandfather's store in the New Mexico backlands in the form of caps and socks and coats – around and around, the circles, Boston, New York, Grants . . .

The Candelarias, the Bacas, Lunas, Sarracinos, Garcias, Moores, Harms, Lees . . . Lagunas, Navajos, Seboyetanos, Lebanese . . .

Grandpa, with his shortened arms, farming, watching, learning the songs of the moon . . . writing his poems to send to Al Hoda, chanting, walking up the road long after sundown to see his fields, his lady, to check to see if the snake he killed that day had died.

And all the time, the memories of the Old Country, the roads he'd taken to trade, to sing at the courts, to visit friends, family.

What did you call your grandpa?

Don Francisco.

What was his name when he first came here?

My grandfather's name was, in the old country way, the name is always the father's first name. This is the son's last name. So his father was Hassen. And for many years in this country that was the way they operated: Elias buHassen.

But further back there in the grandparents' generations, one was a Frenchman. They used to call him Francweh, where the "Francis" comes from. Later on my grandfather and my father, who was already beginning to grow up, decided to change the name from Elias Hassen to Elias Francis. And this is the family tree.

As he speaks, I wonder how Elias buHassen had found Kaweshtima, Cerro Pelone, Mt. Taylor, in all the vastness of the world, and homesteaded on it, on a place called El Dado, "the gift" – a foreshadowing of his tenure in this place, and his last sentence.

When I was a youngster, my father used to take me up there during shearing. We used to shear up there in those days, and these bands of sheep would come from various parts of the country around there. And it was a beautiful location, lots of pine trees. The sheep would stay there all summer and then they'd bring them on down to the east side of the mountain.

There is order in the tale as in the lives. Strangely, in the disjointed tales told lovingly and in laughter, nostalgia, and in the deep silence that lies under such things, a presence. The cassette takes in our voices as we take in the landscapes, the tones, the spirit of that forever space that is the quintessential element of all our lives. I wonder where Grandpa Francis went when he left here. As he was dying, he said, pointing to my father: "Give him . . ." but did not live to finish telling what that gift should be.

I'm curious. I say, How on earth could they ever have found Mt. Taylor, I mean it's a pretty isolated mountain. It kinda sits there all by itself. (No one could have found it.)

You know, when you fly over, you figure – I do, anyway – here's this guy comes over from Lebanon, right? This is a big country. Not only the United States, but he could have gone to Mexico, he could have gone to South America. Canada . . . how on earth did the fellow wind up here? And how does he wind up with a piece of land on Mt. Taylor, of all places? (Why not any place else?)

Well, this was all free country, all free range, in those days, and they used to graze sheep into several counties. They'd go with the sheep. They just used to travel all of it – it was open range – and Seboyeta was a pretty wealthy area there.

They were well-off, they were Mexicans, Spanish people that had come up to settle . . .

The first band of sheep that was brought into New Mexico was brought in to Seboyeta.

Is that right? What? I think, the first band of sheep, the Lebanese man who follows several centuries later, also the first of his kind.

I read somewhere many years ago. They brought those sheep – it was a woman that brought them, Candelaria – and part of those areas then became established as sheep growing areas.

My Dad doesn't seem as amazed by all these things as I am. I see a world I know nothing about except in glimpses and intuitions, but he lived them. The changes came in his time, before mine. I am astounded at the sight, the second-hand revisioning of what had been and might be again – if God is good and this whole thing goes on.

Si Dios quiere . . .

Because the circles define the patterns after all, over time, so it might come back like the grass.

The reminiscences go on.

Grandpa was the best snake hunter in the world, so far as I was concerned. He'd call them by name (he hated those rattlesnakes with a passion), but he'd call them Juanita, or some other name, until he finally got one. The moment he'd get one, because his arms were sort of crippled, he'd kick it, stun it, and then pick it up by the neck. Then the snake would stick its fangs out. Then – and many people don't believe this, but this I saw many times – he'd bite the fangs out with his teeth. He'd get that snake, all that poison in the darn thing, he'd just bite the fangs out. He said this was the poisonous part of the snake. And he'd spit it out, of course, and then he'd wrap the snake around him . . .

When he'd kill one of those snakes, Grandpa used to tell me, "The snake doesn't die until sundown. You can kill a snake but the snake will not die until sundown." So he'd hang them up on the fences in his fields, and the next day he'd check up, and that's when they were dead.

One time when I was just a little boy, Grandma was very ill. Grandpa and I were down in Bibo, and he hunted up this snake. Then he decided – Grandpa always used to joke a lot, to kid a lot, and Grandma wasn't doing very well – to get this snake and get its fangs out. We stopped at his nephew's store there in Bibo and he said, "I need a shoebox, an empty shoebox." So he got this shoebox and put the snake in (and now, of course, everybody's gathering around).

"Now," he said, "I want it wrapped." So they got it wrapped up and we got in the buggy and rode on home. He went up to Grandma's room and said to her (in Arabic), "My dear, I've brought you a present." And he'd sworn me to secrecy not to say anything. Well, Grandma perked up. She opened the box, and that snake jumped up, and she fainted. "I thought she died." He was beside himself. "I don't understand her. I can't figure her out. How come she would faint on something like that? I was trying to make her feel good about something," he kept on saying. Then my father came in and he started in: "By golly, don't do that to my mother," and Grandpa said, "I was just trying to make her feel better!" He didn't do it maliciously, he was just – he thought it would be a good joke.

Well, that stopped the gifts of snakes, you know.

Grandpa had a sense of humor. One that feels strange, perhaps, to modern minds, but different men lived in those times, men whose humor was as unsubtle as their lives – and as vast.

Grandpa used to give oranges to everyone in Seboyeta for fiesta. He'd have them shipped in from California, and on the night of fiesta for his *brina* he'd have these crates of oranges brought in to the *baile* hall.

He'd bring in apples, too, import them, instead of his own apples. And they'd come crated, each one wrapped in paper.

He'd pass out those oranges to everyone, except for one woman. Doña Prometiva.

She's the one who brought me into this world. She was a midwife, a very close friend of my grandmother's. Grandpa would start out purposely on the side of the hall where Doña Prometiva was (my folks always had the place there about the center) and he'd start giving out the oranges. Everybody got an orange . . . kids – the whole works. Doña Prometiva, he would skip her, nothing for her. Then Grandma would start on him, and Grandpa would say, "She doesn't get one. It's my oranges, and I'm not giving her one," he'd say.

He'd take me to Mass with him. He was very religious. And he had that "Irish whisper" that you could hear all over church. This lady, Prometiva, she was the main rezadora, you know, rosary and all that – she was the one that did all that, singing, you know, she did the whole works. And he'd say to me, whispering: "Mira como está rezando. Reza por modos de robarme – por eso reza. Voy a cuidarla cuando viene a mi casa a visitar a su abuela." [See how she's praying there? She's praying how to figure how she could steal from me. That's what she's praying for. And I'm going to watch her when she comes over to the house to visit your Grandma.]

I listen intently, trying to find the shape, the meaning, the person who was my great-grandfather. I'm told he liked to laugh. And he liked to jab people a little, into consciousness perhaps, and he liked to drink. He liked to grow things, and to keep records, and to work. He didn't like to get all fancied up, though the only pictures I've seen of him are in dark suit and hair carefully smoothed, mustaches curled up perfectly. He looks like any American gentleman of that time, however different from mainstream memories his must have been, and his ways.

"Your Grandpa, what were the Christmas gifts he gave you?" my mother asks, prompting during a lag.

Grandpa's dimes. He used to save dimes. Every day he'd put aside twenty cents, two dimes. Every day, two dimes. He used to smoke Bull Durham, but when he got fancy he smoked Camel cigarettes. So he'd fill up these old Bull Durham sacks with dimes. There were nine of us. So for Christmas we got dimes and oranges. And for Easter we got extra dimes because Easter was the big feast. Christmas was nothing. The day Christ was born. The day Christ was risen, that's the big feast they celebrate back in the Old Country. He was on the stone that Christ rose from, and he said that stone was above the earth so much [gesturing]. Grandpa saw that, where Christ was buried.

He hated those Turks and those Druse because they'd killed his oldest brother in the religious wars. He got along with them. He said, "They treated me all right. I used to go to Turkey. I'd take cattle up there and trade it, take wheat and trade it for something else and bring it back. I'd go to Egypt and get into Jerusalem, into the area there."

He was a great friend of Dale Bellamah's great-grandfather, who was an emir. (An emir is higher than a prince.) And he used to be called by the – what was it? – the guy higher than a shah, whatever it is in that area there, a big man. Grandpa was one of the very few commoners that this man would invite, because Grandpa was always a good drinker from the age of fifteen. He could handle his booze. He used to compose these songs, these poems, and he was invariably invited to these high festivities. He used to attend them all. And sing for the guests the songs he'd made up.

In this country he'd compose these poems, and then he'd send them to New York, to Al Hoda, and he'd get the paper and his poem wouldn't be printed, and he'd call in your Uncle Elias Hanosh, who always wrote them

*down real nice for Grandpa, he'd call in Uncle Elias and say, "Look what
these dirty so and so's, what they did to me. Write this letter to them." And
he'd write, cussing them out for not printing his poem. So they'd write him
back that it wasn't a good poem, and Grandpa'd tell Uncle Elias, "By golly, I
know better. I was in that particular area when I composed that poem. I traveled all over. I was in those countries. Those fellows don't know anything, just
New York."*

Sometimes they'd go ahead and publish the poem, and he'd be jubilant.

My father remembers how Grandpa Francis liked to grow things. he
grew fruit and alfalfa and corn, and sheep, cattle, grandchildren, and businesses. He was the best shot in the country and used to take bets on his skill
on his annual trip to Albuquerque. He'd clean up. He liked to raise a little
hell when he got the chance. He was a man who took care where it was
needed, and hung loose when it was time.

He liked to drink, my father says. "He liked his booze, but he never
touched a drop until five o'clock." And then my father tells stories of
Grandpa's drinking, and Grandma trying to keep him away from it. I hear
the voices, the loud people. I see the house full, that big house my great-
grandfather built in the far-away country of Seboyeta, a place never heard
of by the world we live in, however precariously, now.

I remember that house. And the huge gates into the yard. The key that
must have weighed a pound, which opened its lock. (The lock is massive,
rusted iron. It sits on the deep windowsill at my parents' Cubero house.)
Grandpa grew a lot of things in Seboyeta, on the mountain, in the valleys
below its perfect flanks. He grew things in Cebolletito, on the Ignacio Chavez Grant, in Cabezon and Paguate, in Santa Fe where his son went as the
first Lebanese person to hold high office in the United States as a state repre-
sentative. He grew laws and patents, Jido did, and deeds that gave him title
to some of the most valuable land in the world today. And he grew people –
teaching them American ways, teaching them something for another time –
feeding their children as he fed his own. But the land was taken, one way or
another, and the people moved away, and the changes that came to the
world at the same time as his death removed his name and theirs from the
public histories. Still, his life was a testimony to something important –
however ignored.

*My Dad says, Grandpa used to always say, "When I go, all this goes with me." My
Dad thinks maybe it went because Jido couldn't manage so well as Grandpa had,*

that his own nature, so gentle and stern, so progressive, not so wild, poetic, hard-hitting as his father's, was not equal to holding what they, together, Elias Francis & Son, had built.

But I think that it was one of the things about Grandpa that he could see what this world was coming to as is sometimes said, that his lands and what he grew could only have been taken and grown in a special time by such a man; and that with his personal death came another kind of death, the death of a way of life; and that no one could reclaim either.

And this is what they grew, that so amazes me, to think that such things were, and somewhere still are, in memory if not in fact, and perhaps in dreams of a future that is more to the shape of human folk. My father continues into the night:

> *Well, he went to Seboyeta like I said, and he could see that they had to travel fifteen to twenty miles to buy their groceries. Seboyeta, of course, was re-nowned, according to history, in historical books that I've read since then, as a rough area. And not too many outsiders would live there because, from what I read (and I discount it), any killing that had to be done, way back in those early days, they used to hire these people from Seboyeta to do the killing for them. I mean, it was a tough area. Grandpa was a pretty stout person him-self. He wasn't afraid of them, and he made friends with them immediately and they were glad to receive him. They thought it was great that someone would come in and open up a store, and from then he just built up a tremen-dous trade. For miles and miles around they'd come up there to deal with my Grandpa. They used to say that—some of the old timers used to tell me there—the Spanish people, the Seboyetanos used to say: "Me acuerdo de su abuelo cuando llegó aquí. Su tiro con un caballo más chico que el otro—carro viejo—pero aquí puso casa, negocio, y se quedo—que buena ventura para nosotros, todos!" [I remember when your grandfather came in a broken down wagon, one horse smaller than the other one, and he settled here, he's been here ever since, and it's the best thing that ever happened to us.]*

But in their operations in those days they used to run a lot of sheep as well as cattle and stores, and they had a big organization. Elias Francis & Son used to hire around three to four hundred people. They hired from all over the area. All of Seboyeta was on that payroll, and Moquino, Cebolletito, and San Mateo. They hired a lot of Pueblos, too—from Paguate, particu-larly—men like Pedro Lente, Rafael Lente, Andres Garcia, the Sarracinos. They hired people from Albuquerque, from Cabezon, from Guadalupe—a big operation that fed a lot of families—and watched them grow children and grandchildren and now even great-grandchildren who would go into the sheep business, into the cities, even to California.

My father had no education whatsoever, from no place. He never went to the first grade, never went to the second grade, or any grades. Never had the chance, the opportunity. And there he was, el patrón, *the person who had the responsibility of four hundred to five hundred thousand acres of land in addition to thirty or thirty-five thousand head of sheep and two or three thousand head of cattle. He learned to read and write through his own efforts. Spanish – of course, that was his main language – and Arabic, and English.*

In order to be patrón *in those days, he had to be absolute – that is, if a particular individual was working, it was my father's responsibility to see to it that the family was taken care of. If anyone was ill, the* patrón *had the responsibility to see that they went to a doctor. He paid for all of this. He was the best man at more weddings than any person I know of – that's ever lived after that or before him. And he baptized more people in that area there.*

And many of the old timers today, he was their padrino. *That means "best man." It's quite an honor to be a* padrino. *But* padrino, *in those days, meant that for the wedding the* padrino *paid for everything – the* baile, *the food, the* musicos, *the whole works. All the festivities. Toda la fiesta.*

The era, of course, changed when Roosevelt came in, WPA took over, and all that stuff, and eventually they killed off all of this. But at that time, I recall my father (my grandfather had been dead, of course, many years) and I had a lease on the Ignacio Chavez Land Grant from the owners. They were from Nova Scotia. It was leased by my grandfather and my father, and then later on my father included me, so it was Narciso Francis and Son.

So as these times came on, the federal government decided to buy the land. In those days we were in the middle of the Depression. There was no way that we could touch it in buying it. But we wanted to continue operating sheep on it. So they sold it and I came here to Albuquerque. I was already married, and decided to discuss it with the outfit, and I think Briggs was handling it. So I met with them and some government fellows, and I said, "What happened to us? We've been on this land for three generations." And they told me, "We'll give you the first permit and you can run no more than five hundred head of sheep."

In those days, five hundred head of sheep was an income of say about maybe three hundred dollars a year. So I said, "No way can I operate five hundred head of sheep."

"Well, you can have a choice – five hundred head of sheep, or one hundred head of cattle – either one." They told me.

And I said, "Can't make it." But, I said, "What you're going to be doing is putting people out of work. Here," I said, "we're hiring so many people, even during this Depression. These people are dependent for their livelihood on working for us, for my father, and what is going to become of these people?"

"Well, we're going to give them allotments, we're going to get them started," they said.

And I then stated to these people, "I predict to you that within five years there will not be a local person running any stock there."

And it was true.

But, in their operations in the old days, they used to run over thirty thousand head of sheep. They started with a hundred head that they bought and they built them up over a period of years where they were running thirty-two thousand head. And my father, of course, ran the sheep and Grandpa always stayed in the store, and they had land and they bought farms, and he used to do all the farming, Grandpa. So this is how they built up one of the largest operations in the southwest, under the firm name of Elias Francis & Son. Then they built up their operations – they were big in the cattle business, they were on the Board of Directors of the United States National Bank here in Albuquerque. . . .

There were men that were responsible for the wagons. And these wagons in those days . . . I think they always kept about eight wagons, eight teams of horses at the headquarters in Seboyeta. The stable is still there. And each fellow was responsible for that team of horses, and he was responsible for that wagon. And these wagons were always busy, every day. In those days, of course, we used to feed the working people at home, so our cooks would be up, say, three o'clock in the morning, preparing breakfast. Breakfast would be served around four or four-thirty, and then they'd go about getting their wagons hitched. There were people working on the farms, and on the ranches, in the house and the store . . . for example, you have thirty thousand head of sheep, and that required about sixty men the year around, but during lambing it would take ten times that many, so my father and my grandfather were hiring around three to four hundred people. For lambing in those days, you had to give more care. The sheep were in bands, and you had to have somebody there, for example, to take care of the pregnant sheep . . . el pregñador. Then there were the caporales, like, foremen, you know, who would *oversee things. Then there were the cooks, and somebody that would haul water to the camp. And each one had their duty.*

So, the Native people there . . . I think there may be one or two that have permits today. All the rest are gone. Consequently, the towns of Guadalupe, Cabezon were killed off. They all migrated into Albuquerque. There's no one living there now.

Seboyeta, the same thing happened there.

Moquino, I think there were three families, Marquez, two families . . . one family was left there last time I checked. All these were employed by my folks during that era.

They changed the whole picture, the whole strata, the whole thing. So consequently we decided that the only thing to do was start selling out. We cleaned out the sheep end . . . sold them. At that time I think we still had about three thousand to four thousand head of sheep left, and we had to go out of the sheep business.

The other lands, of course, were going. Dad, during that period of the Depression, was trying to settle the estate of Elias Francis and Son, when the Depression hit.

When did Grandpa die? I ask.

Grandpa died in 1931. And he was very ironic, was my Grandpa.

I see the memory, and the knowledge gained leaning out of his face, as he smiles, as the past closes on us, as we remember the present, the small, neat apartment in Albuquerque where Eliatas and his wife now live . . . exiled also from the past and its own turned-over dreams, as he says, "He used to say to me there, it was that last year or so, he used to say, 'When I go, everything goes with me.' And, now, I guess he knew."

One time we were talking, my father and I, about what was going to happen to us, whether it would be awful, the end of the world, or marvelous — the New Age. He told me that he believed that my brothers and my sisters and I, and our children, would see a most amazing era. We would see things that no one had dreamed of. You are entering into an era that will be just tremendous, unbelievable, he said. And that those who didn't believe in this future were just wrong. The signs were there, we agreed (God willing), and the ease and wonder of that coming era would be incredible to behold.

Your children, he said, and you, you'll live to see it. My time is over, I won't. But it will be unbelievable, this is what I believe.

And, like him before his grandfather's death, I guess he knows. Certainly the changes he has seen in his own sixty-three years are nearly beyond comprehension. The Depression, the Migrations, the War . . . automation, electronics. It used to take them half a day to take a wagon of stuff from Seboyeta to the depot at Laguna. I can get halfway around the world in that same time. Grandpa Francis stood astounded at Jido's automobiles . . . I stand amazed at Viking on Mars. So the changes continue. One wonders where they lead.

So, when the Depression hit, Dad and I were trying to settle the estate of Elias Francis and Son, and the Depression was on, and everyone was wanting their money. We could have declared bankruptcy, but my father couldn't . . . no way would he accept that. He thought it was a disgrace for anybody to declare bankruptcy. I was just a young man and quite a bit of the property and the sheep were deeded to me way before my father got in troubles financially.

I owned this land . . . particular ranches in there. And many of the business people in those days would say to me, "You're very foolish, you should let your father declare bankruptcy, and you could utilize and save all this. It's no disgrace." And I'd say, " No way, we've got to liquidate, we have to pay off."

So we started selling off ranches for nothing. Ranches that today are worth millions of dollars. Started liquidating to pay everything off and when we paid everything, all we had left was that lease on the Ignacio Chavez Land Grant and another area and three to four thousand head of sheep. We were clear then. That was about 1939. And then, that deal on the Ignacio Chavez lease was the final blow there, so that's when we completely went out of it. But this is the way it happened. To this tremendous operation.

I wonder if that's the way it happened all over the country: the Depression; the drought of '28. (My father has told me that during that drought he would go out to the ranch and step over dead sheep, hundreds of them.) The allotments. The bankruptcies. The liquidations. The War. So it went.

Now there's a boom out there. Uranium. The oil companies doing their own gobbling, the people, those that are left, or those who inherited land rights trying to salvage something from the past – a rich one, back in the pastoral era of farming and sheep and tough men who could drink hard and work back-breaking hours and still find time for dancing under the moon and singing poems of far-away lands they had actually seen when time held so much promise of good times to come.

17.
My Lebanon

I am Paula, daughter of Lee, son of Narcisco, son of Elias. I am an American of Lebanese descent, cut adrift from Lebanon by the meanders of time, history, place, and the private decisions of my family and myself. Because the course of my family river has been diverse, I have no central myth or legend, no single point of view, to enclose me. I have death, grief, snatches of history, and memory of song. I have tolerance, passion, an oddly persistent memory that can't be mine of a spring graced by the healing power of a female god, a sprite, an ancient waterbeing. I know the sound of *debukke* and oud. I know the sound of finger cymbals. But I don't know how to do the dances, was made foolish at my *lileeah*, my engagement party, by that lack so many many years ago, when I married a Hanosh, my great-grandmother's great-nephew. As her name was Haula (Paula in English), her family in Lebanon was particularly excited by the match. Haula is coming home, they rejoiced. I am told that my picture occupies a place of honor in their home, or did a few years ago, even though I divorced my Hanosh cousin twenty-five years ago. Or maybe the house and the picture have been bombed. Maybe all her relatives are dispersed or dead.

In my mouth sometimes I carry the taste of food, on a tongue that stumbles in saying the names: *kibbe, leban* (or *laban*), *hemos, duele, mamoul, mehle, butujin, risbe habeeb, hibs, cusa mitwe, babaganoush, eftire, kibbe naya, kibbe sinea, kibbe erst, yubra, yuhne, halewe.* Some of them everyone knows: Halvah, for instance, my father calls *halewe*. *Mehle*, that in America is called baklava. *Duele*, dolma, grape leaves. *Risbe habeeb*, rice pudding, rich and sweet, studded with fat raisins, rich with cream. *Hibs*, pita bread. *Laban*, yoghurt, sort of, but also rich, made with whole milk, made with cream. And sour, sour. Best in the summer heat. Or *leban maghtogh*, "mac-tooth" my mother would say, kidding. That you make by taking the *laban* and pouring it into a cloth, like a nice square of floursacking, and tying it up and hanging it over the faucet in the kitchen sink so the whey can drip out. After a time the *laban* gets thick, like cream cheese. Only sour. To spread on *hibs* and eat, maybe with *zaitun*, sour bitter wrinkled olives, like my father, Baiye, and my grandfather, Jidek, did and do. Mostly I don't know how to spell these names, except for a few I've seen spelled in exotic cookbooks or recipes in a ladies' magazine one time. Others are too strange in America, and that's too bad. I can't spell them because they don't spell in English. Not the way I hear them in my ear. I carry a little of my Lebanese people's language in my ear, a few of their stories, their ways, their history both here and in the old country, only a little, but no more. (*Poco, poquito, pero no más*, Jido is saying in my memory, in my ear. "*Pero no más.*")

Lebneni (*lubnaani*); Syrian; Arab. When I was young, I was told that in the East, in New York and New Jersey, they had signs up in certain places, hotels, restaurants, "No Syrians or Jews Allowed." I was told that that meant us, too, because they called all of us "Syrians." I guess there were no Lebanese in the minds of the anti-Semitic sign makers, just as there were no Lebanese for the hundreds-of-years-long occupation and colonization of Lebanon by the Syrians. Indeed, there was no Lebanon for so long that it is still difficult, almost impossible, to find mention of it anywhere except on the news on TV. Does that mean that there is no Lebanon, really?

My Native American grandmother, Agnes Gunn, remembers being excluded from the group at Indian School in Albuquerque, from the group at home in New Laguna: "They used to tell me to go away. They wouldn't have anything to do with me. So, I did."

She went away to Cubero in geographic location. She went away to the home of the German Jew immigrant she married. She went away to whatever version of America she could manage in that tiny Spanish-speaking village, my grandmother Gottlieb who never learned to speak Spanish and forgot as much Indian as she could. Who internalized the scorn and loathing directed against her and against her full-blood mother by their Laguna community, who turned as racist against Indians as she could, for as long as she could. Not because the whites rejected her. But because the Indians did.

And my mother, her daughter, who was not the biological daughter of the Jewish immigrant, but who was his stepdaughter, was stoned by the Cubereño children, her peers, after school. "They used to chase me down the hill," she remembers, "throwing rocks at me, shouting 'Judea! India!' as they chased me." Those children were Mexican-American, Spanish, as they said of themselves in those days, before the new age of militancy and radicalism came into vogue. *La gente. La Raza. "Viva la Raza! Venceremos!"* They have every reason to hate the child they stone. Is she not the enemy? The despised Jew? The loathed Indian? *"Y yo también."*

And me as well. La India. La Arabe.

Like my Lebanese relatives I love the mountains and the sea; like them I am drawn to the madonna, the Mother; like them I feel safest when there is a spring nearby, as there was in my childhood Cubero, a spring I can speak with and know that the sacred sprite who lives within replies. And like them I know that the tradition may change in time and place, but that in essence it remains the same, and that it is in the stories that the sacred essence survives. Perhaps, more than anything in my life, I take that love from them.

So I have much from them. Even my body, which at barely over five feet is not much taller than my grandmother's. My father says, talking about her, "she was broad," he gestures with his hands, "hefty. Like you, and Kathy." Kathy, my sister, is five feet tall and weighs over 150. I am about five-foot one and weigh around 190. When he says that, I am proud, but a little dubious. Not about matching Mama Mina in size, but in face. He says, "You look like my mother." I think, "No, Kathy does, I don't." Because I have heard them saying that one of my aunts looks exactly like her mother, and I know that Kathy looks almost exactly like that aunt. I think my father says that I look like his mother because our dispositions are a lot alike.

My body. From my mother's family I inherit arthritis, sinus trouble, hay fever, and perhaps lupus. From my father's family I inherit size, low blood pressure, a tendency toward diabetes and heart trouble. And thick, thick, curly, almost kinky hair. From them I inherit my skin, a pale olive that turns a lovely brown with the summer sun. I have one far-sighted eye and my father is far-sighted; I have one near-sighted eye and my mother is near-sighted. A little of this, a little of that: a person is made up of too many pieces, a patchwork quilt. A horse designed by a committee. The single most important part of me I inherit from Lebanon: my body. My very unfashionable, unthin, uncool, un-American as it can be; my round, big-breasted body. But even that is half-breed, three-quarters breed, for while its size is of my father's people, and though my hair is thick and tightly curly, almost kinky, I am otherwise quite hairless. Is that Indian? My mother has thin hair on her head, virtually no hair on her arms. She plucked her eyebrows thin when she was in high school in the early thirties and, she says, they never grew back. They are thin. My eyebrows are thin, too. I notice that my mother's grandmother had thin eyebrows, and I don't imagine she ever plucked them. So even my body is part-Lebanese. Though what it matters, I am not sure. I think it matters to me, to know about my own proclivities, inclinations, and dreams. To know whence they are, and in that way, perhaps, to know whence they will proceed. Or maybe it's just that I'd like to know which side I, American mongrel, am on, and whether that side is or isn't "right." To know how I can justify the thoughts and emotions I experience, sometimes overpowering in their intensity, when the subject of Zionism, fascism, genocide, and good guys and bad guys in the Middle East comes up in conversation or on television.

I also have a Lebanese ability to talk, wildly gesticulating. I have a love of loud parties, dancing, drinking, hollering and bonding, and eatingeatingeating. I have a love of full cupboards, laden tables, plenty for all the guests and lots left over. I have an expansiveness, a sense of cunning, a love of storytelling, a love of place, a sense of history, a personal sense, a delight in mystery, a delight in ritual of the Christian kind, a weakness for children, a tendency to humor them, to indulge them, a respect for nuns and priests that comes close to patronizing them. I enjoy doing business, I love to try to get the best of someone in a business deal. I have a pride of heritage and a quick anger, a quick, biting irritability. I have a strong sense of family, of propriety, of place. I have a sense of martyrdom, of melancholia, of great age. I have a liking for difference, a love of complication, a joy in interfamilial conflict, a sense of daring, of adventure, of the folly of humankind. I love to gamble, and I love to win. And I have a huge pile of memories to go along with the pile of memoirs I have also collected and they include the best and the worst moments of my life.

My father has a piece of wood that he says is a piece of the cross that Jesus died on. He says Grandpa brought it from Lebanon. Grandpa used to peddle goods from Turkey to Jerusalem. My father says we are of the House of David, descendants of the same family that gave birth to Jesus. He says that Lebanon was the first nation to convert to Christianity. Long, long ago. Lebanon's patron saint is Mar Elias. According to the story, Elias and Moses joined Our Lord on the mountain peak. And the apostles, overcome with awe, offered to erect a tent to shelter the three, but Our Lord refused their offer, bidding them to simply watch and pray.

Elias, the assumed one, was so precious to the Father God that he did not die. They say he will return to earth in the last days, because like all men he must die. But not yet, they say, not yet. I wonder if somewhere Elias is being born, if somewhere some old patriarch named Elias is declaring himself present, present to preside over the final death of the Lebanese. Of us all.

In the church in Seboyeta, where my father was born and raised, Seboyeta that is nestled in the arms of the Cebolleta mountains on the eastern spur of Mt. Taylor, Seboyeta that is one of the earliest settlements of the Spanish colonization of the northern territories of New Spain, now New Mexico, in that church, one that is very, very old as things in America are dated, hangs a picture of Abraham preparing to sacrifice his son Isaac. But the picture is actually of Saint Elias. Or that's how the story goes, because my great-grandfather ordered a painting of Lebanon's patron saint to grace the church where he worshiped on Sundays and holy days.

In due time the painting arrived, coming from the old country by way of New York, coming west on the train, coming to Seboyeta by wagon from Laguna where the nearest depot was. After such a journey no one questioned what Saint Elias was doing standing over the the prone body of a half-naked youth with a knife poised to plunge into the youth's slender breast. Grandpa had ordered a painting of Saint Elias and, for his money, that was what he got. No one ever questioned it until some young priest, stationed at Seboyeta instead of the sophisticated parish he craved, did. I went to see him because he'd sent word that he had some papers and other things that had been left at the old house in Seboyeta years before, the house that had been bought by the Gallup diocese and was now the priest's house. I wanted to walk around there, remembering. Walk through that old house, look up at the door where my great-grandfather used to sit, now thin air but then graced by a small balcony, stairs leading down to the driveway, gaze at the old store, at the sheds, the stables. Go into the church and sit, and listen, and dream. Maybe talk to some ghosts.

It didn't quite work out that way, though I guess I did talk to ghosts as I listened to the young Anglo priest, bearded and "involved" in the dynamic way the new priesthood often exhibits. He told me about the strange case of the Saint Elias painting, which, he assured me, was not of Saint Elias after all, but of Abraham, the patriarch. He then told me about the superstitious credulity of the local people, the Seboyetanos (descendants of Spanish colonial settlers of the region who were granted possession of the land by decree of the Spanish crown a couple of centuries ago). His story concerned what he called a legend about the miraculous healing of an infant boy, sixty or so years before. The story, he said, was that some local child had had some mishap – something had happened that should have killed him. But the child's grandmother and his mother had taken the baby, wrapped him in a blanket, then crawled on their knees from the church to a shrine some several miles into the hills, praying the rosary all the while. They had begged the Virgin, whose shrine it is, to save the child, and had dedicated him to her for life if she would grant their petition. Well, the baby lived, or so the story goes. And saying that, the priest shook his head pityingly. He thought the story had probably been carried from Mexico, maybe from beyond Mexico, from Spain, a quaint example of folk belief in this modern age. It was, he implied, yet another illustration of the magnitude of the difficulties he faced in this remote place.

I could see that he was university-educated and was quite taken with the sense of himself as folklore specialist stationed in the wilds of New Mexico. He evidently didn't know that the story was quite true. That the infant in the story was my father. That the women – my grandmother and my great-grandmother – had indeed crawled all the way to Portales from Seboyeta, had dedicated the baby to Mary the Madonna, and that the baby had lived. The priest didn't know that after they did their religious best to save the child, they took him back to Seboyeta, and then to the doctor in Albuquerque, who discovered that the immediate cause of his nearly lethal injury – a screw that his sister, then about three, had given him to hold and he, infant-curious, had put in his mouth and swallowed – had passed, like God in the night. The doctor said it was a miracle the infant's intestines hadn't been torn or shredded in its passing.

I do not know where, exactly, the village of my grandparents is. Or if it exists anymore, anywhere at all.

Déjà vu? I know how my elder halfbreed Indian relatives felt. And why a fullblood uncle used to ride on the train, claiming to be Italian. I find myself obscurely humiliated, frightened, grieved, to be one who is identified as the enemy of righteousness and good. I think Uncle Charlie must have felt that way, as many Indians have testified to feeling; because Indians have been so long the enemy of the good as that good is defined by white eyes. And so I can only watch, horrified, as the mobs, the shells, the bullets erupt. I can only listen, aghast, to my professional community as its many members denounce Lebanon and claim the right of the Arab to triumph, denying the right of the anciencientancient Lebanese to live.

Walking to classes is painful. Today small neon-orange stickers adorn the elevators, demanding that the imperialist Israel and the United States get out of Lebanon. No demand was made that all foreign powers get out; that Syria, the PLO, Palestine nationals, the Soviet Union, Iran, or whoever else is in Lebanon minding its business and murdering its citizens at least as much as the so-called imperialists, cease their genocidal war on the people of Lebanon, the people of the mother's breasts, her milk-giving breasts. Lebanon is a cognate of *laban,* "milk." Because the map of Lebanon is the map of two mountain ranges that are divided by a deep valley, the psychic-culture map shows a similar topography: the Lebanese display two towering ranges of knowledge and culture, divided by history, religion, diversity, and oppression. Lebanon, recorded in the Book of Numbers as a land enslaved to Egypt, which quarried stone to send to the Egyptian rulers, carried it out of the quarries through the mountain ruggedness so Pharaoh could have palaces fit for Egypt's might. Lebanon, land of Astarte, Ishtar; whence grieving Isis (EE-Zees) went searching for her lost son, her beloved; where she was consoled by the Goddess Ishtar, whom Isis betrayed. Lebanon, where the body of the beloved Osiris was found, near Byblos, trapped and held within the encompassing embrace of the sacred tree, which was the body of the Goddess from time immemorial. Lebanon, where the children of Mak/Maat lived and live; the children of Mara, of Mary, the children of Mah. Whose isolated mountain springs are still held sacred in her name. Whose descendants, Maronites, still remember the sprites in the mountain pools, the woman spirits who have been their safety and succor for so many ages past, who bear in their name, their race, her memory, her name. Lebanon, conquered by the Aryan Turks, who split the children from the Mother, who stole her male child, her lover, who tore the son from the tree and ripped his body to pieces, and cast the pieces upon the sea; who cast the sacred dogs of the goddess into the sea where they waited long centuries to be restored by Nordic seamen during the Second World War, the war that finally resulted in the liberation of Lebanon, for however brief a time, the liberation of the mountain wild folk, the Lebanese.

I think about the ride up to Los Cerrillos Judy and I took a couple summers ago. I wanted to find the house where my grandmother was raised. The store her father kept. Early that morning my father and I sat and talked over breakfast in my parents' apartment high above the plain. Mother was in her room, Judy asleep. We talk about how he feels now, seventy years old. We talk about how he loses his memory, how it bothers him.

"Are you afraid of getting old?" I ask. Wanting to know, to know something about him, as he is to himself, in himself; wanting also to know for myself, later. So I will know where I am, when I am where he is now. He doesn't answer, just looks at me quickly, in that way he has, eyes darting over to me, away. A bird, perching for a moment on the twig of a thought, then away.

"Your grandmother was raised in Cerrillos," he says.

"Where?" I say. "You mean Los Cerrillos, up in the Sandias?"

"Yes," he says. "Up there. Her father, your Jide Michael, had a store up there. That's where she was raised."

I think this came up because I asked him about his mother. Something I haven't done much because it makes him sad to talk about her. Or it always used to. But now, maybe because he's seventy, he talks about her, mostly without tears. "Was she born in the old country?" I ask, grinning at my joke. "Yes," he says, "She and her brother Uncle Kaiser. They were the only ones born there. But you know, one funny thing. Her other brothers, Uncle George, Uncle Lee, Uncle Johnny, they were born in America, in the United States, but she was the one who spoke perfect American, without an accent. Of course, she was educated here, went to school here. She had a beautiful voice, my mama." He smiles slightly, eyes looking sad, then shakes his head. His eyes gone away from me for a moment, as he remembers a sound I cannot hear, an image I cannot see. I strain toward him, trying. To find what he knows, what he remembers, as he gazes at the room through his childhood eyes.

"After she and Uncle Kaiser were born, they moved to the United States. Had a business in Albuquerque with my grandfather. After a few years grandpa moved to Seboyeta. I guess there wasn't enough business to support all of them, Jide Michael and his family, my grandpa's family. Jide Michael took his sons to Lebanon, to get educated there, to find wives. You know, it was the custom for men to try to marry women from Lebanon. My mama was already married, then. She didn't go with them, of course. But Jide Michael and the rest of the family went, and then they got caught there, in the First World War. You know, after he came back here, he couldn't make a go of it. Not after he got back here, after the war."

I don't think much about what he's saying, just something about how war disorients people. How they sometimes don't recover from the trauma. Later I am reading an article about Kahlil Gibran, the Lebanese-American poet. Who was born in Lebanon, moved to the United States as a young man – thirteen or so. He went back to Lebanon with assistance from an American woman who was acting as his mentor or benefactor, and he, like my great-grandfather Michael, got caught in the "Great War." Gibran seems not to have recovered from it, either. How strange Jide Michael, the fair-haired, blue-eyed grandfather, a businessman, father of seven or eight children (maybe more, for all I know), scores of grandchildren and great-grandchildren, businessman, and Kahlil Gibran, poet, mystic, artist. Both Lebanese Maronites transplanted to the United States. Both harmed, somehow, irreparably, from that struggle, in which Lebanon gained its independence from Syrian dominance under the Ottoman Empire. Mama Mina would have been born under Turkish and Syrian imperial rule of Lebanon. From which her father and mother fled to the United States. So they could live free from fear of beatings, burnings, massacre. They were Maronites, under the nominal protection of the Roman Church through the agency of France, but they were a conquered people, and like the conquered everywhere, they were never free from fear of brutality, of terrorization.

"How old was she when she got married, do you know?" I ask.

"Maybe fifteen or sixteen." He shakes his head, lightly. Not sure. Or sure about the age she was when she married, but not sure how I'll take that. How it sounds.

"How old was she when she died?"

"Forty. She was forty."

"And how old were you?"

"Fifteen."

"She was young," I say. "She had so many kids in such a short time." I feel depressed, troubled. I try to calculate swiftly. Seven children that lived. Nine altogether. Fifteen from forty is . . . I give up the attempt.

"Is the house still there, in Los Cerrillos?" I ask. He doesn't know. It might be. "Wouldn't it be great to go up there?" I say. I tell my mother,

"Daddy says Mama Mina was raised in Los Cerrillos. Isn't that amazing? I didn't know that! Maybe we could go up there, see if we could find the old house, the store."

"Well, why don't you go?" she asks.

"Maybe I will." I say. "Why not."

I used to go up there, years ago. When the kids were small. I went up there a few times to dinner. There was a restaurant that had good food and sometimes a dinner show. I went there the first time not long after I first moved to Albuquerque, on the lam from my marriage to my Sitte's great-nephew. I was living in a sleazy motel, one of those by-the-week places out on West Central, near Old Town. I had gotten acquainted with a guy who was also in the throes of divorce, a guy from somewhere in the Midwest. Iowa, maybe. Indiana. He took me to Los Cerrillos for dinner. Before dinner we went into a store where they sold secondhand and antique things.

As I talk to my dad now, I wonder if the piano I had seen that night might have come from my grandmother's old house. Who lived there now? I remember how much I wanted that piano. It was an upright, and the front was blue mirror glass. The keys were good. I played it a little bit. Of course, I couldn't buy a piano. I lived with my two babies in a cheap motel. I had just gotten a job, clerk in a curio shop – forty dollars a week, maybe. If I was lucky. A piano? But the longing had made an impression, so now, talking to my dad over coffee in the sunstream coming through the kitchen window of their very modern apartment in Albuquerque's northeast heights, looking out over the west mesa to see Mt. Taylor sixty miles away to the west, across the plain, I could remember Los Cerrillos. I wonder why I hadn't known that my grandmother came from there.

It is late August, and the mountain is a study in floral design we drive through. White and yellow, deep gold and dark green, fuchsia and orange. We drive east out of Albuquerque, through Tijeras Canyon, turn right onto Highway 14, past San Antonito. Turn to the right a few miles later, swinging with the highway toward Santa Fe to the north. Past Golden, where the country-and-western twangs out on Sundays at the bar there, and the hip, the cool, and the alcoholics spend a long afternoon drinking and getting stoned in 2/4 time.

I take a lifetime of memories with me on the drive, twenty or more years of drives through this lovely countryside. I take curiosity, the unanswered questions of years with me. I take eyes that look and look at the passing land, trying to hold perfect every blade of grass, every golden or purple blaze of color from the wildflowers, every stone, juniper, pine, trying to find what the land knows, what it remembers, what it means. Every period of my adult life is here with me as we drive, Judy and I, through the Sandias toward Santa Fe. My life rides in my eyes, investing everything I see with a memory, a meaning, a terror, a joy, a grief.

Somewhere is the road that goes among the tall pines where I went with some boy I was dating when I was sixteen. The road to the wilderness, the night, in the snow. Where I was raped, though it took me over twenty years to acknowledge the event. Somewhere else is the road that goes up to the peak, that ends near a path I walked with a man to a round stone building that looks out over the 5,000-foot drop to the plain, the city below, that looks 50,000 feet up to the sky, 50 million million miles to the stars through the openings in the stone. The round stone building where we made love and conceived twin boys. Conceived two, one of whom died. Along here, somewhere, is the place where that man, my last husband, and I saw a light in the sky that was not a star, that was like a revolving spotlight. But out where there were no lights, nor are there any now, so many years from then. The light had followed us back down the highway to where the highway picked up the Interstate at the top of Tijeras Canyon. Odd behavior for a spotlight. It could have been a helicopter, or a plane, I suppose, except that it made no sound. What was most odd about it was that we had driven up there well after autumn dark to see if we could spot a UFO. We had heard rumors about them being seen often up there, particularly from the villages of Madrid and Golden, so we went to see one for ourselves. Who knows. Maybe we did.

And now, so long after, I drive that highway again, counting my life at various milestone, roads that run off here and there, at stops along the way. It's a habit I picked up from my father, and my Jido – this telling my life's stories in terms of the places we drive by. I wonder if I learned to experience my feelings the same way, from those same men. I feel filled with joy because the mountain is so ever beautiful. With melancholy because the thread that holds my life in place here or anywhere is so fragile, so tenuous. So many people I knew in terms of this mountain, these roads, that I have lost. Most of them I've never seen again.

Tristesse. I first heard that word over twenty years ago, when I went to Los Cerrillos the first time. I was with the divorced man from Iowa, or Indiana, or Illinois, the one who was an engineer, who ached for his children, his wife. "*Tristesse*," he said. I forget why he said it. "The sweet sadness." *Tristesse* is what rides with me, in my eyes, in my mind. *Tristesse* is what invests the wildflowered land, the beclouded sky that I look at with significance. I wonder as we go where they went, those Lebneni's who lived here once, who live here no more.

Finally we get there. It's farther from Albuquerque than I'd remembered. It's almost all the way to Santa Fe, through the mountain. We can't find it at first. We pass the turnoff a couple of times before we realize that the road that runs at an angle to the highway we're on leads to Los Cerrillos. I am filled with excitement. Sentiment. *Sentimiento. De me pensemientos.* My thoughts begin to move in awkward Spanish. Primitive Spanish, to be sure. But it is something that always happens when I go home, when I return in fact or memory to my father's house, to his land.

In the village we drive slowly up and down what we take to be the main drag. Now, main drags in villages in New Mexico are not like main drags in the rest of America. This main drag is more like those you see in westerns sometimes. Dodge City, maybe, or *Gunsmoke*. Or some town in that show with Hoss and the rest, only it speaks Spanish and looks as though it did.

Anyway, this is something like those, but the main drag is a wide gravel road. It hasn't been graveled in some time. Unlike many New Mexican villages, though, it has cross streets, stop signs, and even some sidewalks. Maybe because it's so close to Santa Fe. Or maybe because so many Anglo urbanites come up here to browse in the not-quite-quaint shops before they have dinner – if the fancy restaurant that was once here is still in operation. The oldest part of the village sports wooden sidewalks. Made of planks nailed together, raised a foot or so from the ground. Keeps the mud from covering it, makes it easy to dismount.

But we don't have a horse, and neither does anyone else. Or not for riding up to *la cantina* or *la tienda*. After a couple of slow passes, we park cater-corner from the wooden sidewalk, across the street from the few businesses that line the other side of the street. We get out, lock the car. I wonder why I'm locking it. This isn't the city. I don't have much to fear. But I lock it anyway, remembering my insurance man and feeling silly.

The questions haunt me. How long has it been since she lived here? I wonder. I try to spot a building that is old enough, built of adobe and roofed with galvanized steel. Red with age. But I know it's been too long for that to mean much. They'd have reroofed it long since. But I try. There's a building with a faded ancient sign. Circa 1930, at least. There are several buildings that might be my Jido's store. Some that might be the old house. The house that in some sense I come from, but that I've never seen.

"I'll ask," I say. "I'll just go into some store here and see if anyone knows." I do. We do. We go into a secondhand store. It doesn't feature a blue mirror piano. It may be the same one I visited twenty-one years ago with the man from Indiana, but without the piano, I can't be sure. There's a woman tending store, and I ask her if she knows the Michaels, or where they had their store. She's very pleasant, but, of course, she doesn't know. Maybe so-and-so up the block, or down, I forget which, might know. We leave and try the grocery store next door. They don't know either. Spanish-American, Mexican-American, Chicano, I imagine they've lived here for generations, but they don't know. It's been a long, long time since the Michaels lived and traded here, I think. It's not surprising that no one remembers them anymore. I can't even find the restaurant I ate at, so long ago.

We come back out onto the wooden sidewalk. The trees haven't really turned yet, but they have a tinge of gold to them. Or so I imagine them. They toss themselves in the afternoon wind. It's the same wind that she listened to, my grandmother, Sitte. That blew the dust she dodged. Are some of them the same trees? How long has it been, anyway? Over seventy years? Over eighty? She must have been born in 1888, moved from here around 1903. Eighty years, then, since she lived somewhere called Los Cerrillos, though perhaps, probably, it was a different Los Cerrillos then.

She was forty when alone, and surely in despair, she died in a mental hospital in Pueblo, Colorado, in 1928, four years before my parents were married. Such a long time since she felt this wind.

We leave Los Cerrillos. Drive to Santa Fe for coffee. Or not. (I get confused, trying to remember which trip is which, which journey takes me to what place.) We drive back toward Albuquerque, the car behaving strangely. I discover it's because I've had the emergency brake on all this time. Days, probably. Maybe weeks. I release it, hoping I haven't done lasting damage, and we continue toward the city. Along the way we stop and walk around, tasting the mountain with our feet, our hands, our eyes. We take some chunks of a strange stone we find. One that's white and crumbles easily. Hard dirt, caliche, most likely. But it pulls me. I want it with me. We put it in the car to take it to California with us, to the house we haven't found yet. We will have a piece of the mountain in our new life.

Back at my parents' apartment they ask about our trip. My father is in a jovial mood. He jokes around. He knows, far better than I, I suspect, how fragile is the past. How futile the attempt to recover anything from it. And how necessary. His mother lives in his memory, his feelings, his life. And in that way only does she live in mine.

"This is it," a friend said. "This is Rumé." I gaze at the tiny village, almost invisible in mountain mistiness, off to the side in the photograph. There was a picture of the ruin, high atop a hill just outside the village. "That's it!" I exclaim. "That's the place they showed on TV!" I hadn't seen much on the show, though, because the camera was focused mostly on the reporter. I remember his short-sleeved khaki outfit, my frustration at the cameraman. But the magazine spread includes a view of range after range of mountain juniper and other pine trees, sandy rocks, and a small paved road. "No wonder Jido said Lebanon was like New Mexico. No wonder they settled in Seboyeta," I said. "I always wondered how Grandpa found Albuquerque and Seboyeta, in all the world he had before him. Now I know. This looks just like home," I said. Not sure which home I was referring to in that statement. "It's very lovely. In fact, it looks just like I thought it would."

My grandmother, who we called Sitte – meaning "grandmother" in Lebanese – well, actually, my father's grandmother, worked in a silk factory when her husband – my Grandpa Francis – came to the United States that first time. He kept sending money home for her and their son, but his uncle wouldn't give it to her so she was forced to go to work in a silk factory.

My friend Albert described the work of a silk factory to me: "They have huge vats of boiling water. The women drop the cocoons into it – you know, the worm spins a cocoon around itself and it's the thread of the cocoon that is used for making silk. The women put their hands into the water and take out the worms. They have to work very fast, because you can leave the cocoons in the boiling water only a short time, just until the worm is dead. So they would have to reach their hands into the boiling water, over and over, all day long." Albert thinks that the Arab word for "bordello," *karkhana*, comes from *khafanu*, "the silk factory" – because the women worked nearly naked in the intense heat. "Wow," I think. "My Sitte worked in a bordello!" And this thought, obscurely, relieves me of some of that lifelong sense of shame.

Albert's wife Tina tells me about the convent school someone, her cousin maybe, opened in Rumé or near there. She tells me that the woman had wanted to live an independent life, so she became a nun. After some time she found herself unhappy with the order she belonged to, so she petitioned the Patriarch (Lebanese Maronite pontiff) for permission to open such a convent school for working-class girls. She had thus provided young women who worked in Beirut with a place to live, one that their parents would approve of. In this way, she furthered the cause of women's liberation from the constraints of feudal patriarchy. Tina told me the story with relish, delight glowing in her face. Delight, and no small pride. We speculated about whether the woman who founded that convent had been a lesbian, but there was, of course, no way to know. Still, we knew that she had belonged to that obscure but strong sisterhood of spinsters who through the patriarchal ages have helped women retain their sense of independence, of personal strength.

Tina told me over coffee that she had attended convent school, and that Christian women, or Maronite women, at least those whose families had the means, always went to convent school. I remembered my father telling me that his aunts, his grandfather's sisters, had attended a French convent school – that being the kind available in Lebanon. As I said earlier, my family had maintained Lebanese traditions in oddly hidden ways, and so my attendance at convent school in Albuquerque had been traditional. My great-grandfather had made enough money in this country to afford his granddaughters that luxury, and my father, though not particularly wealthy (he had been able to have indoor plumbing installed only the year I was born), still managed to keep his daughters at the convent. I had been told we went there because my aunts had. What I didn't know was that it was the custom, from the old country, honey, to do that. I also understood the anger in my father's voice every time he repeated the sorry tale of Sitte's humiliation at the hands of her husband's relatives. For no daughter of a landed family worked in a silk factory like the poor were required to, yet she, his own beloved grandmother, had been forced to do so. I realized that this had happened because Sitte, born Haula Hanosh, was from a poor family in the village. I knew it because my first husband's father, her nephew, had told me of his childhood and young manhood, when they had suffered greatly at the hands of the Druse colonial armies of the Empire. "Five men work all day eb'ry day in stone quarries," he had said. "Five strong men. And for carrying rocks on our backs for twelve, sixteen hours," he said, emphasizing the point by counting the hours off one finger at a time, "one loaf of bread we take back to family, women, and all the little children. We died of the yellow fever, of diphtheria, of war. We were so glad when war over, and Lebanon was made free of the Turks."

And then he would point to the deep scar that ran down his forehead and down the bridge of his nose so that his face looked eroded, the bone was sunken in a line his finger traced from hairline to cheek: "This I got from the Druse. I was walking home after work one time, I was maybe fourteen, fifteen, and these men jumped me, beat me. They left me for dead. My brother came along and got me, or else I wouldn't be here now."

I realize that my Sitte, this man's aunt, had lived like that; so poor, so without food. She married into a family that would say, two generations later, "We never carried rocks on our backs. We were merchants, traders. We never carried rocks." Except for when we, she, worked naked in the bordello, *khafanu*. Her grandchildren would tell me about her suffering, but would display no understanding of what might have caused it: that because she came from a family that did carry rocks on its back, she was made to suffer physical and social torture at the hands of her husband's relatives when her husband was in America. Were her husband's relatives keeping her in her place? I imagine so, though I can only speculate. I know that later, after her husband returned, he found himself unable to live there amidst the multiple varieties of oppression, so he decided to emigrate permanently. That time he took her and their child with him. Over the years he brought members of their respective families over, and for a long time he was the head of the circle of Lebanese-Americans in New Mexico. After his death, Sitte became the head. She lived to see her son a member of the New Mexico State Legislature, to see her nephews settled and prospering in various villages around the state. To see herself head of the sprawling clan of Lebneni from Rumé, and no one, man or woman, made personal, business, or political decisions without receiving her advice and concurrence. I bet it did her heart good, my Sitte. Maybe she thought about the long road she had taken from desperate ignominy in *karfanu* to being the power center of a large clan of relatives in America in those long nights while I pretended to sleep so I could watch her ready herself for bed, so I could watch her sleep.

My mother says that Sitte always greeted people by saying something that sounded like "S'lem ou klem." It was probably "*Salaam o khalem*," peace and greetings. *Salaam o khalem*, Sitte. *Salaam o khalem*, Lebanon.

18.
Going Home, December 1992

I left New Mexico, my home, almost twelve years ago. I was depressed because the state had voted for Ronald Reagan. My mother called me on election night to crow: "We're so happy!" Her voice betrayed a hint of gloat beneath its familiar warmth. At that time, fury, or simmering rage at any rate, was how I moved from one life stage to another, though it had been a capricious master. It had motivated my writing, my curiosity, and my intellectual pursuits, and it had colored my career and my relationships, often disastrously, for a number of years. That year, just after Ronald Reagan's election, rage moved me to California. On that cold election night, I made my plans to escape the confinements of rage, disappointment, rejection, and fear. On Martin Luther King, Jr.'s, birthday, I headed west along the familiar highway to the Bay area, a song by the Police ringing in my head: "So if you're dreaming about California. . . . "

A small trailer hitched behind my car held some household stuff, my typing table and chair, the three or four cartons of books that remained from thefts and giveaways, sales, and trashing. With me in the car – named White Spirit by the dealer – rode my crystal ball, Mitse; my IBM electric typewriter, unnamed; my lover, M.; and my precious backpack stuffed with poetry and fiction manuscripts, all named though unpublished. And thus, beneath a clear, cold January sky, emboldened by righteous rage and plentiful hope, I set out to seek the American grail in the promised Golden State.

Because my life had changed dramatically in the five years since I had last lived in the Bay area, I wasn't certain what I'd find there, other than a familiar city where gays clustered, where voting Democrat was thought to be somewhat reactionary, where fringe politics and alternative spiritualities thrived. I believed I was heading to California where the Aquarian Conspiracy was alive and well. It was January 1981, and although I didn't know it, California was indeed a brand-new game.

Now it's December 1992. A little over a year ago we buried my mother. For the first time in years I returned to our homelands around Laguna. The day before her funeral, my children and I drove out to Laguna and Cubero, her first and longest home and the place where I grew up. The land was the strongest link between us. We climbed the mesa behind my grandma's house in Cubero, a climb made difficult by someone's addition of a fence just where the sandstone rears up behind my grandmother's rock garden. We performed a small ceremony of remembrance for my mother, burning and then burying the sage used the night before to soothe our grief. Nothing soothes it, really. The hard part is not being able to call her on the phone. In the time I've been gone, a score of family members and several friends have died, and I am not only sorrowing but old. It's strange to be the old folks when you're not really out of childhood, however gray your hair under the wishful red dye.

I had not returned to Laguna or Cubero since my grandmother died seven years before. It was too painful to go where Grandma's chirpy voice no longer greets me with news of scattered family, where there is no cup of her strong black coffee, no Pepperidge Farm cookies stashed carefully against occasions, no little lunch. Too painful to go where there is no tiny Grandma standing at the kitchen door, guiding me with her eyes and voice as I enter her rock garden, disappear behind the pussy willow bush she nurtured for thirty years, and climb toward the ancient sandstone cliffs that were so much my childhood home.

It was only when Mother died that I returned to Laguna, hoping to find her spirit on the mesas above her home, hoping to meet her on an odd volcanic rock we called "the Chair," spewn from an explosion thousands of years ago, landing miles away from the eruption. It was about the size of a Barcalounge, high-backed with an inward-curving seat. It stood sentinel near the highest point of the mesa, and I had spent hours there all through my growing up. I visited it every time I went home. I went to the Chair on the mesa during marriages and love affairs, through breakups, pregnant, with children, alone. I took my best friend there. I took three husbands and two lovers.

So at Mother's death I returned, an aging and grieving woman. Mother wasn't there, only the wind, mysterious in its soughing; only faded memories, great, gaunt vistas, November light, and cold, cold wind. You can see the entire little village from the Chair; you can see eons of Earth's life; you can see millennia of all that is past and returns no more. My mother climbed those mesas in her youth, like her daughter, like her daughter's daughter, like our sons. They were much different mesas then, overlooking a different world.

What I realized on the mesa on that bleak day before my mother's funeral was only that I had not known the woman at all – so private she was, so inward-bound. Who were you, I asked the wind? The silence that holds it in the air was the answer I received: I am myself, and no other.

Mother used to tell me that I might have to go along with whatever was required. I might have to say a lot of things I didn't mean, didn't believe. But, she would say, touching her brow with an extended finger, they can't control what you think: that's for you alone. A few years ago we talked about that privacy. She repeated her lesson, adding: there's a line all the Indian people have that no one can cross. Behind that line I keep everything that is mine, that is me. I don't let anyone cross that line. Maybe we're different that way, she said, pausing. Maybe that's what makes us what we are. It's not the same as "keeping secrets," no. It is simply recognizing that one's self is inviolate; the private soul is private, not public. It's neither commodity nor consumable. It is most like the center of silence that is the always-flowing wellspring of life, like the spring that used to bubble up like a miracle just beyond the alfalfa field that was across the little arroyo from our old house in Cubero – the sweet, sweet spring where every day my mother went to draw water for her family's use.

Now, on this gloom-filled late December day nearly a year since Mother's death and twelve years since I moved to California, I'm heading back down the highway, going home. My stuff has grown by leaps and bounds. Laden with possessions and bills, possessed of three grandchildren all lost to the red mists of their three separate mothers' rage, sans lover, sans mother, deserted by both rage and hope, I make my painful journey home, a wounded eagle returning to the ancient nest. Pursued by tornado warnings, brain-fogged after a night of hurricane-like storms that beat around my daughter's Marin County home until dawn, I turn eastward on Highway 58 toward Bakersfield, toward home, toward Laguna and Cubero. I anticipate driving by the villages just after the new year begins. Speeding by them on I-40. I will remember scores of stories from my life there, the people I knew, very old, lost, dead. I don't think I'll stop. I will speed around them, along the edges. The way of respect, the way of non-violation. My mother's and grandmother's way, the Laguna way. There is still a *there* there, but not one I recall.

I left home premenopausal, debilitated from not-yet-diagnosed Chronic Fatigue Immune Deficiency Syndrome; now postmenopausal, in better health after acupuncture, Chinese herbs, good chiropractic care, and a California-decreed upscale diet. Then, I was an angry daughter determined to flee the redneck politics of my home, my parents, and my bewildered childhood. I return a grieving daughter, a grieving granddaughter, a grieving grandmother, a single, aging woman whose own daughter rages somewhere in the California fantasy I'm leaving behind. My typewriter has transformed into a powerbook, a portable printer, and a PC. My crystal ball is goddess-knows-where, replaced by eagle feathers, my great-grandmother's huge Acoma pot, and a beautiful basket that I think is Pima – or is it Apache? – also once hers. Broke again (or is it still?), I gotta sell them both, soon.

I will miss them, as I will miss the seductive heaps of fresh vegetables and fruit that grace California markets and street stands. I will miss the softly feminine California hills, the redwoods, the fog, the beneficent climate. I have lost much in these twelve years. The edge of the gathering storm I've so far outpaced is a fitting mentor for this newer, older phase. Mournful, sodden, the shaman sky mumbles companionably all around as I drive south, then east: going always brings return.

On Christmas afternoon, just a few days before I left California, a package of photographs was delivered to me at my daughter's home. I reached for one stack eagerly, because the photograph of a man holding a silver-tipped cane strongly reminded me of my uncle Ook, who died five or six years ago. Intrigued, I pulled it out of its covering and stared at it for a time, remembering Ook, smiling, torn. The last time I saw him was in a dream. He was happy enough, once again driving the old milk truck for Creamland Dairies (or was it Valley Gold?) as he had twenty or thirty years before. I guess he wanted me to know he was OK, or to see how I was doing. And I remembered him, a much younger man, dropping by to visit, tilting his chair at the oilcloth-covered table until my mother would say, "It's not a rocking chair! You're going to break it! You're going to fall!" And the time he did fall – *whump!* – flat on his back. And the look on his face, the laughter. "Well, grace, did you enjoy your trip?" When he was ready to go on his way, he'd amble toward the door, saying his customary "See you in the funny papers." I turned the photo over and saw that it had been taken by a Laguna photographer, Lee Marmon, who is my cousin and Ook's, and who took the formal photos for my first wedding back in the 1950s. Of course, the face looked familiar, though at the time I didn't recognize Walter Sarracino, past governor of Laguna Pueblo and also a relative, holding one of the governor's canes presented to the Pueblos by Abraham Lincoln.

I called my youngest son to look. Quietly we went through the stacks together, murmuring. Among hundreds of images were a precious few photos of home. They were, except for my children's presence, the best gift I received, even though I knew that most of the pictures, maybe all of them, had been taken years before and probably chronicled people dead, disappeared, or grown much older than their frozen images from another time. I realize as I drive beneath the lowering clouds that these wonderful photos, static and dead, preserve a subtle lie. Life in its unfolding does not stop, even though life and love both have their finite terms.

I am going home. I left in anger and return in grief. The road that unwinds before me cannot be the same one I took all those years ago. Even the mountains, soaring and serene, the great plains spreading below, the laddered mesas that climb the horizon to meet the rain-blest clouds will not be the ones I left behind. There is a new life brewing beneath the rain-bearing clouds, and I shall drive through the storm all the way to old heart's place, brand-new home.

19.
The Lay of the Land
Geospiritual Narratives and the American Southwest

CUENTOS DE LOS ANGLOS

For the most part, people of the United States have but a general idea of what makes the American Southwest culturally and politically, as well as geographically, a distinct entity within the greater American landscape. Some no doubt see it as depicted in films such as the 1990s *Tombstone*, or earlier movies such as *Stagecoach, She Wore a Yellow Ribbon,* or *True Grit*. In these depictions the Southwest is the West, a land of buttes, mesas, wide open spaces, chaparral, mesquite, redskins, gunslingers, desperados, and Frito banditos. There the language is not necessarily American, and what defines the region is its primal struggle to emerge into the full light of Anglo-American identity after more than a century as frontier. So pervasive and powerful is this media-inspired image of the Southwest that tourists routinely call the State Tourism Bureaus of New Mexico, Arizona, Utah, and parts of Texas to inquire about the monetary rate of exchange, the frequency of Indian raids, and the availability of accommodations with plumbing and electricity.

Other Anglo-Americans equate "the Southwest" with Native American silver and turquoise jewelry, neo-colonial Spanish-American furniture, architecture, a style of dress that is based on Diné fashion of the early twentieth century, Pueblo pottery, Navajo rugs, and green chili in everything from vodka to *foccacio*. These Americans, often among the more intellectual and privileged, believe that Southwest and Santa Fe are synonyms; they perceive the "Southwest/Santa Fe" as a major loitering place for spiritual trekkers, featuring restorative mineral baths, adobe houses floored in saltillo tile, bent junipers, and cliff dwellings in exotic locales where UFOs, Native gods, and spirits still sing and weep among the magnificent ruins of Chaco, Mesa Verde, Bandelier, and Canyon de Chelly, and can be evoked, enjoyed, and videoed. When I decided to move back home and I mentioned it to an English friend, he remarked, "Oh, really! You've moved to the New Age center of the world!" His joke underscored a view that all too many spiritual trekkers and cultural trenders embrace. A young Los Angelena friend of mine was ecstatic on her first visit to Santa Fe. "We had some traditional Santa Fe cuisine for dinner," she enthused. "What was it?" I asked, envisioning some of those superb tamalitos they serve at Maria's, perhaps some real nachos, green chili stew, and, of course, warm, thick flour tortillas made fresh just before serving. "Oh, it was wonderful!" She replied. "We had grilled salmon served with rice pilaf and accented with sour cream and dill sauce and accompanied by tortillas. Delicious!" She beamed with remembered gustatorial satisfaction. I didn't say, "That's not Santa Fe food! That's Santa Monica with a tortilla," but I imagine my face betrayed a bit of my territorial dismay.

Others come to the Southwest because it can be perceived as an excellent candidate for reformation while remaining both exotic and quaint: It's as close to a third world country as one can get while retaining the conveniences, personal and political safety, and the comfortable efficiencies the United States provides its inhabitants. As such, it provides many of the preferred ingredients for the Eastern liberal and radical establishment's favorite pastime, revolution without danger to anyone other than the Natives, whether Indian or Spanish-American.

The regional identity of the Southwest is confluential, for while there are three major contributing groups to its identity, they do not fuse into one, do not melt, but rather retain their separate and unique identities while erecting and maintaining a variety of modes of interchange among them.

There are three cultural bases that define Southwestern cultural identity: the Southwest Native American, distinct in every noticeable way from the generic "Indian" of American fantasy; the Hispano-Mexicano, by which is meant Spanish descent peoples who have lived in what is now the United States for several centuries; and the Anglo-American, which, in the Southwest, includes everyone not belonging to the first two sectors. The American cultural pattern is generally Anglo-American, but it contains visible elements of multiplicit cultural threads originating in western Africa, southwest, southeast, and northeast Asia, and western Europe. Nowhere is the commonality of Anglo-European and other Old World cultures more

visible than in the Southwest, where its presence remains marginal and un-
assimilated at deeper levels despite its evidence in American venues such as
media, finance, and education. It is likely that its greatest impact by far is as
military presence. Fully half of Arizona, and at least one-third of New Mexico is in the hands of the U.S. Armed Forces, and its bottomline economic
presence has been, for over a century, military. Nevertheless, however ubiquitous Anglo-America is at superficial levels, it is far less culturally defining
than the land, the climate, and *los cuentos*, the particular narratives, that
permeate the region in all of its social dimensions. In the Southwest Anglo-
American history is of far less moment than that of the ancients whose presence is recorded in the very rocks, canyons, mesas, and mountain ranges,
and maintained in contemporary American Indian communities in New
Mexico.

What distinguishes the American Southwest from the rest of the country
are its tricultural identity, centered around Hispanic rather than Anglo-
American culture; its position high on the Colorado Plateau; its arid,
mountainous, thin-air brilliance; and, maybe most noticeable, its peculiar
meteorological constitution, highlighted by the vast, deep, and shining
thunderhead clouds. The fact that its identity is almost entirely shaped by
these constituent elements makes western New Mexico the center of
Southwestern America, with portions of Texas, Arizona, California, Utah,
and Colorado as secondary southwestern regions.

There are sources of information that begin with the narratives of the
mesas, mountains, rivers, sky, climate, flora, and fauna far more telling
than maps; an accurate sense of place depends on them. Cultural geogra-
phies, far more than geological or political ones, give rise to regional definitions of use to human beings, so it seems wisest for readers to think of the
cultural dimensions of our "tri-cultural" spiritual-psychic location rather
than of the geopolitical ones.

For true Southwesterners, the land is central to the multiplicit identity
we experience, although we may not always claim it. Given that, the Southwest extends from southern Utah, presently populated by a large Diné community, an even larger presence of Yei (Holy People to the Diné), and Kachi-
nas (Pueblo supernatural beings), Goddesses, and Gods who inhabit some
unknown dimension that corresponds to that area. That presence defines
the entirety of the region known accurately as the Southwest and includes
eastern and central Arizona, northwest and northeast Mexico along with
contiguous parts of Texas, all of western, central, and northern New Mex-

ico, southern Utah and southern California, and the portions of southwestern Colorado and north central Texas that lie adjacent to the Rio Grande.

Drawn in geospiritual terms, a region's identity can be intuited by exploring the Southwestern psychescape. One can readily perceive its particular identity through its characteristic sounds, smells, colors, textures, tastes, and ambiance's both subtle and overt. A major indicator is the kind of social and spiritual structure the local Native people enjoy, a subject best assessed by careful study of petroglyphs and petrograms, samples of the local corn, beans, squash, and chili-based foods, the noticeable influence of Spanish-colonial character, and a particular "cowboy" or Anglo rancher outlook and the accompanying scattering of "Anglo" artifacts of various kinds and degrees of permanence. It might also be profitably seen as a region that has one major factor that, combined with those mentioned above, make it unique in extreme: it was the first place on earth to be nuked.

In a more comprehensive view, the Southwest is that geospiritual space imprinted by the deep understandings possessed and expressed by the ancient ones, and their descendants, the O-o-tam, the nineteen varieties of Pueblo, the Pima, Yaqui, Diné, Tortuga, Apache, Havasupai, Chemahuevi, Yuma, Mohave, Tamara, Kamaii, Ute, Shoshone, and the rest, including the almost equally numerous varieties of Spanish-Mexican Americans on both sides of the political border. Most recently, of course, the multitudinous voices of Anglo-America have been added to the strain, the fiddle adding its songs to the drum-and-flute and the Mariachi guitar. So chantways and dances transpose into *corridos* and wailing Arabic-Spanish-cum-Nhuatl love songs, and bridge into square dance, blue-grass, Celtic Americana fusion. "Just give me weed, whites, and wine," the freeway cowboy/rider sings, "and show me a sign, and I'll be willing to be moving, . . . Tucson to Tucumcari, Tohachapi to Tonopah," "drifting along with the tumbling tumbleweeds." Southwestern Anglos insist "Don't fence me in," but "give me a home . . . where the skies are not cloudy all day." Southwestern Anglo voices are as varied as their earlier non-Anglo counterpoints: pioneer, cowboy, prospector, U.S. Army, forts, ranges, mesquite and cattle, "blue shadows" on the Santa Fe and the Old Chisum Trail, como ti-yi-yippee-yippee-yay, yippee-yay – hi-ya hi-ya hi-ya ho, as the Indian-cowboys/buckaroos-*vaqueros*-sing it. Rangy, tough cowboy ponies and gentle cowboy humor, gun-slinging outlaws, sheriffs and marshals, careful, seamed Anglo ranchers, livestock growers, traders, railroad magnates, priests, preachers, bureaucrats, and shopkeepers.

These are the characters that people the modern American myth of the West, perhaps best depicted in terms of the United States' favorite narrative line. Its roots lie deep in the chronicles of the Celtic riders – knights enlisted in the service of discovery and adventure who wandered from Anatolia, moved around the Mediterranean and into India, while at the same time over millennia moved into southern Europe: Greece, Italy, Spain, and continuing along the trans-Alpine range into Gaul, thence into the British Isles, and on to the Americas. They began their westernmost move soon after their cousins from Italy and Spain/Portugal had begun theirs. Culturally, humanly, the Southwestern region of the United States is the most recent region of Celtic confluence. As such, it is on the threshold of flowering as powerfully as its earlier counterparts, the Levantine, Spain before Ferdinand and Isabella, the legendary Provence, or the even more legendary medieval Eire flowered in centuries gone by. The Southwest is the place where everyone lives: There is no racial or cultural strain not represented within its reflective, meandering borders. Whatever their differences, however great the culture gaps among these diverse strains might seem, they all eat corn, beans, and chili, and in the Southwestern heartland, New Mexico, a side of *calabasitas*, squash, is not unwelcome.

CUENTOS ENCANTADOS

A region's narrative is inscribed in every cultural form, and none is more definitive than its cuisine. Corn, of course, is pure American. It has been the grain staple of choice in this hemisphere for several thousand years. One of the earliest cultivated crops – chili is said to have been the first – its status as a fundamental source of nourishment and prosperity runs so deep that it enjoys hemisphere-wide status as a major archetype in sacred narrative. When Jesus came, the Corn Mothers did not disappear: they just took in another son. They are always associated with the divine twins; it's just that the twins got a brother, another son of the Sun, Oshrats, our father. But the mother(s), the clans, the kins, the people, retained their feminine-valued sense of identity, and, as surely as the Southwestern sun grooves European skin, the idea that nurturing is superior to battling gains sturdy hold in the minds and hearts of southwestern Americans.

Corn, our dear mother, nurtures us in a mythic variety of ways, but for now let us consider the most delicious: dinner. Take a ride up toward Taos from Santa Fe. Take the old High Road and head for Chimayo. There's a restaurant that is a confluential wonder there. You go into a building that looks like a old mountain hacienda – which it is. Somebody greets you, and if you're lucky, you get seated with no wait. It's best to do this midweek, somewhat after peak meal time. You open the menu and as you read from item to item, you realize you died and went to heaven. Someone brings out a basket of corn chips and salsa – a relish made up of chopped tomatoes, onions, garlic, green chili, or jalapeños and dressed in a bit of oil and vinegar in which you dip your chip, take a bite, and start to sweat, swear, and praise all the Saints.

But that's only the beginning: as they say in England, the proof of the pudding's in the eating, and there's plenty of proof to be had when your order is put down before you. Tamales – which are stuffed corn cakes, made of corn flour, filled with meat and thick red chili, wrapped and tied in corn husks and steamed. For those who prefer vegetarian tamales, no problem. The filling might be whole kernals of corn slathered with thick red chili, but the result's the same: sweet corn, spicy-hot chili, flavoring and texture of boiled, then twice-roasted beef or pork that would be falling off the bone if the bone was included. Or you can have a bowl of *posole*, a fiery corn-soup laded with *tamal*, a kind of firm hominy, red chili, pork, perhaps a bit of oregano, *comino*, some salt and pepper, and, of course, plenty of chopped onion and garlic. With this a taco, an enchilada or two, a basket of sopapillas – which in Indian country is bigger and called fry-bread – honey or salt to sprinkle on it, or maybe one prefers a fragrant, fresh pile of white flour tortillas. Slathered with real butter, this incredible version of bread is a sterling example of what can be achieved when two hemispheres combine in savory harmony. Your entree includes *calabasitas* – a fresh vegetable dish composed of zucchini and perhaps a bit of sweet corn, all stewed just long enough to gain full flavor. Mustn't forget the frijoles, pinto beans of distinct flavor. At this exemplary grazing place they are prepared just as they should be, slowly simmered until plump, brown, juicy – no additives but salt.

Most of the ingredients are indigenous, but they are not ethnic. Corn tortillas and corn-based foods are as American as turkey, tomatoes, Coca-Cola, chocolate, and coffee. All are native to this hemisphere – as are some 60 percent of the world's foods – and in the Southwest they achieve their culinary glory. One can end the feast by lingering over a lovely serving of *natillas* – a custard pudding that is Spanish-Mexican in style. Like its cousins crème brûlée, custard pudding, and flan, *natillas* is flavored with cinnamon lavishly sprinkled on top. A rich cup of coffee, almost as good as what we called "sheep-camp" coffee – the kind that stood by the coals all day and had grounds and water added periodically so that, at its best, you could stand a spoon upright in a cup of it – ahh. No need to eat again for a couple of days.

Besides food, which may be the single most definitive aspect of a sense of place, stories provide a deep sense of continuity within a psychespace. A region is bounded, characterized by geographical features, but these features take on a human and spiritual dimension when articulated in language. The smells, sounds, and tactile sensations that go with a locale are as central to its human significance as the sights, and it is within the stories that all the dimensions of human sensation, perception, conception, and experience come together, providing a clear notion of where we are, who we are, and why.

The stories are as old as the land, and as new as one's most recent sojourn to *tierra encantada*, the enchanted land. One of my favorites – loved because it tells as much about the spiritual meaning of place as it tells me about the meaning of myself within the matrix of my people, is the one about the wicked giantess my great-grandmother, Meta Atseye Gunn, told me. When I was about five or six, we went to Albuquerque. My mother drove, and Grandma Gunn and I rode together in the back seat. Driving east on old Highway 66, we passed by old Laguna and she pointed to a couple of very large sandstone rocks – one roughly round, the other rectangular, almost cylindrical. In size the round one may have been five or six feet in diameter, and the rectangular one was the size of a small sandstone house. "That's the head and body of the wicked giantess," my great-grandmother notified me, pointing to the great boulders with her lips. At Laguna it's very rude to point with your finger.

I gazed out the rear window, turning in the seat and kneeling to face backward to eye the indicated monster. She continued, "You know, the old giantess that almost killed the little girl," as though I had heard the story countless times. As Grandma Gunn had many grandchildren and great-grandchildren from her own seven offspring, I imagine she told the story often. But it was my first time. Not at all certain I had seen the exact rocks she meant, I sat back down beside her, saying nothing. I guess that meant she should go on, and she did.

"Once upon a time," she began – she always began stories about the supernaturals that way, it was part of her Carlisle Indian School heritage. She used to tell us stories adapted from Spenser and Tennyson, beginning them

"Once upon a time" as well. It was the proper opening, as I imagine this very proper old Laguna woman, to whom propriety was the secure guiding principle of human conduct, believed, for a story one told to children. So. "Once upon a time there was a young girl who went out to hunt rabbits. She had her rabbit hunting stick, and she went all over the low hills near the village, searching out rabbit holes. Finding one, she would shove the long stick in after licking it carefully, and turn it round and round. If there was a rabbit in the hole, the wet stick would get all stuck in its hair. Then the girl could pull out the stick with a rabbit stuck on it, bash it over the head to kill it, and take it home for dinner." Grandma vigorously demonstrated the actions with her hands, glancing sidelong to ascertain my reaction. "Then, as the little girl was bending over one hole, she heard a terrible laughing, and a big shadow fell over her. She looked up, and there was the giantess, huge, huge, looking down at her. She was very frightened, and she ducked, very quick, under the huge old woman's skirt and ran away.

"She kept running until she found a cave with a small opening that she could barely fit in, and then she stayed there, being very quiet. She could hear the giantess, her footsteps booming and her voice calling, 'Little girl! Little girl! Come here! You have my rabbits! Give them here!' she called. Of course, the little girl was even more quiet. She was afraid to breathe.

"She was crouched in the little cave, pulled as far back against the back wall as she could get, barely breathing, when the giantess found her cave. The huge woman had a long stick, too, and she shoved it into the cave and began to turn it around and around. The little girl drew farther back, keeping out of the stick's reach, but she was even more frightened. Suddenly, in spite of her fear, she saw a small spider on the wall near the cave entrance. And she remembered what she was supposed to do. 'Please, Grandmother Spider,' she whispered, 'please, please help me!' As she called out to the old Fairy woman for help, the little rabbit girl was twisting this way and that to stay out of the stick's reach. But she kept up her prayer. Soon she heard some more noises outside the cave. It was the voices of two young men, and she heard them call out to the giantess. 'You get away from that hole,' they cried. 'There's nothing in there for you!'

"But the giantess didn't heed them. She redoubled her twisting and poking with her rabbit stick, and she was hitting the poor little girl with it. But the little girl was brave and she didn't cry or make a sound. She just kept on dodging the stick as best she could. Soon she saw the shadow fall away from the cave, and she poked her head out cautiously. There she saw the young twins, the ones who always helped Grandmother Spider. They were fighting the giantess in a terrible battle. They were very small, and she was so large, but they had special magic, and soon they defeated her. When the giantess was dead, they split her head from her body and threw them both in separate directions. It's those rocks I showed you that are her body, or what's left of it," Grandma Gunn said.

She didn't say anymore about it, then or ever, as I remember, but every time I pass that spot I remember the little rabbit huntress and how Grandmother Spider and the Little Twins saved her when they killed the giantess. The proof of the story is right there, lying along the now-vanished old road that led from Old Laguna north to Paguate, then on to the eastern spur of Tse'pina, Veiled in Clouds, the old Woman Mountain. That's the one the Anglo maps identify as Mt. Taylor, named after the old Indian fighter and President of the United States, Zachary Taylor, changing meaning, gender, and our relationship to that mysterious, beautiful place. For two hundred or so years the mountain was known as Cerro Pelone, Bald Peak, to the local Nativos because its fourteen-thousand-foot-high peak is above timber line.

Over thirty years after Grandma Gunn told me the story of rabbit girl and the giantess, I learned that the uranium used in the first nuclear bombs was dug up from a spot near the giantess's stony remains there just off the old Paguate road. Perhaps the old woman was getting her revenge on rabbit girl, the Laguna people, the Little Twins (Little Boy and Fat Man?), and the old supernatural, Grandmother Spider, She-Who-Thinks.

Eventually, throughout the 1950s and 60s, the uranium mining industry circumscribed the mountain, and tons of yellowcake were heaped into a bizarre echo of the flat-topped mesas that edge the valleys of the sacred lands. Jackpile Mine, located just outside the Laguna Pueblo village of Paguate, was the foremost supplier of uranium in the world for a long time. Yellowcake blew everywhere during those years of terrible drought. Our dust storms were radioactive, and our death rate from cancer has skyrocketed since that time. But, one wonders – since whatever is on, in, or around was dreamed up by the old Keresan deity, Spider Woman – why would she conjure such terrible deadliness, making it the sacred color of woman, that is, yellow?

Imagine: It was about the time that Grandma Gunn told me the story of Spider Woman and the little rabbit girl, give or take a year, that the bomb was detonated at Stallion Gate about seventy or so miles southeast of Laguna. It was sunrise that day, July 16, 1945, a sunrise that came earlier than the rising sun itself. It was the day the fourth world ended and the fifth world began. That was the time one of the Old Spider's sister-nieces came home. Her name was Sun Woman, and she had long ago gone away, heading east, but they always said she would come back, and I guess that July in 1945 she did. Anyway, that's what they say.

My dad has always called New Mexico "God's Country." When out-of-staters would come by, he'd greet them, "Welcome to God's country." For him, I suppose, the Southwest is western New Mexico. Most of my sense of the region as a never-ending tale comes from him, for he is an inveterate storyteller. My dad is the son of immigrants. His grandfather, grandmother, and father, who was then a young boy, came to the States from Lebanon. They were Maronite Catholic (as distinct from Roman Catholic) and he always bragged that Lebanon was the first nation to accept Christianity. I say this because Americans in general seem to think that Lebanon is entirely Muslim, but that is erroneous. In any event, much of my sense of place, my understanding that I am of the Southwest, comes from his stories and those of his father. They never went anywhere that was not an occasion for a tale. And there are so many, it's difficult to find just one or two, the most telling, the most space-revealing. For it is in the nature of the oral tradition to make significance from story piled on story, without benefit (dubious) of abstraction, theory, linguistic and intellectual alienation. For storytellers like my father, place is more personal than almost anything. Sense of place is about an ongoing relationship, not only of self but of others who have touched one's life. And all those events are cradled in the land. "On that mesa, that's Enchanted Mesa, you know, there used to be thick wooden stakes stuck in the sides. You can't get up there now." Listening, I contemplate the sheer-sided mesa that rises off the flatland not far from Acoma Pueblo. "When I was young, oh, maybe fifteen or sixteen, we climbed up it." Years later I read a thriller novel in which the hero was stuck on Enchanted Mesa, with the bad guys all around, and his buddy flew in, landed on the mesa top, and rescued him. Reading, I imagined the hero, my youthful dad, atop Enchanted Mesa, adventuring.

One story he always used to tell when we went on the annual family picnic to Portales, just above Seboyeta, concerned the sharp incline just before one reached Bibo. "When it would rain, you couldn't drive up it. Your mother used to bring the horses down from Seboyeta and meet me, and we'd ride home." Of course, the road doesn't steeply rise out of the plain at that place any more. Paved, it takes a genteel sloping journey inward, toward the sacred spring sheltered beneath the great white sandstone overhang at Portales. The last few miles are about as rough, though, and during the rainy season that last stretch of road is probably washed out. My favorite family story is about the wild stallion. The hero of the tale is my father, a young family man, who saw a beautiful stallion he longed to own. "I heard that if you shot them, just barely creasing their head, you could catch them when they dropped. But they wouldn't really be hurt, just stunned. So one day old Benino and I went out there. I had my rifle, and finally we found the stallion. We stopped far enough away not to scare him off, and walked close enough to get off a shot. I raised the rifle and took careful aim – I was a good shot in those days – and squeezed the trigger. The horse turned to look at me just then, and the shot got him between the eyes." After all these years, my dad's eyes still get moist with tears, and he shakes his head, sorrowful, full of regret. This is what it means to know the land, to be personally bonded with it, for richer or poorer, in sickness and in health, 'til death do you part – and probably not even then. And it is this exactly personal relationship to place that for me defines *mi pais*, the Southwest, land of enchantment.

This is probably why I fail to connect with the "new" Southwesterners, those transplants who move to God's country and pave it, develop it, merchandise it, commodify it, and, entirely unaware of the land and its actively intelligent presence, attempt to transplant that oddity of spiritual deadness, American culture, to our sacred and hardy land.

I know people who have resided in our *tierra encantada* for two or more generations who think that they're in Wisconsin, or Massachusetts, or anywhere at all. It's as though they brought the concept of franchise hotels with them, before there was such a thing: Stay at HoJo's, and you could be anywhere. But what's the use of being able to imagine you're anywhere, when you are there, here, where there is and I passionately hope will always be a here, there. These people never learned a word of Spanish. Never learned a song, never memorized a *chiste* to lay on their friends, nary a *dicho* among them. They eat chili religiously, and that's that. Imagine! Their children go here and there, trying to find their own souls, as though a soul was a commodity, a consumer good, buyable, sellable, mutually interchangeable with anything at all. These generations-long tourists give birth to the idea that we invent ourselves, and perhaps they do, perhaps they must. Because they seem bereft of that profoundly human capacity to be created in relationship to place. To the smells, the sounds, the tastes, the language, the rhythm that makes one region clearly different from another. *¡Qué lástima!*

Another story, one of my favorites: One Sunday at Mass in the Spanish-Mexican village of Barelas, which is near Albuquerque, one of the old men – a heavy drinker, especially on Saturday nights – had taken his place in the tiny balcony at the back of the church. When the Mass was over, he attempted to descend the steep, narrow stairs and he fell. He landed with a loud thwack. *La gente* gathered around, to see if he was badly hurt, to offer him a hand up. He gathered himself up, and, standing as tall as he could, he regarded the excited crowd indignantly. *¡Cada quién se 'pea como el quiere!"* he snorted. "Everyone gets down the way he chooses." Plopping his hat firmly on his balding head, he stomped – staggering only a little – out the church door.

There are the magical stories, too. One that percolates throughout the region, from Mexico north across the political border, is about *La Llorana*, the wailing woman. I have heard several versions of the tale and have traced its origin to the court of Moctezuma, on the eve of the arrival of the *conquistadores*. As it goes in New Mexico, the Texas borderlands, Arizona, and parts of southern Colorado, *La Llorana* is the ghost of a woman who murdered her *hijos*, her babies. She had them by a Spaniard, an upper-class "don" who later abandoned her to marry a Spanish lady of his class. Thus, she is known to stalk philandering husbands returning home late from romantic trysts, and she is often seen standing on a sand bar in the Rio Grande, near the Bridge Street bridge in southeast Albuquerque. She travels railways and highways and, for all I know, hangs around airports by now; her favorite haunts are waterways. Children are cautioned to avoid arroyos, *acequias* (irrigation ditches), and river banks. Often you can hear her wailing, "*¡Aiii, mis hijos!"* she wails. "*¿A dónde va? ¿A dónde va?* Oh, my children! Where are you?"

Sometimes she visits someone's house, and she is terrible to behold, with her long fingernails and silvery eyes that stare empty of all but eerie rage. She often steals children, and when she succeeds, their bodies are found floating in a ditch, an arroyo, or the river.

¿QUIÉN ES? INDOGERMANIC MYTHOS MOVES WEST
(OR) SHE CRADLES ALL THE STORIES, MYTHICALLY

"Magical realism," as our particular way of perceiving and interpreting reality has been named by literary pundits of the Anglo-European persuasion, characterizes the relationship of humans to the rest of nature for Hispano/Nativos, as the sense of the overwhelming spiritual presence of the land informs all of Native American life in the Southwest. Even though logical positivism, or rationality, characterizes the Anglo worldview, Southwestern Anglo narrative, legendary and heroic in quality and tone, partakes no less of the mystical in its own definitive manner. Perhaps it is the confluence of Hispano-Breton Celtic and Southwest American Indian worldviews given new life by a landscape's palpable presence that revitalizes the old narrative structures of Europe and transforms them. Out West the Ossian cycle takes on a new life, subtly altering *vaqueros, caballeros*, riders, cowboys into supernal heroes – knights and strong, gentle advocates who defend the right and protect the helpless. There are many variants of the old Finnian tales current in Southwestern histories, *corridos,* and narratives; perhaps the cautionary legend of Billy the Kid and the Lincoln County War will do as well as many and better than most. It illustrates the narrative nexus that the borderlands, the frontier, exemplify. It is the one story I know in which every kind and class of human participates, shaped into significance by narrative elements as old as the races – European, African, and American Indian – involved.

Billy the Kid's favorite tune was "The Turkey in the Straw," but he cut a fine figure dancing the rousing Mexican "La Marche," a classic continental waltz, a lively *schottish*, or the Virginia Reel. Deadly and engaging as trickster, the Kid charmed women of all ages, classes, and races; took tender and amiable care of the children; and gained the respect and patronage of the leading men of Lincoln, nearby counties, and south of the border where his ready command of Spanish and his unfailing courtesy earned him affection and respect. He seems to have had a lot of friends, perhaps by virtue of his rigid devotion to the cowboy code of honor: that is, he was uncompromisingly against all that he saw as evil, unsportsmanlike, unseemly, avaricious, oppressive, or merely threatening to those who befriended him.

In another time, perhaps, William Bonney's exploits would have been versed in high epic: a tale of a good knight errant, fondly named Bonnie William, sworn to defend the right and protect the innocent even at the cost of his own life. The mythic significance of the legend of Billy the Kid lies in its descent from legends as old as ancient Anatolia and deep as the multilayered remains of Anatolia's early city Çatal Hüyük.

Forever young and beautiful, James Henry McCarty, a.k.a. William Bonney a.k.a. Kid Antrim, and finally, posthumously, "Billy the Kid," was swept up in the fate of nations. His fame was based on his participation in the Lincoln County War, itself exhaustively chronicled only because of his visibility. The war took place just a handful of years after Mexico had ceded New Mexico Territory to the United States in 1848, in the wake of the United States' Civil War, whose massive energies swept all sorts of men and women west into Indian country, to a region two-thirds the size of England that lay on the southeastern quarter of New Mexico Territory. Lincoln County, New Mexico Territory, was such a crossroads, and its transformation from Spanish/Mexican borderland inhabited mainly by Mescalero (Apache), though dotted by a few cattle ranches owned by old Mexican families and newer Anglo ranchers, into a seething cauldron of investment and progress is one of the region's most famous of mystery tales.

No longer the quiet backwaters of Anglo civilization where the once-fiery Spaniard suffered from the same ditchwater in his veins that marked the passive and long-suffering Pueblo Indians (or so some statesman lamented to the Congressional Record), the Southwest was a singular frontier. There were neither knights to see justice prevail there, nor communities of ordinary people able to live modestly, far from civilization's pall, to halt the voracious westward march of progress. The Law's sneak-attack murder of Billy the Kid, emphatically established a new order. For the kid was a child hero succored by the local citizenry, who hid, loved, and finally mourned him. In the inexorable way of mythic tales, his murder was as inevitable as the English takeover of Scotland, Ireland, and Wales; the Roman-Frankish takeover of Gaul; or the still earlier Trojan/Latin devastation of Phoenicia/Carthage.

From the time of his appearance on the scene, James Henry McCarty was the kind of figure around whom legends grow. The facts about his origins are as much a mystery as those concerning his deeds or the view others had of him. Yet because the verifiable data about him is scant – and what there is was blurred by legend even during his life – this points to a larger fact: Forces beyond the ken of historiographers have much more power to inscribe the land with meaning on a larger-than-human scale than all the bits and bytes of verifiable data.

What is certain is that Billy the Kid, as he came to be known, is a hero who was as mixed a bag as the legendary Finn MacCool. No one knows whether the story of the Kid was merely a product of overexcited imaginations, but it seems sure that its force had more to do with the power of anciently sanctioned narrative to provide strangers in a strange land with a secure sense of home. It is said that his fame comes largely from deeds he never accomplished, that his fame greatly exceeds his actuality, and that the rather homely, buck-toothed, stringy-haired boy was never as gifted, graceful, admired, respected, or murderous as written records of the time, testimony from those who knew him, court injunctions, letters, journals, or newspaper accounts made him out to be. But facts, or their absence, cannot sidetrack the narrative process, for humans, like the land that gives us being, make stories as naturally as we breathe, and, like the land that also gives them being, the narratives obey laws far deeper than ordinary consideration reveals.

If nothing certain is known of this enigmatic man other than his presence in Lincoln County during the trouble, then the last words he is said to have spoken, "*¿Quién es?*" "Who is it?" (Who are you?) take on a profound significance.

The near-cause of the war in Lincoln County was the arrival of a would-be man of wealth and status, twenty-three-year-old Englishman John Tunstall. He soon teamed up with an abrasive Scotsman named Alexander Anderson McSween, attorney and store manager for the town's biggest financial interest, and "boss" Irishman Lawrence J. Murphy and his Germany-born partner, retired Colonel Emil Fritz. An impecunious professional couple, McSween and his wife had settled in Lincoln a year or so before Tunstall's arrival in the late fall of 1876.

Both Fritz and Murphy had commanded Fort Stanton during the years it was being rebuilt after Confederate soldiers had taken it in the early part of the Civil War, while it also served as a center of operations against American Indian peoples. By the time the rebuilding was completed, the Murphy-Fritz partnership was well-established in a large store and brewery. Among their other interests they had secured licensing from the War Department – at that time, the administrative power over Indian Affairs – to operate as Indian traders. According to Nolan, L.G. Murphy & Co. became the "de facto Indian agent." They were also the major source of loans for local families and ranchers, a source of credit for merchandise, and an outlet for cattle, sheep, wool, and such other items as locals had for sale.

So situated, the Fritz-Murphy power over the area's financial and political life was unassailable, at least until the reasonable, well-heeled English stranger came to town and began to build his own empire in competition with theirs. Wild, mountainous, and beautiful, Lincoln County was nevertheless in an area, as Frederick Nolan describes in *The Lincoln County War, a Documentary History* (page 99):

> ... of random violence and danger. To the safety of its empty mountain fastnesses fled the wanted and the hunted, murderers and horse thieves, defaulters and desperadoes from all the surrounding territories ... the absence of law, the presence of godless men, and the volatile mixture of whiskey and deadly weapons created a climate in which any argument or difference of opinion could end in gunfire. It was a place where to kill a man was much less a sin than to steal his horse; and to steal his cattle was not a sin at all.

The further causes of the local war were, of course, the Indian Wars that had raged across the continent for several centuries and would not wind down in the United States until just a few years before New Mexico Territory, divided into Arizona and New Mexico, entered the Union. It was, of course, that larger war that was responsible for the presence of the combatants. The Lincoln County War, a local eruption of a hemisphere-wide process,

> took place at a time when territorial New Mexico in general, and Lincoln County in particular, was a burgeoning microcosm of money-mad, power-hungry nineteenth-century America, America before the dream had soured, America on the brink of becoming a world power ... America in the Gilded Age when the robber barons of Wall Street were the uncrowned kings.
>
> ... They used wealth and influence as a weapon to break any man or group that stood in the way of their ambitions; in their world there were only lions and lambs, hunters and prey. Ordinary people, their rights, and their future, were irrelevant. The only things that counted were money and power.
>
> ... A decade later in New Mexico Territory, opportunities of the kind that the robber barons had grabbed in the early Seventies were just beginning to present themselves. Men like Tom Catron and Steve Elkins, William Rynerson and Lawrence Murphy – aye, and John Tunstall and Alexander McSween – were only emulating, in a cruder way and on a smaller scale, the methods perfected by the Goulds and Tweed. There is no difference at all, except one of location, between the arrogance of "Boss" Tweed's "as long as I count the votes,

what are you going to do about it?" and Lawrence G. Murphy's "It don't make any difference who the government sends out here. We control these Indians."

—NOLAN, p. xi

It is said that Lawrence Gustave Murphy was a strong man: the local law-enforcement officials, including the United States Army by way of its facility, nearby Fort Stanton, by and large danced to his tune. When young John Tunstall—egged on by Murphy's powerful rival John Chisum, the area's pre-Murphy cattle baron—decided to unseat the regional despot, many were rooting for him. Included in Tunstall's cheering section was young William Bonney, who seems to have been an itinerant rider and perhaps gunman. He joined the Tunstall militia, known as the Regulators. Overtly, their purpose was to "regulate" Murphy's excesses by enforcing local laws and bringing violators to the attention of local officials—many of whom were Hispanics. In reality, however, the Regulators mostly settled for protecting Tunstall's interests and bodily well-being. In a narrative sense they functioned like the Highland clans of old: The lord or landowner secured the protection of the clans living within his demesne.

Lawrence Murphy, of course, had his own paid militia whose job was to protect his Lincoln County fiefdom. "Lincoln, the county seat, was the axis upon which the life of the entire area revolved. From here, Murphy and Dolan controlled . . . The Native farmers who relied upon them for the staples of life were as dependent upon them as serfs in the Middle Ages upon their liege lord" (Nolan, p. 99).

The nearest cause of the war was the dispute Murphy had with McSween over insurance money Emil Fritz owed Murphy. Fritz had left the partnership and returned to Germany, where he died; by then, Murphy's financial picture looked anemic, and he was urgently in need of funds. He sent McSween, still acting as his attorney, east to sign papers and collect the money. However, not only did Murphy not realize the several thousands he expected, but every time he made a move to in some way benefit from the German's death, he was blocked by McSween. Of course, McSween was acting in concert with Tunstall, whose economic war with Murphy was proceeding satisfactorily; doubtless, they felt it important that the Irishman's downward spiral continue. Tunstall had secured what had been Murphy & Co.'s exclusive contract to supply Fort Stanton with beef for its garrison and the Agency, a win that must have particularly stung the fort's former commanders, Murphy and Dolan.

The struggle intensified, turning violent. John Tunstall was killed in a gun battle cum ambush in February 1878 by Murphy's men, although he was under famed and feared fighter William Bonney's guard. Five months later, on July 19, 1878, Alexander McSween was murdered on the back steps of his burning home. In his study, *High Noon in Lincoln, Violence on the Western Frontier* (page 2), Robert M. Utley remarks that

> The Englishman's death touched off the Lincoln County War. The Scotsman's death should have ended it, for the rivals were either dead or ruined, and nothing remained to fight about. But the violence and lawlessness unleashed by the slayings of the Englishman tortured the land for months to come, and the Lincoln County War did not finally subside until nearly a year after the Scotsman's blazing end.

The Lincoln County War, a political battle with dimensions far deeper than its innocuous action suggests, was over. Many were dead, a number in prison or on their way. Among the disputants were Irish men, Scotsmen, eastern dudes, cavalry men of African-American descent led by a local law official, Constable Martinez, and even a German national whose return home and subsequent death set off the months-long strife. A Chinese man served as cook and launderer in Lincoln, and a Navajo woman, who seemed to have perceived the Kid to be her child, mourned his death. One of the peculiarities of Billy the Kid's story is that everyone who composed the social landscape of the young United States was apparently in or around Lincoln when the action went down.

In that same July, Henry McCarty-Billy the Kid-Bill Bonney went to his old friends' home in Fort Sumner after escaping from jail in Lincoln. Why he stayed in the area is an unanswered puzzle. Some hold that he was trying to persuade his sweetheart to flee to Mexico with him. As New Mexican writer Erna Fergusson recounts,

> Alone, in stocking feet and armed only with a butcher knife, he was coming to cut a steak off a beef carcass hanging in the entry. In the dark he passed two deputies sitting on the porch.
>
> "*¿Quién es?*" he asked, walking into the unlighted room where Pat Garrett sat. "Who is it?" as though he wished to know which of his enemies was to get him finally.
>
> – *Murder and Mystery in New Mexico*, P. 71

Alternatively, it was a bedroom he crossed, and Pat Garrett crouched near the bed where Billy's friend slept. In any case, he said, "*¿Quién es?*" and then he was blown away.

Now, there are those who say it wasn't Billy shot that day, or that, although wounded, he got away because his beautiful Señorita nursed him back to health, hiding him from the authorities with the aid of her family. According to this version, Billy died a very old man, in bed. One hopes he was not alone. Perhaps, as he lay dying, someone played "The Turkey in the Straw"; perhaps frijoles, chili stew thick with tender chunks of beef, and sopapillas or tortillas, richly laced with lard, were served at his wake. To date, as far as I know, the Kid is not slated to return in our hour of need, but in a few decades or centuries, who is to say? Right now we must ask, *¿Quién es* Billy the Kid? And *¿Quién es* the Southwest?

Notes

Introduction

1. Barbara G. Walker, *The Women's Encyclopedia of Myths and Secrets* (NY: Harper & Row, 1983), p. 453.

American Indian Mysticism

1. Alice Marriott, *The Ten Grandmothers* (Norman: University of Oklahoma Press, 1945), p. 284.

2. Monotheism is not part of archaic tribal belief. Since colonization and Christianization, many or perhaps most refer to "The Great Spirit" as though it was the term their elders had used before history happened to the Native peoples. In fact, missionaries foisted the term on tribal people, even in their own languages. The only comparable term I have uncovered in elder traditions is that of the Ojibway (and, perhaps, akin Algonquin peoples such as the Chippewa). But as I understand it, the term referred to a particular *manitou* (Holy Person or Immortal) who was extraordinarily BIG. Huge. Vast. Massive. That is, the Big Manitou (*manido* or *manidoo*, in some spellings). *Kitche* means "large," "huge," "big," and in eighteenth and nineteenth century usage, "great" was one English synonym for "big" that was usually preferred by gentlemanly Anglo-American writers.

3. Frank B. Linderman, *Pretty Shield, Medicine Woman of the Crows* (Lincoln: University of Nebraska Press, 1972), p. 156.

4. Linderman, p. 157.

5. Linderman, pp. 157–158.

6. Linderman, pp. 159–160.

7. Linderman, pp. 159–160.

8. Marriott, pp. 285–289.

9. Peggy V. Beck and A. L. Walters, *The Sacred, Ways of Knowledge, Sources of Life* (Tsaile RPO, Navajo Nation, Arizona: Navajo Community College Press, Curriculum Development Center, 1977), 101–102.

10. Essie Parrish, as noted by Beck and Walters (*The Sacred*, p. 185) uses "The Creator" in the sense that the "All Powered" or "The Unseen" is used in other traditions.

11. Mountain Wolf Woman, *The Autobiography of a Winnebago Indian*, Nancie Oestreich Lurie, ed. (The University of Michigan Press: Ann Arbor Paperbacks, 1966), p. 61.

12. Mountain Wolf Woman, pp. 61–62.

13. Mountain Wolf Woman, pp. 63–64.

Father God and Rape Culture

1. The volume was published in 1993. *Transforming a Rape Culture*, Emily Buchwald, Pamela Fletcher, and Martha Roth, eds. (Minneapolis: Milkweed Editions, 1993).

2. Michael Baigent, Richard Leigh, and Henry Lincoln, *The Messianic Legacy* (NY: Dell Publishing, 1986), pp. 36–37.

3. Interestingly, the center of major conflict recently in the news as a region claimed by the Iraqis although local Shiite Muslims who actually live there are presently resisting Iraqi claims, which has led to armed conflict. There was some shelling in the region, though not, evidently, quite within the Tigres-Euphrates confluence, during the Persian Gulf conflict in 1991. Maybe the shelling signifies the dissolution of patriarchal rule world-wide. The area is, by many accounts, the setting of Armageddon. That would make the "last battle" more a matter of the death of patriarchal civilization than the end of the world in any total sense.

4. Baigent, et al., pp. 41–43. Emphasis his. It seems a bit strange to refer to a major world religion, one that eventually conquers and dominates a vast part of the planet, as "a cult" as the editors do; the term makes the monstrous seem innocuous and belies the massive destruction, planet-wide, consequent upon that conquest.

5. Ibid., p. 44.

6. Ibid., p. 45.

7. Ibid., p. 46.

8. Libreria delle Donne di Milano, 1990.

9. Angela Miles, personal correspondence, December 11, 1992.

10. *Sexual Difference*, p. 72.

11. Ibid.

12. Ibid.

13. Ibid., p. 75.

14. Fay Sampson, *Herself* (London: Headline Book Publishing PLC, 1990), p. 262.

15. Ibid., pp. 262–63.

16. *Sexual Difference*, p. 138.

17. Ibid., p. 143.

"Indians," Solipsisms, and Archetypal Holocausts

This piece was originally written for *Transpersonal Review* (1993) and is addressed to Transpersonal mental health practitioners and readers interested in that field.

1. The terms "norm," "normative," and "normal" derive from Norman, and refers to the Norman Conquest of Anglo-Celtic England, Scotland, Wales, and Ireland.

2. "White" is used to denote a mind-set or system of mental processes, rather than a racial or genetic identity. There are many Caucasian people and communities who in the past

and at present are as distant from "white think" as any traditional Native American. Some good examples in fiction of this distinction can be found in N. Scott Momaday's *House Made of Dawn* in which the evil beings are, one, the "white man" who, though albino, is full-blood Walatowa and, two, the *culebra*, the Mexican-American police officer Martinez. Then, too, John "Big Bluff" Tosamah, an urbanized Kiowa preacher and peyote roadman is more guilty of "white think" than either Angela St. John, a wealthy Anglo-American woman, or Milly, a social worker of impoverished origins from the South. Abel, the mixed blood protagonist of the novel, is the lover of both of these women. In Leslie Marmon Silko's *Ceremony* the protagonist, Tayo, is a mixed blood, white and Laguna, but he is incapable of "white think," a condition that nearly destroys him. His cousin Rocky, on the other hand, is as much an apple (red on the outside and white on the inside) as any character in American Indian fiction.

While therapists of the Jungian school teach that repressed and unowned misery, trauma, thoughts, and emotions constitute the shadow or dark side of the human psyche, therapists to people of color would do well to see that for their clients the unowned and repressed are more likely to be associated with "light," "bright," and "white," for these signify all we cannot own of our rage and confusion; these are likely to signify all that we would banish from our lives, would avoid and escape, were such possible.

3. David Rockwell, "Digging for Medicine: Bears in Native American Healing Traditions," *Shaman's Drum*, no. 30 (Winter, 1993): 50. This article is excerpted from Rockwell's 1991 book *Giving Voice to Bear: American Indian Rituals, Myths, and Images of the Bear* (Niwot, Colorado: Roberts Rinehart Publishers).

4. Ibid.

5. Ibid.

6. According to Indian history, the inhabitants of the Asiatic subcontinent who are known as Hindu originated in the region of the Caucasian mountains and claim Aryan to be their race of origin. They carefully distinguish themselves from other inhabitants of the region, some of whom are known as the "Untouchables." These were the earliest inhabitants of the region and are dark-skinned. My informant, Dr. David Kaushik, Principal (Professor) of New Delhi University, also said that the Hindu-Brahmans to this day advertise for "wheat-skinned" women for brides. The upper classes don't want the taint of dark skins to mar their status at the top of the caste system in India. It might also be mentioned that Persia renamed itself Iran under the Shah in the 1920s to make its Aryan origins clear. (Iran = Aryan, presumably in Farsi.)

7. Rockwell, pp. 50 and 56.

8. Ariel Spilsbury and Michael Bryner, *The Mayan Oracle: Return Path to the Stars* (Santa Fe, NM: Bear & Company Publishing, 1992). This deck is interesting, but not

Mayan; rather, it is a New Age stew composed of multiple spiritual "traditions" rendered for New Age audiences. Despite the confusion of lineages, it has its finer moments.

9. At various levels we pass laws like "NO Smoking," "Helmets Required," speed laws, seat belt laws, and airport security laws (where laughter and joking around is STRICTLY PROHIBITED), all on the grounds that these measures will lower health care costs. Personally, I wish we could ban white-think on the same grounds! Systematic – and I mean that word in a number of senses – psychological and economic abuse and psychic pollution are the major causes of health problems among Native people, women of all lifestyles, races and ethnicities, "minority" and ethnic men (Jews and Arabs notably among them), most children, and not a few Anglo-European males, particularly those of the gay persuasion.

10. Roger Zelazny, *The Courts of Chaos* (New York: Avon Books, 1978), p. 63.

11. Eduardo Duran, in a lecture at the First Nations Health Convocation, Albuquerque, May 1997, for which Dr. Duran was one of the coordinators.

References

Anzaldúa, Gloria. *Borderlands/La Frontera: The New Mestiza*. San Francisco: Spinsters-Aunt Lute, 1987.

———. "Interface." In Anzaldúa, *Borderlands*.

Awiakta, Marilou. *Abiding Appalachia: Where Mountain and Atom Meet*. 8th ed. (Bell Buckle, Tenn.: Iris Press, 1995).

Baigent, Michael, Richard Leigh, and Henry Lincoln. *Holy Blood, Holy Grail*. New York: Dell, 1982.

Bambara, Toni Cade. *The Salt Eaters*. New York: Random House, 1980.

Belsey, Catherine, and Jane Moore. *The Feminist Reader*. New York: Blackwell, 1989.

Castleman, Michael, in Steven Schechter, M.D., *Fighting Radiation and Chemical Pollutants with Foods, Herbs, and Vitamins* (Encinitas, Cal.: Vitality, Ink, 1990).

Chávez, Denise. *The Last of the Menu Girls*. Houston: Arte Público, 1984.

Christian, Barbara. *Black Feminist Criticism: Perspectives on Black Women Writers*. New York: Pergamon, 1985.

———. *Black Women Novelists: The Development of a Tradition, 1892–1976*. Westport, Conn.: Greenwood, 1980.

Dickinson, Emily. *Complete Poems*. Ed. Thomas H. Johnson. Boston: Little, Brown, 1960.

Erdrich, Louise. *The Beet Queen*. New York: Holt, Rinehart and Winston, 1986.

———. *Love Medicine*. New York: Holt, Rinehart and Winston, 1984.

———. *Tracks*. New York: Holt, Rinehart and Winston, 1988.

Feshbach, Murray, and Albert Friendly, Jr. *Ecocide in the USSR: Health and Nature Under Siege* (New York: Harper Collins/Basic Books, 1992).

Fraser, Nancy. "What's Critical About Critical Theory? The Case of Habermas and Gender." In *Feminist Interpretations and Political Theory*, ed. Mary Lyndon Shanley and Carole Pateman. University Park: Pennsylvania State University Press, 1991.

Gates, Henry Louis, Jr., ed. *Reading Black, Reading Feminist: A Critical Anthology*. New York: Meridian, 1990.

———. *The Signifying Monkey: A Theory of African-American Literary Criticism*. New York: Oxford University Press, 1988.

Gould, Jay M. "Chernobyl – The Hidden Tragedy." *The Nation*, March 15, 1993.

Gould, Jay M., and Benjamin A. Goldman with Kate Millpointer. *Deadly Deceit: Low-Level Radiation, High-Level Cover Up* (New York: Four Walls Eight Windows, 1991).

Kingston, Maxine Hong. *The Woman Warrior: Memoirs of a Girlhood Among Ghosts*. New York: Knopf, 1976.

Lorde, Audre. "The Master's Tools Will Never Dismantle the Master's House." In Moraga and Anzaldúa.

Moi, Toril. "Marginality and Subversion: Julia Kristeva." In *Sexual/Textual Politics*. New York: Routledge, 1985.

Moraga, Cherríe, and Gloria Anzaldúa, eds. *This Bridge Called My Back: Writings by Radical Women of Color*. Watertown, Mass.: Persephone, 1981.

Morales, Aurora L., and Rosario Morales. *Getting Home Alive*. Ithaca, N.Y.: Firebrand, 1986.

Morrison, Toni. *Beloved*. New York: Knopf, 1987.

———. *The Bluest Eye*. New York: Washington Square, 1970, 1972.

———. *Song of Solomon*. New York: Signet, 1977, 1988.

———. *Sula*. New York: NAL, 1973, 1987.

The Santa Fe New Mexican, "Mystery Illness Battled from Worlds Apart, Scientists, Shamans Seek Answers;" Keith Easthouse, "Investigators Lean Toward Virus as Cause," pp. A1–2; AP, "Healers Blame Disappearance of Old Ways."

Schwartz-Salant, Nathan. *The Borderline Personality: Vision and Healing* (Willamette, Illinois: 1989).

Silko, Leslie Marmon. *Ceremony*. New York: Viking, 1977.

———. *Storyteller*. New York: Seaver Press, 1981.

Smith, Valerie. "Loopholes of Retreat: Architecture and Ideology in Harriet Jacobs' *Incidents in the Life of a Slave Girl*." In Gates, *Reading Black*.

Spillers, Hortense J. "'In Order of Constancy': Notes on Brooks and the Feminine." In Gates, *Reading Black*.

Walters, Anna Lee. *Ghost Singer*. Flagstaff, Ariz.: Northland, 1988.

———. *The Sun Is Not Merciful*. Ithaca, N.Y.: Firebrand, 1985.

———. "The Warriors." In Walters, *Sun*.

Credits

Acknowledgments

Thanks to Patricia Clark Smith, Carol Crosby, Laurie Slagle, Karen Wallace, and editors Tisha Hooks, Susan Worst, Mark Waldman, John Gattuso, Michael Steiner, Donald Porter, and Howard Junker, for editorial advice, typing and proofreading, and encouragement.

Index

Note: The abbreviations N.M. and P.G.A. refer to New Mexico and Paula Gunn Allen, respectively.

Budville (N.M.), 185
buHassen, Elias (P.G.A.'s great-
    grandfather) ("Elias Francis"), 3–4,
    193–206, 210–11

Cabezon (N.M.), 201, 202, 205
California, 24, 188, 223–24, 226
Cancer, and Native Americans, 111–12
Canon, literary, 170–71
Cañoncito Navajo Reservation, 184
Carew, Jan, 133–34
Castleman, Michael, 111
Cebolletito (N.M.), 201, 202
Chantway, 54–55, 160
Chávez, Denise, 170
Chemahuevi, 231
Chernousenko, Vladimir, 109, 110
Cherokee, 12, 19, 21, 23, 113–15, 117
Cheyenne, 45, 52
Chickasaw, 24
Chimayo (N.M.), 232
Chisum, John, 244
Christian, Barbara, 152–53
Christianity: Native American, 12; oppres-
    sion of women in, 75; perfectionism
    and, 61–62; in P.G.A.'s family, 104,
    199–200, 210–12, 221, 237; as
    Roman state religion, 70–71, 99. See
    also Monotheism
Cicogna and de Lauretis, Sexual Differ-
    ence, 73–76, 79
Clifton (Ariz.), 195, 196
Communism, 30
Community, 29, 32–34, 47, 177
Concepts, 140–44
Constantine, 70–71, 99
Correo (N.M.), 184
Crane, Stephen, 51

Crazy Horse, 37
Cubero (N.M.), 5, 103, 182, 183, 185,
    187, 189, 208

Darwin, Charles, 149
Deloria, Vine, Jr., 149
Democracy, 142, 148; literary, 147, 150
Dickinson, Emily, 167
Difference: as cultural resource, 78–83;
    fear of, 85; between men and women,
    73–76
Diné. See Navajo
Dinesen, Isak, 98
Disappearadas, Las. See Literature, Ameri-
    can, by women of color
Dreaming, in Native spirituality, 44–45,
    56, 97

Encinal (N.M.), 189
English language, 25, 59
Environmental destruction, 28, 32, 34,
    63, 66, 88
Erdrich, Louise, 166, 170
Ethnic Studies: marginalization of, 132–
    40; questions posed by, 138–41; sur-
    vival of, 143–44
Eusebius, 71

Feminine: as cultural resource, 78–83, 91–
    92; sacredness of, 85–87; subjugation
    of, 70, 88–89
Fergusson, Edna, 245
Food: Lebanese, 207–8; Native American,
    36; Southwestern, 232–34
Four Corners disease, 108–11, 113
Francis, E. Lee (P.G.A.'s father), 4, 101,
    104, 145, 175, 186, 208–9, 224–25
Francis, Elias. See buHassen, Elias

Memory, historical, 25–28, 30, 33
Mesita (N.M.), 104
Messer-Davidow, Ellen, 146–47
Migration: in Keres literature, 1; in
P.G.A.'s family history, 1–4
Milan (N.M.), 187
Milan Women's Bookstore Collective, 74,
78, 79, 82
Miles, Angela, 73
Miles, Josephine, 26
Miller, Alice Duer, 169
Mithras, 71, 99
Mixed-bloodedness: of American Indian
peoples, 6; of P.G.A., 4
Mohave, 231
Mohawk, 135
Moi, Toril, 173–74
Momaday, N. Scott, 7, 134; *The Ancient
Child*, 96; *House Made of Dawn*, 37,
39, 96, 154–56, 158, 159–60, 161–62
Monotheism: and other religions, 85–87;
history of, 70–73, 87–88; misogyny
of, 87
Mooney, James, 114
Moquino (N.M.), 202, 205
Morales, Aurora L., 170
Morales, Rosario, 170
Morrison, Toni, 166, 170
Mountain Wolf Woman, 50–51, 56
Mount Taylor. *See* Tse'pina/Kaweshtima
Multiplicity: in literature, 145–46, 150,
159, 161; of culture, 174–75; of life,
58–59, 63, 168–69
Mysticism, Native American: characteris-
tics of, 40–57; diversity of, 40–41;
pathways, 47–55; training in, 47; vs.
other religions, 49. *See also* Dreaming
Mystics, 47–56

Naotsete (Sun Woman), 90, 106, 115,
116, 237
Narragansett, 36
Native American(s): community, 32–33;
distinctiveness, 12, 93; identity, 6, 12;
invisibility, 36–39; mental health, 93–
100; military service of, 12; mistaken
views of, 8, 12, 33, 44, 93–100; perse-
cution of, 19–21, 26, 28, 29, 32, 34,
38; population, 23, 26, 37–38; poverty, 100; role in American history, 23–
25; speech, 51, 109; spirituality, 40–
57, 85; suicide, 100; women, 79–81;
worldview, 8, 41–42, 44–45, 56–57,
97–99, 172
Nau'sti'tsi. *See* Naosete
Navajo (Diné), 2, 24, 54–55, 108–9, 172,
183, 188, 230, 231
Neidhart, John G., 53
New Age, 84–87, 88, 90, 229; appropria-
tion of Native thought, 96, 97; Christian influence on, 85
New Laguna (N.M.), 186
Nietzsche, Friedrich, 173
Nolan, Frederick, 242–45
Nuclear bombs: effect on culture, 149;
mining uranium for, 2, 101, 102–3,
105, 236; spiritual significance of, 102,
106, 116–17, 236–37; testing of, 4,
101, 102, 149, 231. *See also* Radiation

"Off the reservation," 6
Oglala, 63
Ojibway, 166
Old Man Missionary, 1, 2, 7
Old Spider Grandmother. *See* Grand-
mother Spider
Order, 62–63

72, 78; flaws in, 17–21, 88, 118, 120, 122. *See also* Monotheism; Superiority; Unity

Whirlwind Man, 105, 106

White Corn, 105

Whitehead, Alfred North, 156, 159

Whitman, Walt, 148

Wilderness, 59–61, 63

Wilderness Journal, 59–61

Wimsatt, Margaret, 103

Wolfe, Tom, 150–51, 152

Women: of color, 166–67, 172; oppression of, 73–76, 173, 174

Yaqui, 231

Yellowcake, 105, 116, 236

Yellow Woman, 105, 106, 116

Yuma, 231

Zelazny, Roger, 98

Zuni (N.M.), 100, 188